Manna from Heaven

Manna from Heaven

From Divine Speech to Economic Science

by

Dalton Garis

GR

George Ronald
Oxford

George Ronald, *Publisher*
Oxford
www.grbooks.com

A catalogue record for this book is available
from the British Library

ISBN 978-0-85398-515-0

Printed and bound in Great Britain by Biddles Ltd, King's Lynn, Norfolk

Contents

Dedicated to the Glory of God,
to the defeat of prejudice and ideologies,
and to the unification of all knowledge
under His infinite grace and mercy

Acknowledgements

I am indebted to my beloved wife, Qian Liu, who encouraged me to write and never doubted that the book was in me and would come out if I let it. Wendi Momen, at George Ronald, Publisher, was also of immense help in working to turn a manuscript draft into a published book.

Several books were responsible for instilling in me the idea that in both the spiritual and material worlds identical analytical procedures are employed and that the presence of ideologies is the reason that religion has left off spiritual research and fallen into dogmas and profitless imitation of past forms. Among the most influential in fully establishing this argument are the following.

- The *Kitáb-i-Íqán*, by Mírzá Ḥusayn-ʻAlí Bahá'u'lláh. The logic and evidence supporting its arguments are irrefutable and wash away all traces of the unreal sand castles and idols worshipped till now. With this book the meaning of all past prophetic dialogues was made evident and clear to me. It was this book, more than any others, which opened for me the divine prophethood of His Holiness Muhammad and the miraculous revelation of the holy Qur'án.

- *The Rise of the Gulag: Intellectual Origins of Leninism*, by Alain Besançon, fully explained the character and significance of ideology as a form of belief and thought separate from either science or religion in their pure and unadulterated forms. It proved indirectly that what most people consider to be religious belief is, in fact, ideological and has nothing to do with true belief, which is based on evidence and proof. Once the nature of ideological thinking is recognized it is easy to see how true science and religion are in complete harmony.

- *The Bahá'í Proofs*, by Mírzá Abu'l-Faḍl, showed me that critical analysis is the essential tool of true religious belief and of all life. It argues that the prophetic dialogues were not just true, a priori, but that their assertions were testable and verifiable logically and factually. This was a revelation, to say the least.

Other books and sources are given in the bibliography but these deserve special mention for their influence on the thinking behind this book.

D. G.

Prologue

This book is the result of economic research stemming from explorations into applications of dynamical analysis to individual decision-making. It began with an investigation into the individual self-investment decision and how concepts called the subjective planning horizon and the subjective rate of time preference both rule our daily decisions and largely predict our present and future material states. As the research commenced I became impressed by the extent to which these parameters affect our spiritual states as well and began to investigate the verses of the noble Qur'án and other holy books for their dynamic economic content. Soon I was convinced that the divine dialogues and verses of these books had an unexplored capacity to establish the fundamentals of economic science and also of many financial practices now commonplace. This book shares some of those discoveries, beginning with the idea that there is just rational analysis, that even belief itself depends upon it and that it is a tool of divine speech as well as of scientific investigation.

We will explore the relationships that exist between economics and the teachings of the prophetic dialogues at the centre of those religions that have appeared in the Middle East and Levant regions. It is hoped the same exploration may someday be performed on those religions of the Ganges valley and the Far East, of which I readily admit I lack in-depth knowledge. It is hoped that this brief inquiry will be useful to those wishing to investigate the similarities between economics and spiritual topics.

In our exploration of the relationship between economics and religion much introductory material on current problems in economics is covered in some detail. This is useful in itself and provides the necessary background for understanding its place in a generalized conception of reality. The exposition is analytical but should be useful and readily accessible to people of many backgrounds. I have endeavoured to make the material interesting and clear without burdening the text with unnecessary technicality or glossing over important issues.

The thesis of the book is the following.

- There is an analytical process of verification and falsification, of evidence and logical construction that has been used for about the last 3,500 years or so. This technique, often called the scientific method, is older than science and might have been taught to mankind by the historical religious Prophets. The reason for suspecting this is that it would be impossible for the people either to comprehend their message or to evaluate its authenticity and validity without this method. Their message was very abstract and made a lot of claims for itself and its authors. Without a methodology of verification and falsification it would not have been possible to judge it on its merits.

- Armed with this method mankind was able to analyse the world of the material and super-material, philosophy, metaphysics, biology, etc. This also includes unravelling the secrets that are the subjects of the social sciences.

- Ideology, a way of thinking, a belief system that borrows elements of both science and religion, is responsible for creating a rift between religious dialogues and scientific inquiry. Stripped of all ideologies, both science and the prophetic dialogues are equally logical, falsifiable and verifiable in their tenets and respect the same methods of analysis. This is proved by the words of the historical Prophets, samples of which we will analyse. There then remains just analysis of reality in all of its forms.

- Economics is considered the most quantifiable of the social sciences and in many respects closest to the natural sciences in methodology and positivistic approach. It will be shown that economic principles also share commonalities with the teachings of the prophetic dialogues of religions. The text of the book is organized around this exploration.

Along the way we will enquire how societies change and what are the components of such change.

In developing the discussion of the similarities between economic science and spiritual teachings the body of the religion, with all its traditions, cultural identities and ritualistic practices, is separated from the prophetic dialogues underpinning it. It is the prophetic dialogue that is analysed for its instruction and insight into science and economics and not the religion nominally associated with it.

There is historical evidence that in the early years of a newly-established faith rational analysis did not limit itself to the material world but analysed everything under the heavens and beyond. This work was championed and materially supported by institutions of the new faith and some of that age's greatest scholars and scientists were devoted religionists. The great intellectual rift between religion and science happened later on when religious inquiry was snuffed out and religious leaders turned ever inward and dogmas and the anti-rational ideologies became embedded as religious orthodoxy. But in a repeating pattern, the advent of a prophetic 'Return' rejuvenated intellectual inquiry and reunited material and super-material scientific analysis once again.

This last point indicates logically that ideologies are present in orthodox established religions and abandoned – or abolished – with the advent of the new message. Such evidence affirms the progressiveness and interrelatedness of prophetic dialogues and the religions formed from them. The concept of ideology is key to understanding the arguments of this exploration. A chapter is devoted to its characteristics and the difference between ideology and rational inquiry and testable assertions.

The hope is that the ideas introduced here will stimulate a much-needed discussion on the harmony of science and spiritual teachings. Another volume is planned to explore in more detail a few of the issues introduced here, particularly those involving labour and employment, public goods and externalities.

Dalton Garis
Spring 2007

Introduction

Scientific and Religious Analytical Techniques: A Comparative Analysis[1]

Is it legitimate to discuss religious and divine topics in terms and contexts normally reserved for purely scientific discussions? The answer is, 'Yes'. According to 'Abdu'l-Bahá, 'Furthermore, [Bahá'u'lláh] proclaims that religion must be in harmony with science and reason. If it does not conform to science and reconcile with reason, it is superstition.'[2]

And, further, divine revelation itself was intended to be used as the *Most Great Tool* for critical analysis. What has happened, it is argued, is that over time ideological processes have been inserted into divine speech, which have changed its nature from being a tool of rational analysis into uncritical dogma. To show this we will explore the analytical process employed in science. We then show how this same process has been used by the Messengers of God in their dialogues with humankind, as evidenced by verses in the Qur'án and the Kitáb-i-Íqán. After a careful analysis of the ideology and why its characteristics led to a subversion of the scientific and divine objectives, we show that scientific advancement depends in large part on the stage of advancement of its host-civilization, which in turn depends on the maturation of its religious anchor.

This theme is so important in underpinning this entire book that a fair amount of linguistic formality is used in this chapter. Apologies beforehand but sometimes there is no substitute for a brook-no-nonsense formal treatment so that the legitimacy of the project can avoid constant doubting. If you are already convinced that divine truth is an instrument of supreme analysis, or are only interested in the economic analysis of divine speech, this chapter could be skipped without causing difficulties. Apologies also to those requiring more formalism and for the arguments to be more rigorously proved. Actually, a separate book would be needed to do justice to this theme.

The Common Analytical Framework of Science and Divinely Revealed Speech

Clearly, religion begins with a process of illumination; that is, religions are divinely revealed. This is entirely dissimilar from the process of science, which begins with an insight into the rules of how material creation functions and builds from that. The unity of method in expostulation for both, however, is the same, using similar rational analysis and argument. This unity of expository and analytical method for scientific and religious inquiry provides evidence that both spheres share a common intellectual lineage and common ontological structure.

Elements of Rational Argument

Several common constructions are found in all rational arguments. Their purpose is to eliminate false and misleading conclusions being formed from available evidence. They are largely based on elementary logic. Here are some of the most important ones. *The Bahá'í Proofs*, by Mírzá Abu'l-Faḍl, demonstrates each one of these in far more detail than here.

1) *Proof must relate to what is being proved.*

Being capable of flight is not evidence of skill in orthopaedic surgery because one bears no relation to the other. Similarly, evidence of spiritual authority and ascendancy – the essential condition of divinity – cannot be shown by executing a supernatural act because that is not related to the condition of spiritual supremacy, however impressive it may be to onlookers. This is why the divines refused to work miracles on request, since such things can never prove the spiritual authority they claimed for themselves.

In addition, not agreeing to an arbitrary display of a claimed skill is not evidence that the capacity is not possessed. A judge sent to a district to fill a commission from the central government cannot sentence someone to death just to prove s/he is a judge. That act must conform to the requirements of the situation and not be decreed for the sake of an arbitrary request. And a divine refusing to perform an act arbitrarily is similarly regarded.

> *Lemma: Expertise in one field gives a person no authority or capacity in another, unrelated field.*

Another manifestation of this principle is what we see in popular media. How many times has some scientist come on TV or written in the newspapers about something for which s/he has no special training or gift, resting the arguments on personal authority gained from work in another field? We have seen astrophysicists discoursing authoritatively on the impossibility of the afterlife or the non-existence of God. We also see (at least in America) famous Hollywood actors and actresses addressing the US Congress about food additives and other sciences of which they have none but a lay knowledge. For all their skill in their respective spheres, this gives them no special skill in areas foreign to their study and experience. Being one of the greatest actresses of the 20th century does not make you an expert on food allergies.

An example of this principle is supplied repeatedly in the Qur'án. It is stated that the Prophets and Messengers of God were opposed most often by a community's wealthy and politically powerful, who argued that only the poor and socially marginalized follow the Messengers and none of the wealthy or powerful do. Pharaoh used this argument to convince his subjects that Moses could not have been sent by God, since He was poor, had a speech impediment (Aaron was His spokesman) and was even known to have committed manslaughter some years previously in the marketplace of the capital – while pharaoh held all Egypt in his grasp and was wealthy beyond compare. The implication was that since God had given these things to pharaoh it must mean that pharaoh was a favourite of (the) God(s) while Moses, lacking any temporal authority, unable to express Himself properly, poor and coming from common stock rather than royal blood, could not be a favourite of anyone.

> Pharaoh said, 'O my people! Is not mine the dominion of Egypt, and these rivers flowing underneath me? See you not then? Am I not better than this one [Moses] who is despicable and can scarcely express himself clearly? Why are not bracelets of gold bestowed upon him, or angels sent along with him?' Thus, he befooled his people and they obeyed him . . .[3]

Pharaoh took his great temporal power as evidence of spiritual authority when it could only be a measure of temporal capacity; while Moses adduced spiritual evidence to show His spiritual authority and capacity. It is common knowledge that persons of varying degrees of spiritual capacity possess worldly power and wealth and that their wealth is not, and never has been, a sign of spiritual wealth. In other words, spiritual and material wealth are totally separate and are judged by entirely different criteria.

> And never was sent a Warner to a township but those who were given the

> worldly wealth and luxuries among them said, 'We believe not in that with which you have been sent.'[4]

Bahá'u'lláh develops this theme further in the Kitáb-i-Íqán. For example:

> And now, ponder this in thine heart: Were sovereignty to mean earthly sovereignty and worldly dominion, were it to imply the subjection and external allegiance of all the peoples and kindreds of the earth – whereby His loved ones should be exalted and be made to live in peace, and His enemies be abased and tormented – such form of sovereignty would not be true of God Himself, the Source of all dominion, Whose majesty and power all things testify. For, dost thou not witness how the generality of mankind is under the sway of His enemies? . . . Know, therefore, O questioning seeker, that earthly sovereignty is of no worth, nor will it ever be, in the eyes of God and His chosen Ones.[5]

2) *Results must submit to independent verification.*

This means that results must allow themselves to be independently ascertained, according to accepted standards of evidentiary procedure. Of course, spiritual pronouncements must be judged using proper spiritual criteria and material or time-valued pronouncements can be tested using appropriate criteria for those things. This is yet further evidence that the process of verification is identical for scientific and divine pronouncements, affirming the truth that rational evidentiary procedures and logic are not inimical to divine speech but, rather, are native to it and, in a sense, pre-existent. If mathematics, geometry and economic first principles yield identical results in the verification of an international trade model, for example, then, ruling out sheer chance, this would be evidence of valid scientific verification.

Statements must be *falsifiable* to be considered amenable to proof. Falsifiability means that a statement has in its structure what can prove it false. 'The sun rose at 07:13 this morning.' This is amenable to proof: either the sun rose at that time or it did not. 'The sun is great.' This is not a statement capable of being disproved, so it is not scientific but subjective. The Messengers of God repeatedly blamed the people's denial of the message they had been entrusted to deliver on their literal interpretation of the revealed verses and deliberately ignoring their evident meaning. The Messengers pointed to a pattern of behaviour manifested over centuries, one that is observable and repeatable. Each time another Messenger is sent, another experiment is carried out and the results are always the same.

3) *Results must be replicable.*

It must be possible to replicate the results independently using appropriate procedures. In the case of predictions, these are tested by seeing if the predicted event occurred. Regarding the interpretation of what was actually predicted, we will have much more to say about this – that the evident meaning of the words used must be the measure of whether the prediction was actually fulfilled. That is, if the prediction's words have been literally interpreted, when they were meant figuratively or some other way, it is not a fair test of the prediction's power if the event did not literally occur.

As we shall see, as ideologies fasten themselves onto the body of religion, the literal interpretation becomes the only one acceptable according to the pronouncements of religious leaders, even when its insistence leads to impossible and ridiculous statements accredited to the Prophets and Messengers of God, statements to which even a child would not pay attention.

4) *Lack of data does not invalidate an argument, especially if it is amenable to logical proofs.*

In many of its essential assertions, Einsteinian physics was not empirically testable until recently. Nonetheless, it was conditionally accepted based on its logic and its systematic and comprehensive modelling of what had been observed, even without a body of affirmative empirical tests.

This is also the case with many statements made by a divine Messenger referring to the afterlife and other conditions not directly accessible for testing. But because these statements are part of a comprehensive and accepted model of the operations of creation, they were and remain accepted until data allowing for empirical testing are devised, especially as those things that could be independently verified turned out to be exactly as had been represented by the divine Messenger.

An assertion becomes a structured argument, then a testable hypothesis. A methodology is chosen and a test is made, with the results reported. In many instances, especially during a period in science or religion where fundamental research is begun, the model is purely a logical structure, with no need to go further. If the model conforms to logic and reason then the assertion is proved for the listeners and readers in future times. Later, new methodologies may enable the carrying out of proper empirical tests that generate data for analysis.

These are the main elements of rational analysis. They will be applied to religious statements found in the Qur'án for evidence that Qur'ánic statements are indeed scientific, rational, logical and falsifiable.

Prophetic Speech Debased by Literalism

Comparing religious and scientific statements on any level would seem to be impossible: scientific statements are narrowly literal, while divine speech seems to be open to myriad interpretations. But this objection is internally inconsistent and mostly without foundation. On the one hand it dismisses any attempt to acknowledge the existence of superordinary, divinely-revealed speech while on the other it refuses to analyse the content of that speech or investigate the consistency, rationality, logical construction and falsifiability of its arguments or to independently verify its propositions and predictions.[6]

A far greater difficulty arises when religious authorities insist that prophetic dialogues are to be taken literally in every respect. Such an assertion precludes intelligible discussions of scientific and religious similarities in analytical structures and must therefore be dispatched before moving to compare directly the rational and common structure of prophetic speech and scientific analysis.

A reading of the verses in the Qur'án shows that they fall into several known categories: 1) recitation of historical events, with an analysis of conditions, signs, portents and associated results with respect to spiritual and material outcomes; this is doctrinal, analytical speech; 2) law-giving and rules establishment; 3) exhortations; 4) prophecies, often clothed in symbolic images; 5) mystic alliterations, prayers, etc., which also include symbolic speech; and 6) descriptions of the worlds beyond this material, phenomenal world, which employ metaphors and similes. It is generally easy to separate these different forms of address. For example, while some of the speech is completely literal ('and that you be dutiful to your parents . . .'[7]), references to suns and moons, heavens and earth have numerous meanings, depending on the context established. The statement 'With hands did We construct the heaven . . .'[8] is nonsense if taken literally, as is true of many other similar verses. Therefore, insisting that the symbolic images of prophetic speech were meant to be taken literally, then dismissing them for their literal absurdity, is neither rational nor honest.

Imposing literalism on divine speech is tantamount to voiding its evident and universal meaning. Excessive literalism in the interpretation of the divine verses is a practice consistently and roundly condemned by the Prophets themselves, as verses of the Qur'án testify: 'Are we wearied out with the first creation? Yet they are in doubt as to another creation'.[9] 'And their only response is "Bring back our fathers, if Thou speakest the truth."[10] 'Why hath not an angel been sent down to Him, so that he should be a Warner with Him?'[11] 'As oft as an Apostle cometh unto them with that which their hearts desire not, they swell with pride, accusing some of being impostors and slaying others'.[12]

Without exception, the divine Messengers blame humanity's denial and rejection of every Prophet sent to reinvigorate the spiritual destiny of mankind on people's literal interpretation of the verses clearly meant symbolically. Consider these verses:

> And surely the Hour is coming. There is no doubt about it; and certainly Allah will resurrect those who are in their graves.[13]

> And the Trumpet will be blown, and all who are in the heavens and all who are in the earth will swoon away, except him whom God wills. And then it will be blown a second time, and behold, they will be standing, looking on. And the earth shall shine with the light of her Lord.[14]

These cannot be taken literally, especially when a spiritual and figurative meaning provides a rich tapestry of possibilities while a literal interpretation results in nonsense and silliness. 'On the Day when the earth shall be changed into another earth'[15] again has no literal interpretation.

The following verse represents a complete rejection of the literal interpretation of all the verses of God which, in symbolic language, have repeatedly been employed to foretell the Return:

> And indeed Yusuf did come to you in times gone by, with clear signs, but you ceased not to doubt in that which he did bring to you, till when he died you said: 'No Messenger will Allah send after him.' Thus Allah leaves astray him who is a *Musrif* and a *Murtab*.[16]

Consider what is being alluded to in this statement and the logic it uses. It states that the people of every age have employed a process of acceptance, association, denial, etc., which is anti-rational, and that this is seen again and again, since nothing disturbs its replication. In fact, its replication is guaranteed by the character of the denial and the thinking of the people themselves. Because of the deep-rooted nature of these ideas, when the Messenger returns, all the people deny Him, even though He is identical to the previous Messenger with respect to all His spiritual attributes. 'And never comes there to them a Reminder as a recent revelation from the Most Gracious but they turn away therefrom.'[17] Again, the people come to realize their mistake and thereafter state that, in fact, no other Messenger was or ever will be greater than He was. The new Messenger is mythologized, just as the last one had been because the belief is superficial, a blind imitation of current and past religious practices.

> Then after Him We sent Messengers to their people. They brought them clear proofs, but they would not believe what they had already rejected beforehand. Thus, We seal the hearts of the transgressors.[18]

> And when Our clear verses are recited to them, they say, 'This is naught but a man who wishes to hinder you from that which your fathers used to worship.' And they say, 'This is nothing but an invented lie.' And those who disbelieve say of the truth when it has come to them, 'This is nothing but evident magic.'[19]

This argument is repeatedly made by Bahá'u'lláh in the Kitáb-i-Íqán. In discussing why the Christians rejected the dispensation of Muhammad, He states:

> Inasmuch as the Christian divines have failed to apprehend the meaning of these words, and did not recognize their object and purpose, and have clung to the literal interpretation of the words of Jesus, they therefore became deprived of the streaming grace of the Muḥammadan Revelation and its showering bounties. The ignorant among the Christian community, following the example of the leaders of their faith, were likewise prevented from beholding the beauty of the King of glory, inasmuch as those signs which were to accompany the dawn of the sun of the Muḥammadan Dispensation did not actually come to pass.[20]

A cardinal principle of rational analysis is *parsimony*, that is, if two models are offered to describe the same phenomenon, the simpler one is preferred. Attempting to force these and similar verses into the Procrustean bed of a literal interpretation, when a figurative interpretation illuminates the full spectra of meanings that accords with the spirit as well as the letter of all the other verses in the Qur'án and of other holy books, is scientifically unacceptable. A figurative and abstract interpretation offers valuable results, which literalistic interpretations destroy. The literal interpretation is thus non-parsimonious and a marring of the evident and true meaning of the divine speech.

This is an example of scientific and rational analytical principles being applied to the verses of God, an example of the Prophets and Messengers of God attempting to give logical meanings to the verses known among the people and to anchor their belief in God in rational argument.

> Erelong will they wag their heads at Thee, and say, 'When shall these things be?' Say: 'Perchance it is nigh.'[21]

> We will surely show them Our signs in the world and in their own selves.[22]

As a consequence of interpreting the divine verses in accord with the evident and obvious meaning revealed in the Qur'án, we are granted understanding of this fundamental truth: *the 'magic' referred to by the people when deriding the sayings of the Messengers as recorded in the holy books was, and is, the irrefutable power of rationality and the unanswerable logic of the Messengers' divine speech.* This is shown by the repeated objection of the people to the Prophets for being magicians and sorcerers. We are all familiar with those divine statements referring to the crushing of the mountains, the reduction of the earth to a handful of clay and the establishment of a new heaven and a new earth. What could these statements mean except that the words of the Prophets had some kind of unusual power over their hearers, a capacity to reduce a thousand years of accumulated dogma to a nullity with just one sentence, to convince the listeners that their current religious practices were false and empty, and to demonstrate the truth of God's divine redemptive cause? It is clear that the people were astonished by logic's convincing power and called it sorcery and magic:

> Likewise, no Messenger came to them but they said: 'A sorcerer, a madman!'[23]

> And when Our clear verses are recited to them, the disbelievers say of the truth when it reaches them, 'This is plain magic!'[24]

'And God wipes out falsehood and establishes the truth by His Word',[25] where falsehood means current dogmas and ideologies which hinder the people from recognizing the divine Prophet and the cause of God.

The importance of analysing these quotations is in recognizing that the prophetic verses, having been freed from literalism, represent valid and rational arguments in their own sphere, are fully capable of independent verification and analysis and employ the same rules of argument and rational discourse that are found in science. What ordinarily masks this is the nature of the world being expostulated, that is, the spiritual world, a world of relationships and exchanges between the created and the Creator, between phenomenal and spiritual worlds of being. Even when the people addressed by the returning Messenger were relatively advanced materially and technologically, for them the idea that divine speech was based on logic and evidence must have been mind-bendingly radical, if not blasphemous. For the people living in almost any time, religion was a social institution in which they had all been raised, erected upon myth and miracle, and with which they were content. They certainly did not want someone declaring that He was sent to cleanse it of that foundation and to overturn their comfortable *status quo*. On the contrary, they regarded such a person as a seditious mischief-maker who should be driven out before His radical and subversive ideas took root. Is this not proved by the Qur'ánic verses themselves?

> But when the truth has come to them from Us, they say: 'Why is he not given the like of what was given to Moses?' Did they not disbelieve in that which was given to Moses of old? They say: 'Two kinds of magic, each helping the other.' And they say, 'In each we are disbelievers.' Say: 'Then bring a book from God that is better than those two, that I may follow it, if you are truthful.'[26]

The Essential Complementarity of Prophetic Dialogues and Scientific Analysis

As far as is known, the material–temporal world is devoid of the power of self-analysis. No evidence exists to indicate that a dog understands that the earth revolves around the sun or that earthquakes are the result of tectonic shifts in the earth's crust or that diseases can be spread by micro-organisms. Noting the precedent of religious revelation – that the historical record shows it preceding the development of materially based science and advanced technologies – it is plain logic that the roots of scientific rationality and formal analysis are to be found in divine revelation. This is *Granger causality*:[27] *A* appears and then *B* appears; *B* does not appear when *A* does not appear; and *A* appears before *B* appears.

Again:

- Science deals with process and instrumentality, the discovery, analysis and actualization of material laws, and in immediate causation and association but does not deal in ultimate purposes.

- Religion deals with motive causes and the ultimate purpose of all life and creation, instructing by carefully constructed argument and rational analysis, as shown by the divine texts themselves. Its goal is to effect a transformation in the character of society and a reaffirmation of the purpose of creation.

- Without religion, science and engineering lack the power of ontological reflection; and without independent verification of its tenets, religion becomes tautological and ideological, abandoning real analysis and exchanging it for preservation of ancient and outworn forms. ('Have you not seen those who have changed the blessings of God into disbelief, and caused their people to dwell in the house of destruction?'[28])

The Character of Ideology

So far we have discussed the nature of religion and science in terms of their shared methodology and explanatory purposes. We have made reference to ideologies corrupting science and religion and diverting their nature and purpose, especially with respect to religious dogmas and literal interpretations of the holy writ. But what do we mean by ideology and why is it so dangerous to rational thought? The answer is in ideology's demand for complete and unquestioning acceptance of its tenets without recourse to independent verification of those tenets or validation of the efficacy of its decrees. As is now argued, it goes to objectives: the object of reason is the attainment of truth, scientific or religious, material or spiritual, while the object of ideology is the acquisition of power.

The following discussion and characterization of ideology comes from the pioneering work of Alain Besançon in his groundbreaking work.[29] It is also supported by the works of Heller and Nekrich,[30] by Stuart Kahan in his biography of his uncle, Lazar Kaganovich, the mastermind of Stalin's purges,[31] and by other authors who have discussed and analysed the nature of ideologies both ancient and modern. To this scholarship I have added only the commonly accessible insight that since science and religion share the same expository processes, it must be the presence of systematic and self-maintaining ideologies that has separated them into mutually exclusive camps in people's minds.

Besançon traces the development of modern ideology from the gnosis and the teachings of Mani through various cycles until it reaches a sort of pinnacle as Marxist–Leninism. Since the publication of his work, however, ideology can be said to have developed further, entering new cycles in Saudi

Arabia, Afghanistan–Pakistan, Chechnya and Dagestan, and most recently, in Iraq. According to Besançon in describing Marxist–Leninist ideology (which he declares is ideology in its highest and most developed form),

> Social and political conflict is thus the proof of Marxism. Marxism is the objective reflection in the consciousness of men of the emergence of the proletariat . . . The system is closed because any attempt at refutation reveals the influence of the bourgeoisie, and thus is evidence of the class struggle as Marxism itself defined it. Any contrary argument is thus a fresh proof of the validity of the system.[32]

Ideological results are therefore not falsifiable or refutable. If the ideology attains political and temporal power there will obviously be a huge gap between reality as perceived by everyone and the pronouncements of the theorizing power elite. But this will not result in defeat of the ideology and victory for reality. As just stated, the struggle itself will be given as proof of the truth of the false deity of the ideology. Besançon again:

> But this gap did not stop the Bolsheviks staying in power. On the contrary, they stayed in power because of it. This enormous complex of false analyses, these imaginary struggles between ghostly adversaries, these inconsistent notions of imperialism, this fabulous interpretation of events, none of this did any harm.[33]

> The Government could only act on reality in a destructive way, since it was that real [reality itself] which had to be destroyed before the reality of which the [Communist] party was the repository could manifest itself . . . The duplication of realities, the yawning gulf between the party and society, between the world as seen by the party and the world which society knows, is a constant threat to the legitimacy of the Government's power which rests on the verification of the theory.[34]

Ideology cannot beget anything of itself and exists only in the minds of its believers. Therefore reality and real analysis must be destroyed as they refute the ideology in power. But scientific and divinely revealed arguments, rather than being destroyed by criticism, are sustained and enriched by it, with ideologies and false results being expelled and purged over time from the body of scientific or religious exposition. This is evidence that both science and religion, in their capacity as tools of rational analysis, reflect a reality that is not dependent on people's belief for its existence.

Indeed, people are dependent on understanding reality for their existence. The Messengers return to mankind to restore the primacy of intellectual inquiry and to re-establish the truth that *only rational analysis survives and is true* and that divine revelations, in their utilization of irrefutable logic, reason and truth, are the first-best weapon against the false deities of ideology. 'Say: the Truth has come and the falsehood can neither create anything nor resurrect.'[35]

Is there any question, then, that the return of a divinely appointed Messenger of God would be marked for elimination by the power structures by any means at their disposal? The record of events as recounted in the Qur'án and the other holy books testify to this reality. An insight into the thought process of such a power elite has been suggested by Fyodor Dostoyevsky in his unfinished work *The Brothers Karamazov*. In the chapter 'Pro and Contra', one of the principals, Ivan, is relating to his younger brother a poem he is working on about the return of Christ and His subsequent arrest and interrogation by the Grand Inquisitor of the land. The polemic of this Grand Inquisitor is so powerful and evocative of totalitarian credos that the Grand Inquisitor and his dialogue have taken on mythical dimensions over the years. These lines capture the thinking of the ideology's *will to power* and control, one that is foreign to both science and religion. The quotation is long but, more than anything else, it relates the character and identity of ideology and that its goal is to supplant the true reality it cannot fashion and remake, and to replace it with its own vision of reality. As you read this, see which mass movements share these goals and this thinking.

> Canst Thou [Jesus] have simply come to the elect and for the elect? But if so, it is a mystery, and we too have a right to preach mystery, and to teach them that it's not the free judgement of their hearts, not love that matters, but a mystery which they must follow blindly, even against their conscience. So we have done. We have corrected Thy work and have founded it upon *miracle*, *mystery*, and *authority* . . .
>
> . . . Oh, we shall persuade them at last not to be proud, for Thou didst lift them up and thereby taught them to be proud. We shall show them that they are weak, that they are only pitiful children, but that childlike happiness is the sweetest of all. They will become timid and will look to us and huddle close to us in fear, as chicks to a hen. They will marvel at us and will be awe-stricken before us, and will be proud at our being so powerful and clever, that we have been able to subdue such a turbulent flock of thousands of millions . . .
>
> . . . Yes, we shall set them to work, but in their leisure hours we shall make

> their life like a child's game, with children's songs and innocent dance. Oh, we shall allow them even sin, they are weak and helpless, and they will love us like children because we allow them to sin. We shall tell them that every sin can be expiated if it is done with our permission, that we allow them to sin because we love them, and the punishment for these sins we take upon ourselves. And we shall take it upon ourselves, and they will adore us as their saviours who have taken on themselves their sins before God . . . The most painful secrets of their conscience, all, all they will bring to us, and we shall have an answer for all. And they will be glad to believe our answer, for it will save them from the great anxiety and terrible agony they endure at present in making a free decision for themselves. And all will be happy, all the millions of creatures except the hundred thousand who rule over them. For only we, who guard the mystery, shall be unhappy . . .
>
> . . . What I say to Thee shall come to pass, and our dominion will be built up. I repeat, tomorrow Thou shalt see that obedient flock who at a sign from me will hasten to heap up hot cinders about the pile on which I shall burn Thee for coming to hinder us, for if anyone has ever deserved our fires it is Thou. Tomorrow I shall burn Thee. Dixi.[36]

The ideas in this extended quotation from a literary work may seem bizarre, too extreme. Perhaps; but my guess is that it is closer to a true description of many mass movements than we may at first wish to believe. It captures the rationale of many orthodox religious structures as they are presented to us today. When these words were written in the late 19th century they presaged in their essence the mass movements of the 20th century, fascism and communism, and the recently emerging radical religious movements of Judaism, Christianity and, most notably, Islam. These thoughts are offered here to act as a characterizing capstone to our analysis of ideology so that its potency to wield power in the political and religious sphere and its goal to completely subvert science and religion to its own ends is not underestimated, nor the necessity of sending to mankind a fresh revelation to rub out the ideological gods humanity has come to worship.

Ends and Means

Nothing quite shows the contrast of science and religion on one side and ideology on the other than an analysis of their respective goals and whether means determine their ends or are justified by them. Both science and religious teachings hold that *the means determine the end result*. In science this means that good scientific methodology validates research results while a bad scientific methodology will invalidate results. Religion acts identically in that it teaches by example, by rational argument, and not by recourse to extraordinary events such as miracles to convince.

History (and sadly, current events) details many episodes of religiously inspired persons committing acts so atrocious that only if they believed that the end justifies those means could they have countenanced them. Yet in the revealed verses of the Messengers of God no statements can be found which declare that the end justifies the means. Indeed, divine revelation declares first and foremost that the means determine the end pursued. 'There is no compulsion in religion.'[37] In fact, the verses of God inform us that we become exactly what we do, what we sacrifice our God-given resources to become. But the extent to which ideologies root themselves in religion is the extent to which means-justifying is carried out.

Ideologies also exist in science, of course, in the form of deep-rooted biases which subvert and nullify its explanatory value. The beginning of this chapter cited the example of science generally refusing to analyse the verses of the Qur'án for their rationality and falsifiability or to independently verify the social states under various scenarios predicted by spiritual principles and laws. Scientists have relegated all divinely revealed verses to the position of a special discourse and have followed the religionist doctors in declaring that science stands apart from such discourse and can have little useful to say about it.

At the highest levels scientists may themselves act as priests, enforcing traditions in a guild of dedicants. Observe a commencement of college graduates, their attire, hats and gowns, etc., and see how closely they resemble the medieval attire of scholastic monks. Not only is this evidence of the religious antecedents of modern science but it is also illustrative of how, over time, any paradigm becomes received wisdom, accepted dogma, opposing independent examination of its tenets rather than championing it. This is well explained and developed by Kuhn in *The Structure of Scientific Revolutions.*

A Comparison of Scientific and Revelatory Goals

What are the respective objectives of science and divine messages? One possible answer is that science seeks to know while the divine message, which later becomes an organized, self-sustaining religious cause, seeks to affect a reformation in thinking. But are these actually two separate goals? For example, whatever science discovers is tested for utility and applicability to solving problems and enhancing life in intellectual, emotional and physical ways. Later, engineers devise new technologies, goods and services from the initial discoveries, be they natural laws or new materials. Commercial and educational enterprises develop to carry on the work, whose goal is to change the nature of life as it is lived. The divine Messengers have acted in exactly the same way as pure science in this regard, revealing laws and explaining how spiritual creation operates. Later, religion organizes this opus into an institution with strategic and tactical objectives for transforming the spiritual character of humankind.

The relationship of religion to science is that of generator of its initial impulse. Religion seeks to explain and science seeks to know. Science is encyclopaedic in nature, dedicated to analysing and describing the material, temporal world, including human relationships in all their causes and effects. Stripped of ideologies it lacks a political agenda *per se* and seeks only to understand. Blind to the harm or benefit of its own discoveries, it relies upon religiously derived ethical sets and moral philosophies to light its path and on engineering to translate its findings into useful goods, services and social policies.

Both processes similarly rely on mankind's unquenchable desire to discover, comprehend and manipulate universal laws in order to improve the experience of living. In that context, it is misleading to insist that the purpose of science is purely encyclopaedic while that of religion is transformative. Taking into account derived science and engineering, commercialization and institutions for learning and knowledge dissemination, science is as transformative in its purposes as religion; and in light of the clear statements of the divine Prophets and Messengers themselves, religion is just as encyclopaedic, even scholastic, in character. What the divine Messenger does is to reveal laws of spiritual life and instruct mankind in their applications; religion then organizes this into institutions capable of self-preservation. This is no different from the scientific paradigms and schools analysed by Kuhn, which are also for the purpose of self-preservation.

We have this general result: the purpose of science and divine speech is to disseminate knowledge to the world, which has the latent capacity to transform life for humankind. Perhaps this is what is meant by 'the creative Word'? And further, neither the scientist nor the Messenger has a plan to acquire power. Rather, it is the utilizers of their respective outpourings who will accomplish that: religion is established by authority of the divine message and institutional science and technology from the research scientist. For better or worse, and drawing their authority from the root discoveries, it is scientific and religious institutions in society that display a desire for political power, the better to influence the direction of human advancement.

The Rational Process of Religious Renewal

Another objection to asserting the commonality of scientific and religious rational structures is based on how each renews its central principles and goals. In fact, the process is identical. In each sphere the outworn paradigm is sloughed off and the underlying core truths are again revealed. The arguments discussed above showed not only that religion is renewed from age to age with the coming of a returned Messenger but also gave the purpose for such a return: to blot out ideologies and return religion's analytical capacity so that mankind can continue to advance socially, spiritually, morally and intellectually, as well as materially and technologically.

Assume that religion and science form one continuous body of knowledge, i.e. that there is just *knowledge* in all its myriad and manifold forms ('And verily, this your religion is one religion . . .'[38]). Therefore, we see divine truth spreading at various times from different centres in the world through the ages. As with science, divine revelation has followed a pattern of advancement wherein the divine teacher has invariably announced the appearance of yet another divine teacher 'at a time appointed'.[39] The appearance of a succession of divinely appointed Prophets and Messengers is how the cause of God itself is revised and renewed from age to age.

And when these new institutions attain temporal power the religion will begin, after its golden age, to go into decline as the result of ideological inroads and the self-sustaining capacity of all paradigms, religious or scientific, which vigorously defend themselves from agents of change, until finally being overthrown from without.

> And when there came to them a Messenger from Allah, confirming what was with them, a party of those who were given the scripture threw away the Book of Allah behind their backs, as if they did not know.[40]

> Then do you believe in part of the scripture and reject the rest?[41]

The cause of God, being a continuous revelatory process whereby it is impossible to accept one Messenger but reject others, is therefore fully capable of renewal by its own divine agents. 'No distinction do We make one another of His Messengers.'[42]

Whatever proves the validity of one proves the validity of all and whatever argument can be used to reject any individual divinely appointed Messenger is equally applicable to all the others.

> And when it was said to them, 'Believe in what Allah has sent down,' they say, 'We believe in what was sent down to us.' And they disbelieve in that which came after it, while it is the truth confirming what is with them. Say: 'Why then have you killed the Prophets aforetime, if you indeed have been believers?'[43]

This is one of the most reiterated of Qur'ánic themes, as shown by the number of surahs and verses devoted to it and, as can be seen, it is based on irrefutable logic and rationality.

One of the objections levelled against Jesus was that He did not fulfil all the laws of Moses but, rather, moved to annul two of the most influential Mosaic laws, divorce and the Sabbath observances. But these objections ignored the reality that *the purpose of the appearance of a new divine revelation is to effect a change in the practices and thinking of the people so that they may continue to develop and advance according to the divine purpose.* If the Messengers of God in every age were to sanction the beliefs and practices current among the people, the cause of God could never advance, which in turn would mean, as demonstrated below, that civilization could never advance. This same objection is levelled against every chosen one sent to fulfil the promises of rebirth, return and renewal, as described by the verses of God recorded in all the holy books, of which the Qur'án provides the most thorough and complete record previously seen.

> And if the truth had been in accordance with their desires, verily, the heavens and the earth, and whatsoever is therein, would have been corrupted![44]

> And verily, this religion is one religion . . . But they have broken their religion among them into sects, each rejoicing in what is with it.[45]

For example, according to the Surah of Hud (Surah 11), the Prophets of God have appeared successively, each inviting the people to abandon what had become for them a ritual preservation of an ideological creed, without any true spiritual life – a creed which holds that once upon a time, long, long ago, there was a magical period when a Messenger of God appeared who worked many miracles and gave many signs, left humanity with a book and departed. Now we all await the destruction of the world, as promised by a literal interpretation of the verses in the book the Messenger left with us.

But instead of the expected end of the world, the Surah of Hud says a Messenger appears, inviting the people to a new faith, confirming the core truths of their current religion, comprehensively explaining the true meaning of the verses of the divine book in their possession, providing a new set of laws and ordinances that promotes economic, spiritual, social and material advancement and revitalizing the cause of God.

> And there came indeed to them their Messengers with clear proofs; but they were not such as to believe in that which they had rejected before.[46]

> And when it is said to them, 'Follow that which God has sent down.' They say, 'Nay, but we follow that which we found our fathers following.'[47]

Rather than fulfilling what the people expected of them, the Prophets and Messengers propounded new teachings, annulled laws laid down by the previous divine Manifestation, rejected as invalid many of the current religious practices and, using alliterative speech, established the signs and portents that would herald the advent of yet another Messenger, who would in turn repeat the process; that is, reject existing religious practices that had been perverted by ideologies and condemn their exponents, restate the divine purpose, establish new ordinances and laws as He saw fit, lay down the requirements of a true seeker after truth and propound the appearance of signs signalling the advent of yet another dispensation from God to follow.

> O children of Adam: If there come to you Messengers from amongst you, reciting to you My verses, then whosoever becomes righteous, on them shall be no fear, nor shall they grieve.[48]

> And nothing prevents men from believing when guidance has come to them, and from asking forgiveness from their Lord, except that the ways of the ancients be repeated with them . . . And We send not Messengers except as givers of glad tidings and warners. But those who disbelieve dispute with false argument in order to refute the truth thereby. And they treat My evidences and that with which they are warned as a jest and mockery![49]

Furthermore, by propounding a new set of laws and ordinances the Prophets and Messengers declare that they are not changing the cause of God in the least.

> That was the Way of God in the case of those who passed away of old; and you will not find any change in the Way of God.[50]

Rather, they are re-establishing it and returning mankind to the path of truth, away from ideologies that have no existence and toward the *and* of rational analysis, the reality of truth.

> Whatever verse do We abrogate or cause to be forgotten We bring a better one or similar to it. Know you not that God is able to do all things?[51]

Because it is God's divine revelation, His divine speech, which is given to us and forms the basis, as we shall prove, of the progression of human civilization, this knowledge is not of our own creation and therefore cannot be renewed by us. In that sense its renewal is from the outside – exogenous to human endeavours – but endogenous to the covenant of the Messengers.

It is a mistaken characterization of knowledge itself to believe it is man-made and therefore amenable to our own efforts at renewal. It is no more ours than the Will of God is ours. Sunspots may be shown to affect business cycles but business cycles cannot affect sunspots, no matter how much the data is tortured to give evidence for it! The Prophets and Messengers criticize mankind for its own attempts to revise the religion of God, which just turns religion into sects, creeds and political institutions alien to the purpose of unification that is the basis of every divine message – unification of peoples, of collective endeavours, of law and economies, of science and religion itself.

> He has ordained for you the same religion He ordained for Noah, and that which We have revealed for you, and that which We ordained for Abraham, Moses, and Jesus, saying you should establish religion and make no divisions in it.[52]

But unlike science and religion, the experience with ideologies is that they have no ability to be renewed over time because they are not founded upon real analysis. Therefore exposure to reality can only cause the ultimate extinction of ideological pronouncements. Recall the last time you tried to convince a racist of the falsity of his position. It is likely that logic and reason had no effect on his or her position since it was based on belief and not truth – either you believe in it or you don't. As previously quoted, 'Say: the Truth has come and the falsehood can neither create anything nor resurrect.'[53]

The Motive Force behind Scientific Development

Two things suggest that divine revelation itself gives rise to new sciences and technologies. The first is the Qur'án and its divine verses:

> Alif-Lam-Mim. This is the Book, whereof there is no doubt, a guidance to those who are *Al-Muttaqun*.[54]

In addition to those verses already cited, there is this:

> Verily, We gave life to the dead, and we record that which they send before them, and their traces and all things We have recorded with numbers in a clear Book.[55]

Thus numeracy is native to divine revelation just as literacy is. And how could mankind know a thing that is unknown by his Creator or have a capacity which God lacks?

The other source of this evidence is the historical record. That such renewal of the religious cause and purpose induces vastly expanded scientific research and discoveries is shown by historical developments arising after the appearance of a new divine Messenger. Consider the degraded state of peninsular Arabia in the 'days of ignorance' just prior to the advent of Islam, its level of commerce, statecraft, arts and literature, jurisprudence, science and technology, education, medicine, agriculture, etc. and what obtained in the centuries following. There is simply no plausible explanation for the dramatic improvements in all these attributes of civilization in the absence of the appearance of Islam. The growth path Arabia was on was basically flat, became exponentially positively sloped after the appearance of the Prophet Muhammad, then tailed off in later ages to assume the sinusoidal shape customary as the graphical profile for the spread of a new paradigm.

This discrete revelatory process would seem to be in strong contrast to the continuous analytical process of science, with each generation of scientists building on the discoveries of the last. Its agency is the ordinary but gifted human and not a divine Messenger or Prophet. The scientist studies and analyses creation and thereby adduces its laws and principles through inductive and deductive processes. While often claiming divine inspiration, scientists make no claim to being divine Prophets but are themselves followers of one of the established religions or go their own eclectic way.

But science's seeming continuity, moving smoothly from one discovery to another, is deceptive because most discoveries are made within the shelter of an established paradigm powerful enough to defend itself and shelter its researchers, until it is finally overthrown and its inhabitants scattered. This is not a continuous process at all but only appears so from a distance. Moreover, scientific analysis is a derivative process, the culmination of divine revelations that revolutionize social institutions and cause civilizations to rise and fall. Science operates within these civilizations and is therefore dependent on the appearance of successive religious revelations as its generating impulse.

Assume that the changes to peninsular Arabia over the past 1,500 years is a specific example of the general principle that *a region's cultural, scientific and material development is dependent on the character of its religious expression.* Besides the changes to Arabia and later to North Africa and Asia with the advent of Islam, there are the earlier examples of Israeli Palestine after the appearance of Moses, Rome after Constantine and Christianity, and India, China and central Asia after the appearance of Buddha. There are many others.

In these examples a new and progressive religious dispensation gave birth to an outpouring of scientific and cultural developments in that land and beyond. Each case also demonstrates the reverse situation: that as the religions associated with these regions turned away from the fundamental and underlying principles that motivated constant improvement, analysis and spiritual and material development, and turned inward, this caused an identical effect in society's scientific and cultural striving. Consider the early days of the world's established religions, when their followers dedicated their lives to the investigation of the spiritual, metaphysical and material universes, documented findings, established colleges and universities in science, philosophy and engineering, recorded new discoveries in books on anatomy, astronomy, geography, history, the natural sciences and mathematics, catalogued and collated the great discoveries of the past, endowed libraries, established research chairs and added to arts and literature, etc. and contrast this with what obtained in their latter days, when discovery and scientific investigation, inventions and industry turned into pure scholasticism as the religion used monasticism and withdrawal from the world as a measure of personal piety. The following examples offered here in support of this argument are examined in full in 'Abdu'l-Bahá's *The Secret of Divine Civilization.*

Early Judaism after the Exodus. The early state of Israel became the dominant political, economic and cultural power in the lower Mediterranean under Kings David and Solomon, influencing the entire region with trade, commerce, philosophy, jurisprudence and law, statecraft, technology and advances in warfare. There is evidence that the Greeks travelled to the kingdom of Israel, and thus inspired, returned to found their world-famous historical schools of mathematics, science, philosophy, statecraft and metaphysics.

Middle and late Judaism turned inward, abandoned those things that made it great, became disunited and occupied itself with endless and dissipating ideological and theocratic disputes (*fitna*). Suffering from sectarian strife and disunited at its core, Israel became easy prey for its neighbours: first Babylon, then Rome completely subjugated and destroyed it. It would be over two thousand years before another state of Israel would appear on the world's political landscape.

Early Christianity. After Constantine ascended the Roman throne and Christianity became the state religion, Rome became the dominant religious, cultural, economic and intellectual power, exceeding its previous glories, most particularly in the wisdom of its political and juridical order. And in Europe and North Africa, Christians were at the centre of political organizing and unifying efforts and were known for their advanced statecraft, their arts, sciences, etc. People after people, when freed from their native and stultifying creeds, added their unique talents and abilities to the Christian religion and its political domination.

Later Christianity. The mighty edifice of Christianity was irrevocably split into two parts, the Eastern Orthodox and Roman Churches, with a later irrevocable split between Catholics and Protestants. For over a thousand years Europe descended into its dark age of monastic scholasticism and did not emerge until after the Crusades through the influence of Islam, while in the Eastern Orthodox realms a similar intellectual decline was seen. The rise of Islam circumscribed the temporal power of the Eastern Church and reduced Byzantium's influence. Finally, the Holy Roman Empire was reduced to a few acres in the centre of Rome under Pope Pius IX.

Early Islam is justly famous for its scientific discoveries, its mathematics, geography and astronomy, its universities and the range of its cultural diversity. To the previous list must be added advances in economics and trade, jurisprudence and investment law; banking and contract law; the intimation of the joint stock company; insurance, taxation and transfer payments;

and many other specifics in macroeconomics and public finance. In fact, the concept of the nation was a teaching of Islam, as was the concept of the public institution supported by general taxation and the rule of law as abstracted from the power of any leader or kingdom. Minority religions were tolerated if they paid a tax to the state.

Recent Islam.[56] As the historical record will clearly show, recent Islam has experienced what can only be honestly described as a great 'falling off' as compared to its early centuries. Theologically it has turned inward. From being expansionist, it has become isolationist in character. From being guided by the most erudite and knowledgeable in its vast community, it now must look outside for such guidance, as many of its intellectuals and scholars have been driven out by intolerant creeds. From its political and temporal leaders being esteemed throughout the world for their wisdom and understanding of statecraft, its leaders today struggle to understand the globalized world, a world that is a natural extension of Qur'ánic teachings and which has actually adopted in many of its particulars and in all of its overarching principles the teachings of Islam, even while – sadly – the traditional Islamic countries of the globe struggle to accommodate these same teachings.

> And the Messenger will say: 'O My Lord! Verily My people deserted this Qur'án.'[57]

While we can argue over the details and specifics, and while there are a few notable exceptions, the broad trend of a relative failure for most Islamic nations to thrive cannot be denied.

> That is so because God will never change a grace which He has bestowed on a people, until they change what is in their own selves.[58]

This sweeping statement would be difficult to accept were it not so obvious to even the most casual observer.

> See you not that We gradually reduce the land from its outlying borders? And God judges and there is none to put back His judgement, and swift is He in reckoning.[59]

There is no evidence that the causality of religion on national development runs in reverse – that a nation's development is responsible for the appearance of a divine Prophet. In fact, the Messengers of God have always seemed to appear to a people or nation in the nadir of its history, when its fortunes have been reversed, its past glories forgotten and its life force spent. (Only later are the surrounding developed nations that circumscribe the recipient community co-opted to facilitate the spread of the new religion but the recipient community itself is usually on its last legs when the Manifestation appears to them as the return of the previous one.)

In every case of a nation or region becoming dominant, where the source of its inspiration is known, its rise can be associated with its adherence to a divine teaching in its ascendant developmental stage, a teaching either addressing that nation directly, as in the case of Moses to the Jews, or indirectly, as in the case of Rome and Europe from the influence of Christ's teachings, and of Asia with Buddha and later with Islam. In those indirect cases, where a nation, by virtue of judicious borrowings, equals or exceeds levels of past glories by regional rivals, the reason is its adoption of spiritual or philosophical teachings currently unknown to it and which offer renewal of long-dormant capacities. Rome started as a hegemonic empire, dominating the Mediterranean and much of the Middle East after the defeat of the Carthaginians and all other regional powers that stood in its way. It inherited the polytheism of Greece but also its philosophy and material sciences, which had themselves reached their highest expression after Greek philosophers travelled to Israel during the time of Solomon to learn from that nation. In a subsequent age Rome reinvigorated itself with the teachings of Christ under Constantine. A similar story can be told for Persia, China, Korea and India. The Inca and Aztec civilizations mirror the relationship of the Romans to the Greeks.

Furthermore, the falling off of these great powers can be associated with a decline in their spiritual fortunes, when religious expression ceased to act as an instrument of analysis and of scientific and philosophical advancement and had been debased into particularism, dogma, fanaticism and strife.

> How shall God guide a people who disbelieve after their belief, and after they bore witness that the Messenger is true, and after clear proofs had come unto them?[60]

The Hebrew Bible describes the rise of Israel under the generations after Moses and its subsequent decline from internal divisions and excesses and rejection of the teachings of Moses, until local rivals were able to eat away at its territory.

> See they not how We gradually reduce the land from its outlying borders? And Allah judges; there is none to put back His judgement; and He is swift in reckoning.[61]

Finally, Rome under Tiberius utterly destroyed Jerusalem and extinguished the kingdom of Israel. For the next two thousand years the Jews were persecuted and without a homeland.

> And for every nation there is a term appointed; when their term comes neither can they delay it, nor can they advance it an hour.[62]

Those areas of the world not directly receiving a revelation from God nonetheless experience its influence as reflected light, so to speak. Ancient Greece is an example. The Athenian Socrates is known to have visited the kingdom of Israel during the time of Solomon and was influenced by its monotheistic teachings. Pythagoras followed a similar path, as did Herodotus. Ancient Rome built up its own jurisprudence on the bedrock provided by Greece in many respects, which in turn was influenced by previous developments in Israel.

The Reformation is largely credited with giving a generating impulse to northern and central Europe's development in scientific, technological, economic and political realms. At one time it was northern Europe that borrowed from southern Europe and Moorish (Islamic) Spain but the borrowings were reversed in later centuries. A similar story could be told for the development of Central and South America and for the Indian subcontinent of Central Asia.

The case of religious influence in China is interesting. Owing to its philosophical and religious teachings, primarily associated with Buddhism, China became one of the most powerful nations in history, making contributions in every branch of knowledge – philosophy, culture, economics, exploration and statecraft. But Buddhist practice, with its intellectual and philosophical richness, turned ever inward and monastic and ceased to offer useful guidance in statecraft and secular spheres. After the Confucianist spiritual and moral revival had spent its force, China fell prey to internal schisms and warfare. Finally, it was possible in the 19th century for a small number of Britons to take over its capital and in the 20th for Japan to conquer, sack and pillage it. After the rise of Maoism and the defeat of all its opponents by 1949, with its unique mix of native Confucianism, Hegelian and Marxist dialectics and reconstituted Leninism, it again became a world power, if only militarily. With a measured and rising adoption of western capitalism in production, labour management and financial institutions – institutions the wellspring of which is Islam – it now is fast becoming a true world economic super state. The credit for this turn of events is in its shifting and pragmatic philosophical alignments, as shown by its ancient and recent political and philosophical declarations. But the spirit of nationalist purpose is now very strong in China. It remains to be seen if this becomes transformed into a general spiritual philosophy of statecraft and governance.

The social and economic set of attributes required by nations today is far different from those needed in the past, when it was still possible to live relatively isolated from the great currents that transform the world. That older derived philosophies of national character and striving have produced less than stellar results in modern times is not evidence that they lack efficacy but only that the world has changed and so must our approach to governance and collective leadership.

Conclusion

This chapter has explored the unity in purpose, methodology, means and ends of scientific and religious ways of investigation and analysis. It argued that both use the same methods and have complementary ends, which include explaining their respective worlds in their own respective terms. It has shown that both assert that the means employed determine the ends obtained. Because divine teachings predate science and advanced technology as far as is known, it is evident that the Prophets and Messengers of God themselves inculcated the scientific method and evidentiary procedures, which were later utilized by mankind as tools for analysing the phenomenal world.

It also argued that ideological thought processes, by inserting themselves into religion and science, are responsible for their separation and mutual exclusivity. Ideology has been discussed at length to provide an understanding of its relentless and corrupting will to power. Its morality is whatever helps the cause of ideology to get and maintain temporal rule, that any means can be utilized and are justified in pursuit of this exalted goal. The accumulation of ideology in human minds necessitates the constant reappearance of divine Messengers sent by God to rejuvenate and restate the divine purpose and to set civilization's advancement on a straight path once again. Since subsequent revelations comprehend all past ones, the religious process continues to advance in sophistication, complexity, flexibility and its capacity to address the changing conditions of humankind. The divine message continues to be responsible for motivating the scientific, political and economic progress of human society.

These arguments for the pre-eminence of divine speech in the progression of the human world were supported with historical examples tracing the dispensation of religious teachings and their associated effect in the rise and decline of national and regional fortunes. Even the reflected light of religious revelations was shown to be responsible for national advancement. It is hoped that this chapter has been able to establish an acceptable basis for the existence of a unity of expository process for science and religion. Establishing the argument that religious and scientific means of revealing truth are practically identical has the effect of rending the 'veils of glory' surrounding divine speech, veils which have prevented a fuller understanding and appreciation of divine revelation and its applicability to the human world.

It is now possible to rationally interrogate the verses of God as revealed in the Qur'án with respect to their economic teachings and to follow their dispersion into the larger society, Islamic and non-Islamic, without being burdened by false assertions that divine speech is not amenable to such an inquiry and that employing such a process in analysing divine speech is inappropriate and unfruitful. Establishing the argument that religious and scientific means of revealing truth are practically identical has the effect of rending the 'veils of glory' surrounding divine speech, which have prevented a fuller understanding and appreciation of divine revelation and its applicability to the human world. The hope is that this will open up Qur'ánic dialogues to a broader context wherein they find applicability and where their pre-eminent influence in the human world can better be appreciated and analysed.

1

Economics in Science

Those with a little experience working professionally in the sciences live with it but the uninitiated are always surprised to discover that the natural and physical sciences have not exactly rolled out the welcome mat for the social sciences, such as economics, sociology, anthropology, etc. Physical sciences have criticized the social sciences for not really being sciences at all. Economists themselves have worried about how scientific their science is. Gunnar Myrdal wrote a classic paper that asked 'How Scientific are the Social Sciences?', arguing that they can never provide the type of certainty in results of which the natural sciences are capable. Karl Popper, the Nobel-winning philosopher, has discussed this at length in numerous articles and books, such as *The Poverty of Historicism*. The natural sciences utilize carefully controlled experiments to analyse creation. Because economics is not experimental *per se* and deals with the unpredictable world of human activity and actions, it finds itself periodically attacked as unscientific. That would explain the entrenchment of all forms of higher mathematics and statistics into economics, even beyond the point of diminished returns with respect to useful gains in understanding economic phenomena. It is as if this alone would provide it with a legitimizing mantle, a way to say 'Me, too!' to the other branches. This use of mathematics in all its endeavours and pronouncements, or the need to prove all economic results mathematically, can distort any science and is not always necessary or without cost. It is also tautological: mathematics is a language and there is as much bad maths as good maths in science.

This chapter discusses how economics fits into science, what makes it a science and how it has changed in recent decades. We are not going to get too technical but we do need to understand how economics analyses the world and what tools it uses. This will help us to see how it can be used effectively to analyse the Holy Qur'án with respect to its economic content. Here we will talk about how science, and economics in particular, used models to simplify and abstract what it is interested in from the complexity of the real world. We also need to make sure that economics is not confused with some of its derivatives, such as marketing, finance, trade, etc.

It turns out that economic phenomena are far too complex for full representation using standard mathematical applications. Economic systems are not often smooth and continuous but rather characterized by volatility, discontinuities and abrupt changes. Under these circumstances standard mathematical tools, such as differential and integral calculus, are of limited use, being able only to illustrate some of what is happening under very restricted circumstances. Basing economic theories on such results yields little useful information, even if it is tractable and the mathematics is easy and well-mannered. This is being discovered after much pain and many reverses in the confident policy suggestions based on standard academic economic research.

Of course, economics established much of its fundamental insights using integral and differential calculus; in fact the economic cosmology familiar to most persons, such as the marginal revolution in economics, has been a great step forward in our understanding of economic phenomena. The difficulty is in what qualifies under these results. Many instances exist where the use of differential calculus has given misleading results. But thanks to advances in computer power we can now use more sophisticated and appropriate mathematical techniques, including fractal analysis and many nonlinear and discontinuous system analytical techniques. In addition, this is providing better social and political policy results.

We are also going back and testing some of our most cherished 'first principles' to see if they really are as good as their advertising says they are. Without getting into specifics, the results are mixed; but happily, the process of discovering and rooting out systematic errors and critically testing our model assumptions is being carried out by economists themselves, for the most part, and this is hopeful news. Let's look at some of the elements of scientific modelling.

For something to be scientific its findings must be arrived at using proper principles of proof, evidence and falsifiability of results. What is required, in other words, is that its findings be in the form of testable hypotheses, presented as a logical construction or model.

The Introduction analysed the process of knowing and how science interrogates the world to come up with durable and useful results, results that form the basis of applications that enrich our lives and advance civilization itself. Now we must know something about scientific modelling and causality and how economics is firmly established in this process. Then we can understand what is a science as a specific branch of inquiry having its own explanations, methodology, etc.

What is a scientific model? What makes a good model? A scientific model is a working explanation of reality. Sometimes it is a generalization of something observed. An apple falls from a tree, so I generalize that all apples fall from trees, then that all things fall earthward, etc. We see that a young person left to fend for himself after his family unit has broken down has become unruly, rebellious, untrusting and morose, is in trouble at school and that his planning horizon has attenuated. Based on this observation we generalize the following: young people whose families have been weakened and where they have been left to find their own way without daily adult supervision and intervention in their affairs tend to become more and more uncivilized, become incapable of learning in a structured environment, are rebellious and exhibit signs of depression and paranoia. They also become more now-centred and self-centred. If, after gathering appropriate data and testing it, we find this statement (called the experimental hypothesis) to be *not incorrect*, then we accept it as a useful model of this situation until a better model comes along to displace it. All models have certain things in common. They all rely on assumptions and these assumptions say under what circumstances the model's results can be relied upon. A 'robust' model is one that gives appropriate and useful results even when important assumptions have been relaxed. For example, the principle of the conservation of energy found in Newtonian mechanics and encountered in high school physics classes relies on the assumption of there being no friction, air pressure, etc., that act to 'leak' energy out of the system. Monetary economics, the branch of economics that studies how much money an economy needs at any time, subscribes to this same principle of conservancy, even while admitting the existence of 'leakages' such as hoarding, currency destruction and other ways that money is just lost in the economy. Otherwise it maintains that 'what goes in must come out' somehow and all of it must be accounted for.

This same conservation principle is asserted in religion, of course. In their statements and dialogues the founders of religion and Prophets assure us that all our deeds are recorded and that whatever we have done will be shown to us in a record after this life is finished. They have said that this is true even 'to the extent of a mustard seed'. However, since what is being preserved begins in one dimension and is preserved in another entirely hidden from us here, the process of convincing humans of this principle of the conservation of deeds and actions is complex and challenging, to say the least.[1] The Prophets succeed in convincing their listeners of this and of other things where there is what might be termed a 'data problem' by the use of models constructed of logic and rational argument. This was so successful that the people hearing logical arguments for the first time called them 'magic' because of their power to convince. 'And when Our clear verses are recited to them, the disbelievers say of the truth when it reaches them, "This is plain magic!"'[2] Parables are models.

Einstein also used logic models to advance his theories. They were accepted tentatively until technology finally advanced enough to verify his arguments empirically.

Must the model be judged on the reasonableness of its required assumptions? Generally, no. A model's value is based almost entirely on how well it predicts the behaviour it describes. In the physical and in the social sciences a good predicting model is superior to all others. Knowledge of this enables us to understand how science and religion advance. Over time models get replaced with better ones, ones that predict more accurately and do it more simply and explain ever more phenomena in use. We still teach Newtonian physics in every university, even though it requires certain assumptions to work. These assumptions are usually not met in nature but it hasn't caused much harm. Later on, engineers learn probabilistic techniques to make sure that the elevator is, in fact, up to standard and the refinery will not blow up.

When a set of related models are combined into a generalized approach to a wide array of problems it becomes a *paradigm*. According to Kuhn,[3] the paradigm acts to shelter its models and makes some of the research easier by relieving the scientist of the constant burden to demonstrate every aspect of a proposition in order to obtain needed funding, for acceptance in peer-reviewed journals, and to found and defend a life's work of research. In this way some things can be accepted as self-evident and not in need of further testing. Thus once we accept the primacy and infallibility of the Prophet of God based on the evidence, for example, we then are willing to accept those things not accessible to direct proof. And once we accept a theory of market behaviour, it is then possible to form models based on its results and demonstrate by proof only those aspects of the model that are new or previously not demonstrated.

A paradigm goes through its own ageing process. First, it is fought by the *status quo* before being accepted; then it experiences its golden time of creativity as its explanatory power becomes better understood. The paradigm becomes ever more successful in explaining an increasing array of issues. Eventually, its *status quo* reputation becomes unassailable, a sort of 'received wisdom' above the need for testing and a fortress of thinking against any challenges based on new information that may dispute its findings. Researchers apply its world view to everything. But there is a clear danger of the paradigm overreaching its scope, declaring to be now 'explained' what in fact might be pure speculation. Broadening the applicability of the paradigm increases the danger of bad science and the need to test it in use, even while the perception for such need is fading. Thereafter, the paradigm's usefulness declines. Instead of advancing the science, it begins to exist only to advance the personal interests of its practitioners and 'true believers'. Logical flaws creep into the research, adding to the doubtfulness of its findings. In the meantime, models that do not fit into the paradigm, and even seem to disprove all or parts of it, are ignored until finally the accumulation of 'super-research' models overwhelm the existing paradigm and completely displace it. Thus Ptolemaic (geocentric) cosmology was replaced by Copernican cosmology, Newtonian mechanics by Einsteinian relativity – and one religious world view by another, more dynamic and modern one.

The phases of religious development and religious revelation show this process clearly. The Prophet, through dialogues and actions, exhortations and patterned living, attracts a limited number of followers who proceed to establish this as a new belief system, a spiritual paradigm that largely replaces the old. The best and the brightest, both young and old, rush to learn this new system and devote their creative energies to researching its various aspects. Institutions are established to safeguard its structure and spread its findings far and wide. Eventually a world civilization is generated from this system, since it offers advancements in all phases of social discourse over what it replaced. In other words, it offers better answers and its models predict better, make 'more sense' and are less restrictive.

Over time, however, ideology and orthodoxy replace its original energy and freedom, beginning with the rejection of the progressive and continuously inventive and innovative nature of divine revelation underlying the basis of all religious appearances. A rigid hierarchy is formed to defend the paradigm against 'heresy' – actually, to defend the interests of its practitioners, who seek only the continuance of their prestige and perquisites, all bestowed upon them by the exalted status of the existing paradigm-power structure. What had been the cause of human advancement becomes the cause of its retrogression.

Finally, another Prophet appears to reinvigorate societal life and restore its purposeful development. Another (religious) paradigm is formed from these new and potent models of reality and the pattern is repeated. As in religion, so it is in science and in economics.

Grouping paradigms, methodologies and, most importantly, topics for critical investigation yields a distinct science. Biology studies the physical properties of animals including humans, physics studies the mechanics of physical systems in space, large and small, and economics studies human transactions in exchanges, large and small. Religion and related studies analyse the laws pertaining to the non-material aspects of the human condition. In each case the object is to explain reality in terms of the science in question and to derive its fundamental laws and principles.

Using this definition changes the purpose of religion as generally accepted. Here it means *a branch of rational inquiry and discovery dedicated to uncovering and applying ontological and spiritual laws and principles pertaining to non-material reality and its associated transactional behaviour.* The identified source of its often abstract, symbolic and minimally constructed material is taken to be the source of reality itself, i.e. God, in the form of a specially appointed and prepared human mouthpiece. Evidence for this is to be found in the dialogues that comprise the source material for the associated paradigm. This is a very sterile-sounding definition. Of course, religion is much more, or much less, for each human being. It is personal and involves the deepest and most fundamental of human understandings and relationships. Not surprisingly, many have the same feelings about what science is or aspires to be in its ideal state. This is not as bizarre as it sounds when we remember what a gulf exists in most person's minds between these two worlds. It has been a millennium since a major religion dedicated itself to rational inquiry and provided a welcoming and stimulating home for scientists. Since then scientists have had to go their own way and so invested material science with all the home-like characteristics needed to make of it a full life, in need of no outside support except funding from sympathetic power structures.

Economic science in its modern (western) form is said to have begun with the publishing of Adam Smith's *The Wealth of Nations* in 1776. Previous to this there had been significant research into various aspects of the national economy, such as the quantity of money and banking systems, wages and returns to capital, undertaken in Poland, France, Germany and elsewhere, with some originating with Aristotle. But Smith, known as a political and moral philosopher who emerged as perhaps the most distinguished thinker of the Scottish intellectual renaissance of the 18th century, created a model of the entire national economy and treated practically all its known aspects. The book discussed employment and wages, rents and capital, international trade and the firm, governmental economic objectives and many other things. It also characterized and defined the actors in an economy and explained why they were there, what they wanted and how they were expected to act in given circumstances. There is not a lot of higher mathematics in *The Wealth of Nations* and Smith is not sparing with his characterizations of what he considered economically or financially short-sighted behaviour, for two reasons. The first is that mathematics in its modern form, using calculus and other advanced techniques, was just becoming formalized. Calculus would give economics several key insights into transactional behaviour and also equip it with facile tools for analysis. But this was some time off in the future and awaited a comprehensive treatment by Marshall and others.[4]

The second reason for the lack of moral detachment in the book is that economics was thought of as part of politics and moral philosophy and not a distinct branch of science. As such, economic writings were supposed to be prescriptive and directed to opining on the direction society should take. Today this is called 'normative economics', as distinct from 'positive economics' which is considered free of prescriptive recommendations. Critical analysis free of moral pronouncements in the spirit of chemistry or physics was as yet expected of the new subject of economics and it was not thought of as necessarily explanatory in nature. But *The Wealth of Nations* would change that by putting on display the analytical potential of this new branch of inquiry and moving it beyond a mere descriptive presentation.

Nineteenth-century Europe and England would become fecund suppliers of economic ideas and principles. Scientists and others would expand on Smith's work, developing the analytical potential of economics and establishing its scientific foundations. The great John Stuart Mill wrote several comprehensive works on economics. Among many contributions to the science, he suggested a principle for quantifying human wants. Contemporarily, Thomas Malthus described population growth and food sufficiency problems and thereby set out one of the national economic challenges in the starkest of terms. Here benefit–cost analysis was showcased and established itself as the analytical heart of economics. It also enabled economics to distinguish itself as a distinct branch of science, with its own vocabulary and utilizing the best traditions of mathematical modelling and critical analysis, rather than merely a political movement. It employed cold logic and refused to go beyond benefit–cost analysis into prescriptive exhortations. It was aided in its establishment as the benefit–cost analytical tool for human conditions by contemporaneous political movements in England and elsewhere, including the work of Herbert Spencer, who also influenced the models of Charles Darwin (even though the reverse is falsely believed).

What to do with the information economics came up with was to be strictly a social/political decision and could have nothing to do with scientific inquiry. By this time the word 'economics' was popularly coined, just as, say, 'ecology' would be popularly coined in the early to mid-1970s in the United States and elsewhere.

The recently codified mathematics of the calculus, with its ability to model how things changed from one state to another and to express this as a rate, and even to relate these rates in a quantified system, opened many doors in economics. Mathematical modelling of economic principles began to accelerate and the idea of marginal valuation – the value of the next unit of something produced or consumed (the next dollar earned, the next worker employed, the next truffle eaten) – began to take centre stage: the first derivative of a function represented the instantaneous rate of change with respect to a controlled value, giving economic modellers an appreciation of shadow prices and other technical elements. Really good answers, answers to some of the trickiest and oldest economic puzzles known, were being solved and explained using new mathematical tools. Also about this time market structures began to be analysed for attributes that included efficiency, efficacy and market power. Concepts of monopoly (single seller), monopsony (single buyer) and pure and perfect competition were developed, as well as the nature of public goods.

The real change in the study of economics, however, had to do with its formalization by the end of the 19th century. The nature and timing of this change has meant defining what economics would and would not attempt to explain. Defining its boundaries of inquiry very early in its progress as a science, legitimizing some lines and declaring others to be 'out of bounds', has had a profound effect on the direction economics has taken over the last century. The reason is that economics – and social science in general – is still discovering its potential for explanation. Deciding on its boundaries of inquiry and methodology at such an early stage is thus premature and potentially harmful to its development. Indeed, scientists who extended the range of economic inquiry into areas of life hitherto off-limits, so to speak, have won many of the Nobel prizes for economics. Economic analysis has been used to model the family, racial prejudice and discrimination, art, sports and entertainment, advertising and the nature of bureaucracies. The point is that it is not likely that we can know the developmental direction for a science in so short a time from its inception, especially when the world is in such flux and so many new paradigms in all sciences are replacing previously unassailable ones. But there is still strong disagreement about what economics should and should not investigate or what methodologies are appropriate, even among all those methodologies capable of yielding repeatable results. One area of dispute is the degree to which economic phenomena can in fact be modelled using the elementary tools of differential calculus. The assumption which must hold is that the processes to be modelled are continuous. This is exceedingly hard to verify beyond carefully defined sets of possibilities. Where this assumption does not hold, differential calculus results are inappropriate and misleading. The misapplication and brave acceptance of differential calculus results that are inappropriate have been the cause of overextending model results where they do not hold and promoting derived public policies that are not warranted nor supported by the science. These actions have reduced respect for what economics can do well and surely and diminished its prestige in the public's mind. Compare the number of jokes dealing with economists with those involving practitioners in the other sciences, such as physics, chemistry, etc., and the situation becomes clear. Only statisticians attract the same kind of unwanted attention.

The Process of Economic Analysis

Economic inquiry almost always involves *benefit–cost* analysis. This is the process of defining and summing appropriate costs and benefits involved in making a decision or following a certain policy. This can be a trivial process or enormously complex, depending on the definition of the costs and benefits involved. Another complexity is introduced when decisions have effects over time, so future values and the future importance of things must be accounted for somehow. What are the costs and benefits of building a new state school in a region? Should the money for its construction come from borrowing or from increasing taxes? What about the benefits and costs for a new bridge expected to have a useful life of a hundred years? How would we arrive at the correct balance between work and leisure? Should more food be grown in favour of producing more cash-yielding export crops?

These things form mainstream economic analytical subjects. But there are other possibilities where the employment of benefit–cost analysis would be appropriate and could give useful insights into many social problems. What are the social benefits and costs of advertising directly to children and treating them as adults in the market? What about universal healthcare, global warming and women's rights? Finally, what about the economics of spiritual and religious pursuits?

Before closing this chapter and moving to the main body of the book, a few words should be said about the tools of economic analysis and its methodology. Broadly speaking there are three.

The first tool is empirical/statistical data analysis. Cross-sectional or time series data are collected and properly interrogated using statistical methods to arrive at useful conclusions about what has happened economically, e.g. has a tax break resulted in increased investment? Was American slavery really unprofitable? Has the Clean Water Act worked as intended and what are its benefits and costs to businesses and the public? Compared to other methods and depending on the statistical technique employed, statistical analysis introduces fewer behavioural assumptions. While such introductions would not ordinarily trouble practising social statisticians, they might cause non-scientists to question the results. The display of specialized and highly refined knowledge required for statistical analysis usually works to allay such public questioning, however, often for good reason.

The second tool is mathematical programming, where a mathematical model of the hypothesis is devised having all the essential elements needed for the analysis. Here, explicit assumptions about personal behaviour are built into the model. For example, it is assumed that the market agent (a person, business, government, etc.) wishes to maximize utility, however defined. This says that the business wants to maximize profits or market share, output from inputs, sales, etc., the person wants to maximize income, consumption, security or some other chosen value of happiness, and that the country wants to maximize exports or border security, etc. Parameters and variables are decided upon and mathematics is used to solve the system.

The mathematical algorithms used to solve the system are *optimal-seeking*, meaning that they are designed to find the extreme value – the largest, the smallest, the cheapest – and can find these answers with respect to a set of constraints. So we can say, 'Maximize profit from food production subject to the need to grow corn for the dairy cows, where each unit of corn sold earns this much, every unit of milk earns this much and where available land for corn production or for dairy is as given.' Again, 'maximize national security, given this number of troops, this size navy', etc. Often it is desired to achieve several goals at once, so weighted values are selected to give due importance to the achievement of each goal. This is goal programming (GP) or multiple objective programming (MOP). Many other types are used as well: integer programming, where fractions of units are disallowed; network programming, finding the shortest route through a network, subject to the need to visit specified locations, etc. Facility location, plant layout, the journeys of travelling salesmen, bulk deliveries, logistics in general – all these problems are solved with this method.

More complexity is added when things are specified across time periods or where things must be phased in over time. For example, when growing crops or raising children, certain things must be ready for use at specified times, and if not ready, the whole enterprise may fail to produce satisfactory results or actually produce unwanted results! These problems are called dynamic and a special mathematics has been devised to handle them.

As we shall see, one particular method for solving dynamic problems – Optimal Control Theory – can easily be adapted to modelling and solving many societal problems, such as how much capital a community should form and maintain over time in order to sustain a specified level of economic growth or consumption. Reformulated, it is equally capable of modelling drug addiction or investments in children or other family and social welfare issues. Optimal Control Theory is a branch of the calculus of variations. Unfortunately its formulations and analysis are accessible only to students of high level mathematics. Graphical techniques are available to display some of its results, however, but this too requires an understanding of advanced mathematics.

Finally, the nature of the problem to be analysed could be such that it is best to devise a computer program to mimic its attributes. Computer simulation has been used to solve many complex problems having statistical, mathematical and other aspects combined. Computer program code is written representing the system to be analysed, whether a factory, a farm, a college, a market sector or another economic system. Subroutines or separate blocks of code perform certain functions then return control to the main program. These might include adding statistical or probability characteristics to the result or performing mathematical programming on a previous result. Then the system is run many times, perhaps thousands of times, to simulate time in use. Results are then analysed.

At the heart of each of these tools are assumptions about what reality is and how it works. This may seem tautological – using tools with embedded assumptions about the subject under analysis – and that charge cannot entirely be dismissed. The situation is made more or less unsettling by observing that in this way economic science and religious dialogues are very closely associated, not just in sharing the same process of rational inquiry but in what they both assume about human behaviour and motivation. Thus economic analysis has as its foundation the pronouncements of the Prophets of God. The remainder of this book analyses these assumptions and this relationship.

2

Life as Economic Science

In the last chapter we looked at economics and its emergence as a science on its own. Here we look at the economic world view, which we need to understand in order to see how it analyses life.

What is Economics?

Economics is the analysis and modelling of *the exchange* in all its possible aspects. The context is in attempting to achieve unlimited wants with limited resources. It can model any exchange where benefits and costs can be specified, even where not quantifiable. In this sense there is no decision you can make that is entirely free of economic consequences. Any stock entity, money, time, sunlight, attention span can be treated as a resource from which benefits must derive according to some plan or behaviour.

While based on the individual acting in a market, many of the most important economic results have to do with group activity: the theory of the firm, consumer behaviour, international trade, unions and management, investment theory and national economic growth. By modelling group behaviour many of the results are useful and insightful but not all of them.

Of the numerous contributions to our understanding of reality given to us from economics the following stand out as particularly important.

Marginality

The concept of marginality mentioned in the last chapter has enabled us to appreciate how economics understands the way all rational decisions are supposedly made. When we decide to do or not to do something, what is considered exactly? It turns out – and this has been repeatedly shown – that we do not consider total costs or benefits of every decision but only consider the value of doing something in relation to what has just been done or experienced. In other words, we analyse marginal values, not absolute values. We are not talking about wisdom here, just how most people in most circumstances really decide to do things. Of course, wise people are more concerned with total costs and benefits of every decision but most people are not wise or are not wise all the time. When we see children and teenagers deciding to do things, it is striking how much they use marginal rather than absolute values in decision-making. And that, of course, is the problem!

What are these marginal values and how do they differ from total or absolute values? The marginal value is your valuation of something with respect to what has just occurred or will just occur. For example, how much are you willing to pay for a drink of water? It is needed for life itself, after all, but what you care about is how thirsty you are *at the moment of the offer*. If you are very thirsty at the time, you demand a lot; if you have just had a drink, then maybe nothing is fine. This decision process takes place continuously in our lives, whether it is to watch TV for one more minute, based on the benefits and costs of doing so, to get up and get going or to turn over and get some more sleep, etc.

Costs with respect to what? With respect to the next best use of the resource or opportunity in question. If it is a moment of time, then the cost of doing one thing is what else you could do and the benefits you are giving up by not doing it with that available moment. Thus the cost of fixing your bathroom sink depends on what else you could be doing with the time and how much your time is worth in its next best use. As a day labourer for $11 an hour, it is a money-saving plan to fix your own sink; as an orthopaedic surgeon at $1,200 an hour, it makes no sense at all, except taken as recreation. The decision to fix the sink also carries the risk of harming the tools of your trade, i.e. your hands and eyes, which you use daily in your work as a surgeon.

Such a decision-making process is not guaranteed always to yield the best results – far from it. In fact, such marginal thinking is the very reason young people are likely to commit themselves to actions which, though pleasurable now, may have devastatingly high costs later on in life, costs they fail to consider because they are not 'wise', that is, because they do not consider the future and the total or absolute cost or benefit of present actions.

It is a cliché that most of the genuinely precious things in life have high initial costs but yield surpassingly large bounties in the future, while things offering pleasure today often demand that a high cost be paid later. This is like the New England joke, where two farmers are chatting.

'The weather is good this spring.'
'Yeah but we'll pay for it.'

Economics can show the devastatingly high cost of marginally based impulsive behaviour but it cannot tell us what to do. Its only statement is to encourage 'efficiency' in the use of resources, so as not to threaten the existence of the system itself. Applying this principle says: Do not just knock someone down who makes you angry because this threatens the system; you go to jail or could be killed in retaliation. But are divine teachings prescriptive? Certainly, in the same way parenting is. That is, the parent knows that we are free to make any decision or take any action we choose but that there will always be consequences which must be experienced. The divine Messengers, therefore, explain what those consequences will be and encourage us not to do things that threaten the system's survival or its quality of life. Assume you want to avoid difficulties; then you should follow these instructions carefully. This is the process.

The teachings of God, as revealed in all the holy books, encourage absolute value thinking, that is, the total costs and total benefits of a thing must be considered. These teachings force far-seeing thinking, which is called wisdom, i.e. the ability to see the total benefits and costs of any action. Every private decision has public consequences, whether trivial or profound; spiritual thinking forces us to take such consequences into account in all our actions and decisions.

Let's detour for a moment from our main theme to see an example of marginal thinking costing us real money. Do we spend differently when we use a credit card rather than cash? Some economists maintain that the rational market agent will eschew the use of credit if its cost adds so much to the cost of the good that the purchase would be 'uneconomical'. But here is an example of marginal values being considered rather than absolute values. (Certainly one would expect economists to be free from committing such a mental blunder!) The credit is more likely to be treated as a *sales coupon* in use where the item considered for purchase is the thing of importance, while cash in the hand will certainly be thought of in terms of *all the other things it could be used for,* keeping the buyer's attention on the cash itself rather than the potential purchase item. Thus with the credit card the focus is on whether to buy *this item* or not buy it, while with cash the focus is on what *the money* can best be used for. The experience is that those using cash are generally more thrifty than those using credit and have less of a tendency to buy on impulse. And this result flows directly from applying the principle of marginality, which has been demonstrated using economics, to human behaviour, empirical test results and mathematical proofs. Graphical analysis can also be employed to illustrate marginal principles. All that is needed to produce the present result is to understand how a dollar of credit is viewed in immediate use compared to a dollar of cash.

Utility

Utility is the economic word for material and/or non-material benefits, happiness or bliss; and maximizing utility is what all life does. It is, however, a mistake to think that utility derives only from material consumption, selfish aggrandizement or acquisitiveness. It can just as well be the satisfaction of self-sacrificing behaviour, asceticism or the joy of dispensing justice or telling the truth, or the elation from discovering the solution to a complex and challenging problem. Depending on the individual and the circumstances, maximizing the experience of any of these altruistic and positive joys could be the goal. The personal tastes and preferences of the individual will determine this. And these in turn depend on the upbringing, genetics and environment existing when that person was maturing. The following must be clearly understood at the outset of any discussion of utility. *The concept of utility exists between two absurd and useless extremes.* At one extreme utility is capable of quantifying the interpersonal strength and importance of human wants and thereby applying mathematics to derive some kind of personal or aggregated social value function. This is impossible. Such things like utility are only partly revealed to the person himself; how much more hidden from others they must be. Furthermore, the idea of a closed form mathematical utility function is equally absurd and preposterous. Wants are just too dynamic and changeable, always depending on the context in which things are measured.

The second extreme is that utility can be abstracted to include practically any kind of human want and, by extension, explain the motive behind any kind of human behaviour, since it can never be ruled out that whatever was committed must have been done to maximize personal utility. Even if technically true, and its opposite cannot be conclusively proved, such derivations are essentially useless, non-instructive and tautological, a trivial exercise.

Between these two worthless extremes sits a useful abstraction capable of modelling behaviour comparatively and explaining a lot of otherwise puzzling human actions. Particularly useful is the concept of marginal utility, as explained above and developed further in the following pages, and that we care more about something's immediate effect and less about its total or overall effect. There is a vast social science literature empirically documenting this finding.

It is one of the main contributions of economic science to human understanding to have discovered that the abstract concept of utility can informatively be used to model the complexity of human motivation in many circumstances. Utility is a deconstruction of the assemblage of the myriad wants, needs and desires abiding in a region between brain and heart. As such, it can be represented as a variable and used in mathematical and statistical analysis. While measuring ordinal utility (that some activity represents some number of 'utils') is a fiction, measuring cardinal utility (that *this* is preferred to *that*) is obviously possible and very instructive in empirical practice. It is frankly hard to imagine how social sciences could have advanced as far as they have without the instrumentality offered by the concept of personal utility.

This concept finds further use in aggregated form as social utility, an abstraction of social wants and demands. It finds application in deciding how a society will likely make saving and spending decisions in war and peacetime. For example, for whatever reason, in some – but not all – countries, sports heroes are paid more than college professors, a reflection of a public consensus that sports entertainment is worth more than education.

Of course, society never really decides things in such a stark form because total values of such decisions are usually hidden and hard to conceive. But it doesn't matter: the sum of all such decisions will determine how much a society dedicates to the needs of production and how much to consumption and enjoyable pastimes. Compare China to the United States in this regard: the Chinese save about 40 per cent of their income, while Americans actually have had a negative savings rate lately, that is, they spend even more than they make over time. In China, consumer spending comprises about 25 per cent of the gross domestic product (GDP), with production and other expenditures comprising the rest, while in the US consumer spending is over 65 per cent of the GDP. And this difference is the result of the collective aggregated taste and preference set for each nation, which comprises the respective social utility function. So, what happens if Americans stop buying things they don't need? The economy goes into a slump. What about in China? Not much, because they sell to everyone else and their domestic consumption is not a very large factor in the sale of most produced goods in China, which are destined for export. This is useful information based entirely on social and personal utility functions.

If the object of economics is to explain the world in its own terms, the object of economic activity is said to be *individual utility maximization*. The evident simplicity of this statement can be very misleading and deceptive because it seems to enshrine selfishness and hedonism above all other personal goals. But that is definitely not true. When we work in groups, for example, our personal goals are subsumed within the goals of the group and our happiness and satisfaction derive from the success of the group enterprise. We see our greatness in the achieved greatness of the group, be it the family, the school, the corporation, the nation, the cause or humankind in its entirety. As social beings, and as history will attest, our need to derive positive utility from the achievement of group goals is very strong. Ordinarily, we think of selfishness as doing things for yourself with no thought given to how our actions might affect others now or later. Wanting to help others because it makes us happy, wanting to die a martyr for a great social or religious cause, giving all our money to charity – these actions are not usually thought of as selfish behaviours. Only in its all-inclusive and trivialized sense can these actions be called selfish. Even so, some argue that they display 'enlightened selfishness'. I reject this characterization as demoting every human action, however pure and sincere, to the hard-wired stimulus-response level of scorpions. Evidence will show (though not presented here) that humans exist at the nexus of the material–spiritual universes. Defining all our actions according to one set of criteria is presumptuous and grossly misleading.

The Concepts of Public Goods and Externalities

Ask economists why a government is needed and expect to receive a variety of answers. Some will contend that its sole purpose should be to provide third party guarantees for exchanges and nothing more. Others will declare that it must take responsibility for guiding the progress of the national economy and for the security of its dependents. Why this broad range of responses? It has to do with the nature of what are called public goods and externalities.

Some of the most essential goods and services we require include such things as roads and highways, laws and policing, educational infrastructure, national defence, sewerage networks and utility grids, clean water and air. These can never be supplied to us by private enterprise or ordinary market activities. Unit pricing relies on a unit of production being related to costs of production and per unit value in consumption. But some goods do not allow this kind of calculus. There may be no way to measure their actual value in use. In fact, there may be no one-to-one relationship between a unit of cost and a unit of associated benefit. Economics is responsible for discovering the nature of such goods and showing how they must be supplied. As time passes and the world becomes more integrated, the need to understand and arrange for the supply of these essential goods increases. Indeed, the prosperity of the world will depend to a large degree on assuring their presence.

What is the unitary per capita community benefit of a unit of national defence, a mile of road, an hour's worth of a family crisis worker or a graduating high school class? Such goods will never be supplied to the public by private agencies since their value can never be directly quantified and related to the cost of supply. Indeed, there is no way to directly charge users for receiving these benefits. The goods in question are called public goods, not because the public supplies them but because they all share two characteristics. One is that the number of users or the number of times the public good is used does not diminish the amount available. National defence is not divided among the persons using it, where one person being defended reduces the amount available for others. The same is true with available knowledge: your use of it does not reduce its amount for someone else to use. Such a good is called *non-rival* in consumption.

The other characteristic of a public good is that it is impossible to exclude someone from using it. For example, all persons in a state are protected by its armed forces, whether or not they wish to be protected or agree with defence policies. How could someone supply such a good when users who do not pay cannot be excluded from using it?

Arguably the most important public good is the system of jurisprudence, the various laws that exist to regulate human activity and actions, including regulating practically all transactions of tangible value or price. As we shall see, no exchange or transaction is possible without the presence of such a system. But since it is derived from an even more fundamental set of teachings – divine teachings from the Messengers of God – the system of jurisprudence is maybe the second most important public good. The Most Great Public Good could therefore be the divine Revelations of God, from which all other things flow in the fullness of time.

Economics analysed the properties of public goods and showed that their supply must be arranged by a collective body and paid from tax revenues. Today, the need for public goods is not disputed, nor the need for a central government to arrange for their purchase. What is still debated is the quantity of public goods that is required at any time and their overall importance to the proper functioning of the national economy. However, there is no doubt that where public institutions and goods are lacking, the economy will underperform.

Another so-called market failure occurs when a market exchange affects those not involved in it – the public consequences of private decisions. Second-hand tobacco smoke is an example. You make the private decision to light up and it has the external consequence of choking the person next to you. Or a factory makes paper and pollutes a nearby stream, making trout fishing impossible and causing other unpleasantness to persons neither working for the plant nor using the paper it makes. Another example is where a person is inoculated against the flu, paying for it himself, to the benefit of those nearby. Left to private markets, the transaction having the negative spillover effect would not be curtailed because its cost is not figured into the price of the good purchased, since not only is the effect external but so is its cost. In the case of the positive externality, the good is under-consumed because its benefit to others does not reduce its private cost.

Economics has studied such situations. In both positive and negative cases the problem is that there is a difference between a good's private price and its public value. What is needed is some way to internalize the externality's cost or benefit and have this reflected in the private price to the consumer or producer. The conclusion is that government could be useful in solving such problems. Economics discovered that the external effect must be assigned as the responsibility, or property, of one of the parties in the exchange. That way a cost can be assigned to it to reduce its presence or a payment offered to increase it where it is beneficial, like the flu inoculation. Today externalities receive much attention from economists and from litigants. The principle of public benefits and costs flowing from private (including corporate) decisions is used to disentangle environmental issues, to pass better property laws and as a reason why otherwise private but risky behaviour should be regulated or outlawed by a central authority. It explains why motorcyclists should be required to wear a helmet and why taking dangerously addictive drugs is illegal.

So we return to the question: what is the proper role of government in the economy? And our answer must include arranging for the supply of needed public goods and adjudicating externalities. For some economists, that about sums up what government should do but, as we shall see, more comprehensive roles are now envisioned, including government making basic provision for all its citizens and dependents and entering into collective security and trade agreements with other states. Basically, this extends the menu of what should be considered public goods or goods having important externalities that society ignores at its own risk. Since an educated populace promotes economic growth and higher levels of production and consumption possibilities, government has taken the lead role in arranging for the supply of education as much as possible. And all advanced economies but one – the United States – have thought it wise and cost effective to arrange for the public provision of health services for their citizens and labourers. Also, public transportation has been addressed by many governments. Many other things are now considered the natural responsibility of governments. This is a big change to what obtained a hundred years ago, when the list of public goods supplied by governments began and usually ended with jurisprudence.

Government therefore functions in a *facilitative* capacity in economic activities. It is therefore a cost to society and must be supported from the produced wealth of society. Here then is the source of all the argument about the size of government and privatization initiatives. If allowed to become too large government costs will become greater than the facilitative benefits of economic activity. But if allowed to become too small, government cannot perform its essential supportive role and the economy will underperform.

Deciding whether government is too large or too small at any time is the source of many arguments within the economics profession and outside it. But the teachings of God revealed in the holy books record with precision the role and responsibilities of government. We ordinarily think of Judaic law and Islamic law as the chief sources until now of divine pronouncements on the correct scope of government. But Confucianism, Daoism, Buddhism, Zoroastrianism and Hinduism all have discussed the proper role of government and rulers.

So now we have established the role of economics in governmental analysis and the role of government in divine teachings. This establishes another bridge to an economic analysis of divine teachings. Not only can it be useful in understanding the economic content of divine Revelation as applied to the individual but also on the benefits and costs for governments functioning in accord with divine teachings.

3
The Spiritual Nature of Economic Investigation

So far we have discussed some of the ways science does its work, how economics fits into the scientific tradition and methodology and a little about what economics has discovered about our lives as lived. We now expand this to fill in the blanks of economic science and the science of purposeful living. After all, the agenda of life is the agenda of economic science, as will be shown.

We now begin the analysis of spiritual laws as they operate on the material plane using the analytical tools of economics. With the development of the marginalist paradigm and the facility offered by utility theory, the specific qualities and nature of the laws indicated and developed in the dialogues of the Prophets is capable of scientific deconstruction, analysis and a surprising amount of quantification. As a practical matter, this takes place in the context of benefit–cost analysis.

Economics is responsible for the development of many useful metrics, familiar to many of us, such as consumer sentiment, income demand elasticity, labour efficiency, and many more. A *metric* is a measuring device, most often an index, so that disparate quantities can be compared for their relative value changes. There is a branch of economics called *cleometrics* which uses historical data to test various claims about what was important in history; for example, the economic impact of commercial railroads in the 19th century, the development of the American and Canadian West to world wheat supply, or the probability that Peninsular Arabia could have risen so high and so rapidly in the absence of the advent of Islam. Econometrics is a branch of economics that uses structured regression analysis and other statistical tools to test variables in an economy, such as GDP, trade balances, demand, the effects of taxes on supply, etc.

If we apply economics to investigate spiritual things and explore its similarities to divine speech as revealed in the Qur'án and other holy books, is this just business as usual for economics or does it merit its own category? 'Spiritualmetrics'? Divine economics? But all knowledge is divinely inspired if it is traced back far enough. Spiritual economics is imprecise. The economics of spirituality is also inaccurate. Suggestions are invited. After all, there is no body of results that stands as a record of previous accomplishment in this field. We are just beginning and have not arrived at a new paradigm. For now, spiritualmetrics, until a better term is devised.

The translation into the material plane of essentially infinitely-valued and unknowable speech containing spiritual laws and ordinances constitutes the collision of the absolute and infinite with the ephemeral, the contingent, the evanescent and the dependent. Humans embrace the infinite by stages, revolutions, reactions, revisions, metamorphoses, and with doubts, troubles and deep concerns over the whole process. Economics, the science of life itself – of life lived – teaches that this human accommodation with the infinite is like a system that is constantly being revised. On a practical level, with respect to the individual action or decision response, *solutions to problems are characterized by what is called in mathematics a saddlepoint, an optimization within a system of constraints.* That is, pleasure is maximized *subject to* the constraint that immorality not be committed; or discomfort is minimized *subject to* the requirement that the goal (knowledge acquisition, work production, character perfection) be attained. When time is an argument the saddlepoint solution gives way to a saddle*path* solution, where the set of all best saddlepoints is found.

Our first application of spiritualmetrics analyses things in time and shows how that mysterious entity which, according to available evidence, exists only in the material plane, is relative in ways that Einsteinians could appreciate. We will see how the perception of time changes as the amount remaining changes and how the process of deciding what to do with the time remaining is a straightforward application of marginal utility analysis in the presence of what are called stock effects, explained below. In order to do this we assume that spiritual laws do in fact operate on the material plane in the sense that intellectual perceptions informed by spiritual teachings are fully operational here and these perceptions, as common experience and the writings of unnumbered religious followers, converts and students will attest, are subject to spiritual laws. The following situations are directly or indirectly treated by the Prophets and Messengers of God, whose often astounding insights into these situations provide the first best approach to their management.

Stock Effects: Subjective Measurement of Time

In life we fulfil unlimited wants from limited resources, broadly defined. We receive bequests of time, inner resolve, health, humour and intelligence while coordination, sense, endurance, some tendency towards baldness and socializing capacity have been given to us by nature and events, and we can use all these things to fulfil our dynamically plastic set of goals. While still young so much time is available to us that it hardly seems to act as an absolute constraint on our life-system at all. This is called the *stock effect.* In the last chapter we saw how marginal valuations for all our decisions can lead to unwise and ultimately costly decisions because they leave out total costs and just look at the value of a thing based on what we just did or how we feel right now. So an impulsive decision could meet the marginal value requirement but flunk the total value requirement, to our loss. Youth are practically defined by their inclination to decide things on impulse.

One theory is that when we are young we think we will live forever, time will never run out, our health will never decline and old age itself is inconceivable as a condition of life. The same type of thinking affects nations, who think they will never run out of educated workers immigrating from overseas, and with the world when it believes the fish in the sea will never run out, or the cheap oil we have grown used to, or the oxygen itself. This type of thinking is called a stock effect and means that there is currently so much of something, running out of it is unimaginable. In 'Proverbs of Hell' William Blake said, 'Bring out number, weight and measure in a year of dearth.'[1] What makes it hellish is that it is a trap. Rather, 'bring out number, weight and measure in a year of plenty' and thus reduce or eliminate years of dearth. The stock effect is what fools the soul into thinking that what is can never be exhausted, even if fixed in amount and even if being drawn down inexorably. Stock effects are almost omnipresent in daily experience. They are represented by the spendthrift credit card holder, the business or government addicted to borrowing, by the smoker contemplating the carton of smokes sitting on the table like a cornucopia of contentment, the 'endless summer', the unlimited time remaining to get to the airport as you lie in bed and the drinker with a weekend's supply of forgetting-juice. What strings all these examples together is the total submersion of time within the subjectivity as conceived in the mind.

In a famous paper for the scientific journal *Science*, Garrett Hardin in 1968 described what he called the 'tragedy of the commons'.[2] The commons refers to the common grazing property that existed in many places in North America and elsewhere before land was fenced off and privatized. The 'tragedy' is that, left to its own management – that is, *no* management – the land will be over-grazed and become worthless.

This is an example of the public good referred to in the last chapter, only in this situation it acts as a public good as long as there are not many users of the resource. But as that number increases the good becomes 'congested', that is, rival in consumption, being used up faster than it can recharge and rejuvenate itself. Finally the system collapses.

And of course the rate at which time *itself* is being used up is an example of the ultimate stock effect. Benoit Mandelbrot, in his book *The (Mis)Behavior of Markets*, states that markets are not just volatile in prices but actually turbulent, that is, there are long periods when nothing happens and markets are calm, followed by other times when things happen quickly and time is compressed in the minds of traders. This is another example of subjective time and each of us can relate many instances of time seeming to change values of quantities at different occasions in our lives.

This subjective relationship with time, resulting in part from the stock effect, leads to a primary deception that is central to the life condition.

Stock effects – the deceptiveness of having a large sum now which must last over an unknowable period – is closely related to another deception. Call it the *network effect*: achieving a highly satisfying result only to have it become worthless when opportunities suddenly change.

Perhaps you remember being in school and waiting for the last bell of the day to grant your release. You might have been in 'home room' pretending to study while thinking only of getting out. Then your teacher, in an act of inexplicable kindness, gave you the task of taking the erasers *outside* and banging them free of chalk dust. Compared to sitting at your desk this was like heaven! Going *outside,* to be in the fresh air and weather, your eyes freely wandering to trees, roof lines and the shapes of clouds; your ears, instead of being attuned to the closed-in sounds of milling feet on waxed floors, shuffling papers on students' desks and the sound of silence punctuated by throat-clearing and nose sniffling, partake of the faraway sounds of children playing somewhere, of birds in consultation and of railroad trains signalling their departure to far-off places. Yet with the sound of the final bell, your nirvana had suddenly turned into purgatory. The dusty erasers that had just liberated you from sitting at your desk now shackle you and the work of cleaning them has become a torture devised by some brutal judge. What a difference in an instant of time. But what had actually changed? Nothing you were doing, only the possibilities of the moment.

Life is lived in stages and its benefits are judged moment by moment against all possible alternatives, with current benefits being the result of what has been done in earlier stages. There are many ways to represent this situation using programs and solution algorithms from operations research, called dynamic multi-stage optimization techniques. The key to success in any of them is not to fall into the network trap of choosing a first-stage solution because it has a good immediate result, when actually a broader view would show it to be sub-optimal. So many life choices are this way.

The Prophets have also devoted considerable space in their expositions to this phenomenon. By their use of various symbolic constructions we are repeatedly warned against the network trap and the dangers of the stock effect in our subjective thinking. And really, anything offering immediate gratification coupled with high future costs is an example of this network or multi-stage optimization problem, motivated by stock effects short-circuiting our rational thinking capacity. The Prophets also repeatedly warn us that our lives will pass away before we realize it. These prophecies also say that our days are numbered, that there is a set time for each of us and when it is spent, we die. In sum, they confide to us that,

> The world is but a show, vain and empty, a mere nothing, bearing the semblance of reality. Set not your affections upon it . . . Verily, I say, the world is like the vapour in a desert, which the thirsty dreameth to be water and striveth after it with all his might, until when he cometh unto it, he findeth it to be mere illusion.[3]

Similar wording can be found in every known holy book recording the teachings of the Prophets of God. From the Qur'án: 'And the life of this world is only an amusement and play. Verily, the home in the hereafter – that is the life if you but knew.'[4]

Elsewhere we may read that our allotted time in this life is a preordained measure, like having good eyesight, numeric ability or having a 7¼ inch hat size. We may also read, however, that we are 'contingent' beings and that we therefore depend on some causality for our initial and continued existence, that therefore 'things happen', as they say, and that this may radically change life expectancy. For example, quitting smoking and taking up exercise may extend our lives, all else being equal, just as the bus we didn't see will flatten us and shorten it. They also mention the inevitability of death, that 'every soul will taste of death, then to Us shall you be returned'.[5] 'Wheresoever you may be, death will overtake you . . .'[6] and that we'll be there for our own death, even as we were not there, in the sense of being conscious, for our birth.

The Subjective Planning Horizon

Accomplishing any productive activity takes time and planning. At different ages in our lives we plan to do different things. At advanced ages people usually do not choose to learn another language, earn a PhD or start a business having a five year payout period, for the obvious reason that these things take time and a great deal of energy and discipline. With life's finish line in sharp focus and youth a muddled recollection, such activities are not taken up as often as, say, writing, socializing, meditating and travelling because the time remaining for life is now clearly limited. Conversely, all these difficult things just mentioned are readily taken up while young and there is plenty of time both to accomplish them and to recover from any costly mistakes their accomplishment, or the failure to accomplish them, might entail, materially and psychically. Businesses are started, languages are learned and PhDs are earned.

Ordinarily the planning horizon is relatively long towards the beginning of life, once the person has matured, and becomes shorter – at least in terms of limiting material activities – as the chronological time for natural death is approached. (This, of course, is one of the reasons for the stock effect and is inversely related to it.) Most enterprises capable of generating great value take time to plan, organize and execute. Controlling for all things else, the highest sustained income levels are possible only for those people having years of training, experience and expertise. The so-called new economy does not change the calculus that wealth creation is possible only from the pre-existence of capital resources, especially human intellectual capital, which takes years to form. And this, in turn, assumes the existence of social institutions capable of inculcating them in the individual.

The longer the time horizon used for planning the multi-stage life process, the more scope there is for productive and creative enterprises. This works for national economies as well as for individuals. Economics uses planning horizons in its calculations in a very formal but straightforward way. The subjective planning horizon is the limit of the summation of all benefits and costs, or the limit of the integral of these benefits and costs for a given activity. They bracket the time period in which all costs and benefits will occur.

The perceived length of a person's planning horizon changes as his or her life situation changes. Further, the abstraction of future time and future possibilities are learned concepts. Where children are carefully nurtured and cared for, their planning horizons are extended to include years and decades. But if they are neglected and their immediate situation is unsafe and uncertain, and no relationship between actions taken and results experienced is established, then planning horizons never extend much beyond a few days or weeks, or in the extreme, beyond a 24-hour day.

Even when a properly developed individual possesses a long planning horizon, severely negative circumstances may shorten it to a day's length and it may never extend further again, even after things return to 'normal', without formal intervention techniques. If the individual's daily circumstances become less certain, if safety and security are threatened and the person feels in constant danger, then the planning horizon will shrink to a few days or even a few hours, since only in this time frame can any planning be useful. Again, if dangerously addictive drugs are ingested for a period of time then the life plan reduces to procuring a subsistence amount of the drug and all other goals are subsumed within this one. Many drugs cycle through the body within a day, so this becomes the user's planning horizon; other drugs, like the opiates, take longer and two or three days might be required, thereby extending the planning horizon appropriately.

A time frame of hours or days precludes the creation of productive processes. While people can and do work productively for a few hours a day, this assumes the prior formation of some enterprise the person can fit into as needed. But under circumstances which diminish the planning horizon significantly, only consumption is possible, not the creation of productive enterprises that form wealth and value. The full destructive impact of drug addiction is now shown: lives so controlled are reduced to consuming what they themselves and others have previously created while being incapable of creating or producing any additions to the store of wealth from which consumption is made possible. In this sense, drug addiction is the purest form of consumption imaginable because even the self is slowly consumed.

Planning horizons can also be extended under certain conditions. When the individual welds his or her will with the will of a larger entity, be it political, intellectual or spiritual, then this becomes in large part the planning horizon used and the individual one, while still there, plays a lesser part in decisions. Thus a corporate executive plans his or her life around the plans of the corporation, the sports fanatic around the playing season of the team, the scientist around grant funding, etc. An author may plan his or her life around the completion date of a particular work or when a series of works will have been completed. A craftsman working on a cathedral that may require a century to complete has an even longer horizon, as does one engaged in spreading a new message of God over the earth. We might ask, what is the planning horizon for a Prophet of God?

Actually, it seems that all material benefits are experienced in a 24-hour day. After that time the process is repeated. We rise in the morning and all our bodily needs must be attended to just as yesterday; we recall the new car sitting in the driveway; again feel the flush of happiness when our boss said that because of the great job we have been doing, he is going to give us a 10 per cent raise in pay; and we also recall the shame and conflict when we showed the new car to our spouse, who had other plans for those funds. We live in the day and all material characteristics of our life end with sleep and begin again upon rising the next day.

Advertisers are aware of the power of planning horizons in decision-making. By inviting us to shorten ours, they hope we will save less and spend more. Consumerism depends on attenuating our subjective planning horizons by various inducements.

Intellectual and spiritual life is not so regulated by 24 hour cycling, and if the intellectual and spiritual sides of our personality have been developed, our lives are lived on a more continual and transcendent plane of being than what obtains for a life lived purely on the material plane. For people involved in intellectual and spiritual pursuits, their subjective planning horizon is much longer than for the pure materialist. In any case, this subjective planning horizon is consistently dependent on circumstances; when these change, the planning horizon changes. The drug addict, whose planning horizon is the length of time to obtain the drug of choice and for whom nothing exists beyond that time period, experiences a lengthening of this time frame when getting clean of the drugs. Plans are made that include weeks, then months, then years.

Children also have a very short planning horizon which, where proper training and care are given, is extended into years as the individual child matures and becomes older. Why this fuss about planning horizons? Because a population with long planning horizons is capable of planning and executing great things, things that take years and decades rather than weeks or months. Ask, 'What is the planning horizon of an elected politician?' Short planning horizons are often harmful to the long-term development of the individual, to the nation and to the planet.

Taking the extension of the planning horizon as useful in itself, the introduction of religious experiences and consciousness into the individual psyche can extend planning horizons even where nothing else has been able to do so. By accepting that there is a life after this one, that its realization is inevitable and that its condition for us depends on our present actions, planning is thereby extended to cover the entire life, from the present to the very last breath. Bahá'u'lláh states,

> How often hath a sinner, at the hour of death, attained to the essence of faith, and, quaffing the immortal draught, hath taken his flight unto the celestial Concourse. And how often hath a devout believer, at the hour of his soul's ascension, been so changed as to fall into the nethermost fire.[7]

Common experience provides many examples of people who had been of little practical use to the community or to themselves and whose actions might have been destructive, who were transformed into useful members capable of carrying on productive activities and supporting themselves and others after coming into contact with religion.

The point here is that whatever else religious conversion means, by extending planning horizons from myopic to cosmic the individual is enabled to view life as possibly more than just consumption so that it now includes production, creativity and purposeful action extending over years or decades. The extension of the subjective planning horizon was necessary for this to have occurred. Also possible with long subjective planning horizons is the cultivation of wisdom, which allows the individual to eschew behaviour having small current consumptive pleasures but large future costs, in other words, to avoid the network trap. The enormous costs entailed in many dangerous activities are often not experienced for years, long after the event's consumption value has been reduced to a nullity. Wisdom protects the individual from such things by enabling him or her to visualize all future costs in the present circumstance. And long subjective planning horizons are essential for wisdom to form. In fact, it could be argued that having a long planning horizon (and a low rate of time preference, defined below) is tantamount to wisdom, by definition.

Lessons are Learned Only within the Planning Horizon

Suppose it is desired to effect a change in a person's behaviour by imposing corrective actions. Whatever the subjective planning horizon is, changing behaviour means that the full costs and effects of taking certain actions must be experienced within that time frame. If those effects occur beyond this frame then they cannot make an impression and behaviour will remain as before since those effects will be seen as random events rather than as the direct result of actions taken previously. Therefore, whatever extends subjective planning horizons tends to result in the generation of solutions to problems and whatever attenuates them tends to create problems.

To summarize, life engages us over a long time frame. It is a multi-stage process and without a long subjective planning horizon its true quality can never be fully understood since its lessons transcend the mind set of life lived in a few hours or days. The harsh results of failing to heed its unfolding lessons are viewed as random events, with no connection to past actions. This is suffering at its worst: when there is no way to learn from life and mistakes are repeated indefinitely until all hope of ever improving one's lot is lost.

Consider altering the behaviour of a child. Children normally have very short planning horizons, just a few hours or days, depending on age, temperament, conditioning, etc. In order to get his attention and change behaviour, the altering condition must be placed so that it takes effect within the planning horizon of the child; otherwise it will be perceived as a random (negative) event, entirely misunderstood and unrelated to any actions previously taken by the child. The reward or punishment must occur, therefore, within the next few hours for a child having a planning horizon of just a few hours. Criminal justice systems for juveniles fail to change behaviour because, among other things, their findings take so long to occur, far longer than the planning horizon of the youth in question. So the results are seen as so much negative randomness, like bad weather or an unexpected death in the family, and unrelated to anything the youth may have done.

Where longer planning horizons exist (hopefully possessed by the parents!) it is not necessary that rewards and punishments occur so soon on the heels of the associated behaviour. Just the fact that they will occur is enough to elicit the sought-after behaviour. The fact of its eventuality is identical to its actuality in the mind of a person with a sufficiently long subjective planning horizon. No need, then, to actually show the person what is 'behind door no. 3'. All that is required is that some degree of certainty exists that the event will in fact occur.

As for the Individual, So for the Nation

Training of the individual is, of course, a core issue in prophetic dialogues. Child-rearing and education bring this together in a forceful way, requiring society to decide how vast resources will be dedicated. Because the benefits of education take years to accrue while the planning horizon of the students is normally much shorter, there is no way for children to appreciate the necessity of schooling other than an abstraction lacking in certainty of positive outcomes flowing from this seeming drudgery.

For this reason the schooling of children is compulsory in most advanced and advancing countries. Even the children's parents may not appreciate education's value if children have always been looked upon as a resource for the parents, old age security, so to speak. In that case children are not invested in and social capital flows from the children to the parents, a socially regressive direction. Eventually the system will fail and that economy will collapse. Where children are seen as an investment, fewer children are born and social capital flows from parents to children, a socially progressive direction and one that enables intergenerational economic growth. Economics has taken on the role of applying arithmetic results to social sums and quantities. If fertility rates increase and more children are born to each family, even if this results in more hands to care for the current generation, what will they eat? It also requires that puberty occur at an ever earlier age to accelerate the childbearing process before available capital is used up. This is a Ponzi scheme, a pyramid scheme where current holders of rights are granted them by future members, a sort of 'bigger fool than I was' scheme. It is precisely how a speculative bubble is constructed.

In what has just been demonstrated, fundamental laws of the material plane were employed, including the calculus of economics and simple arithmetic. It is certainly impossible for a society to advance if social capital is passed from children to parents. The most that can be achieved is a kind of stagnation, even in the face of rising fertility rates. It is no different from wondering how long a crop can be harvested from ground that receives no fertilizer and is systematically disinvested in over time.

The Subjective Rate of Time Preference

We have established by logical argument and illustration the necessity of long subjective planning horizons for activities of building, producing and behaviour refining. But a long planning horizon alone will not guarantee that such activities occur. The Messengers of God attempt to extend our planning horizons into another life, a life after this life. By insisting that all will rise after physical death and will be repaid for our actions – that is, that the quality of the next life is dependent on our actions in this life – the Messengers encourage us to develop spiritual and moral attributes that will assure a good afterlife experience.

> Say: 'Short is the enjoyment of this world. The hereafter is better for him who fears God, and you shall not be dealt with unjustly even equal to the spot on a date stone.'[8]

But that is not enough; we need patience and the Messengers tell us to develop it in ourselves. Patience is a quality having profound economic and financial effects on our lives. If the planning horizon is lifelong but the individual has no ability to be patient and work for a long time before results accrue, little can be accomplished. A ten-year investment plan is conceived – say, college followed by medical school and residency – but if the individual is not capable of going without sleep or of giving up weekends and evenings of fun and entertainment, then the investment plan is doomed to failure.

How many times have we acquired a book on mathematics or some foreign language we dearly want to learn? After a few weeks or months, however, the book is moved from the desk to the living room table, thence to the office and finally to a bookcase where it gathers dust, its encouragingly worded spine a constant reproach and reminder of our weak resolve and lack of grit. (Oh, the shame!) This is all too common, however. We may even be in that number who have earned an advanced degree after years of sacrifice but are now unwilling to ever again be subject to the tyrannical discipline certainly required to really gain the new knowledge we seek. What is being discussed is what economics has named the *subjective rate of time preference.*[9]

Specifically, the subjective rate of time preference measures personal patience in a very formalized and quantifiable way. It models personal patience as a discount rate, similar to an interest rate on money, whereby future values are arithmetically discounted when arriving at their present value. For people who are very impatient for things, the discount rate, call it φ (the Greek letter theta), is high, meaning that future things are not worth as much as they are seem to be in the present. Such people do not become interested unless the future value is very large, a lottery jackpot for example. People with more patience have a lowered discount rate so that future values need not be so large to attract attention.

To illustrate, the value of $50,000 five years from now at a high discount rate of 25 per cent is just $14,510.40 in today's money, while at the lower discount rate of 4 per cent it is $40,950.16, almost three times as much. For the impatient person 14 grand is not worth spending five years worrying about; but for the patient person it is not $14,000 but actually $40,000 and 40 grand certainly is of importance. The greater the patience, the greater the perceived present value of future rewards; and the less the patience, the smaller is the perceived value of future rewards. For those subscribing to this calculus, great rewards in this life await in the form of detachment from present states, as more importance is attached to future states or even future lives. By such means we can overcome the need to achieve immediate gratification all the time. Thus freed, we are capable of working towards a goal, of investing and producing goods and services for ourselves, our families and our communities, of forming human capital and thus transforming ourselves into people capable of solving complex social and personal problems and of achieving the highest level of life lived. From this human capital stock, consumption is made possible, with its enjoyments and pleasures.

More important is the associated love for production – work itself – that may result from engaging in this essentially spiritual process.

But without being freed from the need to fulfil our consumptive wishes moment by moment, productive activities, with their initial difficulties and their requirement for patience and endurance, are clearly impossible for anyone. And without the capital formed from production there is no basis for consumption.

Life experiences can either increase our valuation of the future or reduce it to zero, that is, we put no stock in any future plan coming to fruition. Secure upbringing and surroundings in the early years of life, coupled with a systematic and comprehensive range of rewards and punishment, are thought most responsible for creating both low subjective rates of time preference and long subjective planning horizons. Conversely, forms of systematic or prolonged insecurity seem to be most responsible for increasing the subjective rate of time preference (impatience) and reducing the length of planning horizons.

Community Trends in the Subjective Rate of Time Preference

Such a formalization of subjective patience enables a mathematical treatment of many interesting problems. Among them is how various investment schemes will be perceived by individuals and the public at large. If the public is impatient for fiscal results there will be little desire to spend tax dollars or bond issues building new schools, even while increased taxes or bond issues for a new sports stadium or casino resort may experience little resistance. However, perceptions can be changed. If the government spends sufficient time to effectively educate the public to its present and future needs, with pictures of little children outside decrepit school buildings, with additional camera shots showing broken toilet fixtures, stained ceiling tiles and dark stairwells, the school bond issue may fly through with full public support – especially if we cut ahead in time and show young men and women dressed for success, passing under the ivy-covered archway entrance of a private college, or men under guard in orange jumpsuits with 'Prisoner' stencilled on their backs passing under an archway announcing that 'All visitors must submit to a full body search'. Perceptions can change, all right. It is exactly such stark comparisons that the Prophets of God present us with in their dialogues and verses to get our attention and motivate us to change our behaviour. 'Market agents respond to incentives,' say economists and say the Prophets of God.

The ability to change public and individual perceptions through exposure to new ideas suggests that social institutions play a large role in forming public tastes and preferences, especially tastes and preferences associated with work and effort. The ability to endure the wait for investments to pay out their benefits is essential if necessary projects are to be undertaken. Schools were just mentioned. Also important are other forms of public goods investments, such as transportation, communication and healthcare infrastructures. All these things take time to build and show results while requiring the sacrifice of current funds. But governments can mandate the necessary funds with public approval, or even without it for short periods when necessary. However, it is in individual endeavours that the subjective rate of time preference becomes the determining factor to what life will be lived and what accomplishments will be achieved. This result will be determined solely based on individual free choice. What is already indwelling will determine the result.

With so much at stake, it is no wonder that the individual decision-making process is carefully scrutinized in economics.

Spiritual Impacts of These Elements

What is significant in these observations? Trivially, there is the nature of the elements themselves as they pertain to the subjectiveness of time as an amount, a frame for activity and as the future itself. Beyond this, however, is how changing individual and collective perceptions of these elements can lead to changes in behaviour directly affecting the future possibilities of the society and all its members. Is it any wonder, then, that the Messengers of God spent so much time and effort in trying to get us humans to extend our planning horizons and to learn patience? With respect to the subjective rate of time preference, for instance, this element is responsible for the rate of growth possible within the limits set by the existing planning horizon. It is like the planned trajectory for a rocket ship headed towards a pinpoint target in the vast emptiness of space. It turns out that slight changes in these initial conditions will have profound changes on the flight of the rocket ship, even forcing the abandonment of the initial target in favour of another, less ambitious one closer in. This system perfectly models the individual in his quest to achieve all that is possible from his initial endowment. Changes in early childhood change the life trajectory, making some things possible while ruling out others. Societal growth acts in the same manner. Like the spaceship, optimal growth requires that available resources be used at all times in their first best use where possible, that needed capital be formed and maintained and that consumption spending be subservient to the needs of production which makes consumption possible. What is called the *Turnpike*

Principle dictates that for a community to succeed it must identify the optimal growth path as early as possible and stay on it as long as possible.

As mentioned previously, subjective planning horizons, the length of the time frame we use to plan our life stages, are often amenable to alteration by circumstances. And as presently explained, the subjective rate of time preference measures the degree of intertemporal patience, which, being formed at the nexus of the individual and his environment, is also amenable to alteration. In a previous chapter we discussed the rise of the Islamic civilization in the midst of a people regionally notorious for their treachery, tribalism, ignorance, brutality, savagery and cruelty, even burying their unwanted daughters alive. These people of Peninsular Arabia comprised loose tribal confederations. Their lives were arranged about pastoral and agricultural needs, harvests, trade, war and raiding soirees, marriages, etc. Few fixed settlements capable of supporting commerce on a continual basis existed, with permanent building structures often inherited from the cultural and material output of a people long vanished.

Within the analytical context of the subjective rate of time preference and the subjective planning horizon, their level of civilization and lifestyle was not conducive to low rates of time preference or a long planning horizon. Also, their utility functions were now-centred and ego-centred, linked only to the immediate family, clan or tribe. There was no concept of the future as such extending much beyond a few months or years. Their religious practices were imitative and lacking in meaningful analytical structure. Under these circumstances, with an attenuated planning horizon and a large subjective rate of time preference, coupled with utility functions intergenerationally and intertemporally disconnected, there was no scope for civilization-building, artistic development, advanced commerce or the construction of all other advanced social institutions. How, then, was it possible, after the appearance of this one person, Muhammad, for the swift development of all these civilized attributes they would soon display, including universities, hospitals, artistic institutes, transportation hubs and international commerce, a standing army based on universal conscription and with advanced methods of warfare, the establishment of many public institutions, including universal taxation, both positive and negative, and a codified system of jurisprudence?

From what we know now, the acceptance of Muhammad's divine cause entailed a critical analysis of His dialogues and of the sophisticated social models they implied. This in turn necessitated abstract future considerations with models of future states being linked causally with present actions, the reduction in the subjective rate of time preference (increase in patience) and the expansion of subjective planning horizons. Utility functions – those things inside each of us that register happiness or sadness, rejection or acceptance and contentment – were also revised to become interpersonally and intertemporally linked – people caring about each other and being happy in seeing others happy – in keeping with Muhammad's exhortations, now accepted as binding on all societal members. Thus the present generation sacrificed for the sake of other citizens, and for those yet unborn, bequeathing to them a wealth of recorded knowledge and a growing set of intact and maturing social institutions dedicated to safeguarding the rights of the individual while energetically encouraging group production and enterprises on a national level. The development of the Middle East after the appearance of Muhammad and the institutionalization of Islam as the state religion is a matter of record. Even those nations that refused to accept Islam borrowed generously from its techniques in statecraft and this too is a matter of record. We are thus presented with a 'treatment–result' experiment over time, providing the basis of what is termed by statisticians *time–series analysis*. Its use in the analysis of historical events and epochs is called *cleometrics,* as mentioned in the beginning of this chapter. But even in the absence of formalized analytical methods, casual observation of such unprecedented events as the civilizing of Peninsular Arabia and the nations of the Middle East, Asia and beyond, forces us to conclude that there must have been something extraordinary in Muhammad's words to have caused such tumult and social revolution in so short a time. With what we know of the requirements for productive enterprise then, whatever else the dialogues were responsible for, they must have had the effect of promoting long subjective planning horizons and low subjective rates of time preference and in forming intertemporally and interpersonally linked utility functions which, when maximized, would result in the enrichment of the individual, the family, the community and the nation. This is just one example of the spiritual–social significance of utility maximization, subjective rates of time preference and the subjective planning horizon. As to the spiritual significance of marginality and the insight that 'all decisions are made at the margin', this underpins the entire edifice of human volition. Just because an individual overcomes impulsiveness and learns to control his/her passions is not to say that utility is not being maximized marginally. What has happened is that the individual can now partake of the joy that comes from learning a new science or from being able to give up selfish action for the sake of making dependents happy and secure. Decisions are still made instant by instant and weighed on the basis of what actions provide the greatest utility within the set of all possible actions. Moreover, as the subjective rate of time preference shrinks (patience increases), future values equate more closely to present ones, thereby equating total and absolute values with marginal values.

We have this interesting result: As the subjective rate of time preference shrinks, future values equate more closely to present ones and marginal valuations approach total valuations, reducing the difference between marginal and absolute valuations. (Hurrah! The marginalist revolution is safe!) As this is an immutable and fundamental human characteristic and will occur in any case, what affects individual and social outcomes are the development of individual utility functions linked intertemporally and interpersonally. Then the natural tendency of the individual will be to make others happy and to produce benefits for future states, all in order to maximize his/her own happiness. The lesson is clear: Utility maximization never disappears from the human condition. 'For self-love is kneaded into the very clay of man, and it is not possible that, without hope of a substantial reward, he should neglect his own present material good.'[10] Also, 'And human inner selves are swayed by greed.'[11] Our only chance for advancement, therefore, is to cause to be developed in each person utility functions that, when maximized, lead to socially and spiritually beneficial behaviour. Since utility functions are the actualization of individual tastes and preferences, it is then obvious that societies must be concerned with doing everything possible to encourage the formation of socially beneficial sets of individual tastes and preferences, respecting what is possible within the developmental capacity of each person.

A further lesson is drawn from what is known of the formation of taste and preference sets, that *they are formed in the earliest years of human life*. Since the family is the dominant social institution for the individual in these years then, logically, society must assure the provision of familial support both materially, in the form of adequate physical sustenance, and non-materially, in the form of social, cultural, intellectual and communal capital, if it wants to increase socially constructive behaviour. Such systematic provision is supplied within the words of the Prophets, in symbolic, in abstracted and in clearly evident forms.

***

In this chapter we have bridged some of the fundamental components of economic dynamics with the message of the Prophets of God. These have included marginal analysis, utility maximization, the subjective planning horizon and the subjective rate of time preference. We then saw how each of these elements works in human individual and social life. Finally, we described their spiritual characteristics, which, when known, made it possible to understand how the prophetic dialogues were capable, by their own unaided influence, to establish a world civilization by a previously unknown and barbarous confederacy of nomadic tribes. We coined the term 'spiritualmetrics' to describe analysing economics for its spiritual content and prophetic speech for economic content, and both as they lead to sustainable dynamic human system development and maintenance.

In what follows much more will be said about the formation of spiritual characteristics, their analysis and how changing them in various ways can result in 'something wonderful'!

4
A Brief Analysis of the Exchange

Without trivializing it, the exchange is the most basic of human activities. In economics we ordinarily think of the exchange itself rather too formally and the requirements for an exchange not formally enough. But describing its characteristics and its requirements is where economic science has had marked success over the past one hundred years. We need to understand the characteristics of the exchange because of its omnipresence. We exchange when we spend money or time or concentration. And if we choose to do something then we are choosing not to do something else at that time. In fact, whenever and whatever we decide to do with ourselves, we are choosing how to use some resource we possess, even if it is just our time and thought. It is true to say that the Prophets and Messengers of God have been sent to the human tribe in order to regulate and sanction what and how it exchanges.

This chapter will discuss both the exchange's characteristics and its requirements. At the end we will have a definition of the exchange that covers most human activities, even very private ones, and a formal idea of what is needed for there to be an exchange and from where those requirements are normally to be found. Finally, exchanges are discussed in the context of markets. Then we can appreciate the enormous scope of the record of divine speech received from God throughout our history and how it has facilitated and enabled our material and spiritual development.

Generated from a successful exchange is the idea of value, or price, as *information*. Exchanges are important for this reason: that they supply this information so all may know what something is worth, broadly defined. In this sense, an exchange using money as the medium, and where some commodity is bought and sold, is a small but important subset of ordinarily occurring exchanges. The word 'transaction' is used interchangeably with exchange throughout.

Exchange Requirements

Exchanges are events, an occurrence in time and place. It is not necessary, however, that both parties of the exchange be present at the same time and place. A 'sell' order can be posted for some future date, for example, and both time and place may separate the persons in the exchange. Exchanges exist in a market, an arena or context where they occur. They may or may not offer a formal structure for exchanges. Exchanges require three things to make them possible: 1) there must be the right to transfer some kind of property or thing possessed from one party to another in the exchange, 2) there must be rules and regulations agreeable and acceptable to both sides and 3) both sides must obtain some benefit, i.e. mutual benefits must be generated from the exchange. These elements both constrain exchanges and make them possible. Let us examine each in turn and look closely at its characteristics, its source of supply and what it says, and does not say, about the nature of exchanges.

Transferable Property Rights

This means that the seller has the right to transfer ownership of the traded property to another party in the exchange. We have all heard the joke about the naive person who buys the Brooklyn bridge. The joke is that s/he should have known that the bridge is not the property of some person who can sell it for any price. It is the property of the City of New York. So, the buyer was fooled because s/he bought something that cannot be sold.

Now imagine that you have just left work and you are met by a person offering to sell you a Rolex watch for $50 cash. What is the problem here? 1) It might not be a Rolex, since a genuine Rolex ordinarily costs over $1,500 used (is the second hand rotating in that jerky fashion characteristic of quartz movements? Is the watch a little light in weight?) The watch could be a fake, in other words. Or 2) it is a real Rolex. What is the problem then? It is probably stolen property. The seller does not have the right to transfer the property. And if you purchase the watch, you are liable for arrest and prosecution for accepting stolen property. (And never mind telling the presiding judge that you didn't know it was stolen: 'A genuine Rolex for $50? Take him away, bailiff!')[1]

Mutually Acceptable Rules and Regulations Governing the Exchange

This is the requirement that some form of contract exist between the transacting parties in the exchange covering possible and imagined contingencies. When you buy something in a shop or supermarket, or even pay a cab fare, you get a receipt. This acts as a *conditional sales contract* and records the fact of the transaction. Such receipts may be implied and are not always written down. Cultural assumptions may preclude their use or there might be too much to specify for a formal contract (though as time passes more contracts are formalized). In any case, we can think of the things such a typical contract would cover: quality, return policies, method and timing of payment, dispute resolution, etc. These rules must be agreed upon by both sides or one party will refuse to transact, because it has become too risky, for example.

Mutual Benefits from the Exchange

Both sides of the transaction must derive some tangible or intangible benefit from the transaction or the exchange will not occur. This seems clear enough but this fact can have strange-sounding implications. For example, if you willingly borrow money at a usurious interest rate the statement can be made that since you did this willingly, then you derived a benefit and regulations against usury are not needed. Mutual benefits were obtained, after all. What is wrong with this conclusion? It may mask the reality that even if coercion was not used, the lender may have had far more knowledge of the situation than you, the borrower, for instance how the interest compounds, etc.

This is called exploitation,[2] which means that something is not paid what it is truly worth. It explains why some markets are sternly regulated as to what is allowed to be exchanged and under what conditions. For example, borrowing money requires that 'full disclosure' be made by the lender as to the effective interest rate on the outstanding principal, payoff restrictions, etc. (In the United States, auto leasing rules are far less restricted and customers often do not know how much the lease is actually costing them.) Obtaining complex services, such as legal or medical, are often thoroughly regulated. Years ago I needed an operation on my right hand. I was 17 years old at the time. The doctor and I discussed various surgical possibilities and their associated costs and benefits, both physically and financially. Finally I chose what operation I wanted from the available alternatives, and haven't regretted it. But such negotiations would never be possible today in the US! My limited ability to foresee the implications of the available choices and negotiating with a surgeon who was expected by training and office to have such knowledge put the doctor in a principal–agent relationship with me. American law would never allow it today. You might conclude that such regulatory intrusion is what's wrong with American medical practice now but few people, I think, would be willing to return to the unregulated lending practices of old.[3] With everything there are benefits and costs.

Clearly, this idea of an exchange and its requirements goes beyond the usual supply-and-demand discussion. The exchange in the present context is an abstraction covering virtually all human activity, material or even spiritual, since we live in a temporal universe wherein we must choose to devote time to whatever we do. Thus whatever the Messengers of God have to say about our activities – our exchanges – is, by being central to the exchange itself, leveraged so as to have extraordinary effects on human outcomes and futures. Altering exchange characteristics alters the hub of the wheel of civilization itself.

Now consider the source for each of these exchange requirements. The mutual benefits provision is obviously decided by the traders themselves. So this value is endogenous to the exchange, i.e. fully contained within the exchange experience. But what about the first two requirements, the transferable property rights and the mutually agreeable rules and regulations? These are not supplied by the traders themselves. As parties to the outcome, neither is really capable of enforcing these exchange requirements to the satisfaction of the other. So an outsider – a third party – must supply these regulations and enforce the transferable property rights.

The need for third party governance of exchanges takes us into 'market existentialism'. There are those who believe that everything can be provided by markets alone. Over the years these theorists have given us a copious literature in support of their belief, with Nobel laureates in economics among the authors.[4] But this extreme position masks the need for third party governance in every exchange – and where is this third party to have come from? And since it provides a necessary and valuable service, and therefore costs something, how is it supported? The simple answer is government.

Some maintain that government is needed to regulate those things markets cannot handle, such as the supply of public goods and the adjudication of externalities (discussed in the previous chapter). Granted. But what are rules and regulations if not public goods? Their use does not diminish the amount available for others (non-rival in consumption) and within their juridical boundaries people cannot exclude themselves from being subject to them (non-excludable). The system of jurisprudence is therefore a public good that cannot be supplied by ordinary market mechanisms.[5] In fact, it is supplied by a monopoly: the government of the land.

This system of jurisprudence could be called the 'second most great public good',[6] since it is essential for any exchange to take place and embodies in its workings the will of society with respect to its expectations of how goods and services are to be produced, exchanged and distributed among its members. In this way the system of jurisprudence reflects the acquired knowledge of whatever has been learned from all sources, current and historical. These include scientific, cultural and religious sources, to name a few.

The root-source of transactional jurisprudence is, of course, divine speech, as sent down to us from the Prophets and Messengers of God. For instance, Mosaic laws, particularly the Ten Commandments, revealed over 3,500 years ago, have established themselves as pre-eminently useful and practical, so much so that every nation on earth has some semblance of these commandments codified into their civil and criminal laws. With the appearance of other Prophets in the Levant and elsewhere, Mosaic law was often the starting point for developing additional or enhanced legal codes. That they find themselves operationalized in modern societies, often with little or no alteration, is evidence of three things: 1) the original law was transcendentally sound, 2) societies avail themselves of various sources in determining and codifying rules and regulations affecting a comprehensive set of social interactions and 3) markets, being the arena for fundamental social interaction, are regulated by society to reflect its various goals. These include, in the case of institutional maturation, how the wealth of the community – and wealth produced therefrom – is to be distributed.

Later, various social choices for wealth distribution and the principles on which they rest will be examined. For now we note in passing that economics establishes that enterprises, when successful, pay returns for all resources used (that all resources are just exhausted). One intellectual difficulty has been in defining which resources these are. The direct contributors are obvious but it can be argued that indirect resources must also be rewarded from the profits, i.e. those things acting as resources for the resources, a set of factors ordinarily not appreciated for their essential contributions to any enterprise. These may include the schools where the inventor was educated and where all the workers, researchers, helpers were trained, the government whose laws regulated the production, provided the property rights and covered all transactions with adequate contracting, including for trademarks, patents and copyrights; the transportation, communication and information infrastructures, etc., etc. Enlarging the scope to include returns to these factors obviously results in enriching the supply of public goods and reducing the profits that would be held privately.

***

Even while most exchanges are regulated by the government in the form of the system of jurisprudence and contract law it provides as monopoly supplier, it doesn't always happen that way. Often the central government is weak and incapable of enforcing its laws. In that case some other agency will step in to guarantee the exchange particulars. This might be the Mafia or a quasi-governmental entity such as Hesbollah, which, in addition to pushing its political-religious agenda, supplies goods and services to the population, which the central government, for various reasons, cannot supply in adequate measure or acceptable cost. In fact a test of government strength is the extent to which the Mafia or another substitute entity is capable of inserting itself into guaranteeing exchanges. Compare the Russian market experience in the last two decades with that in a western or central European country or Japan and China. Also compare government supply of essential goods and services to the poor in southern Lebanon and the Palestinian territories, where reliance is placed on quasi-governmental Islamic groups rather than on the central government.

The governing body regulating the transaction will require payment for the service it provides. In the case of a government it may levy a sales tax on the exchange. In a way this is eminently fair: government has made the trade possible, providing facilitative regulations and enforcing its legal requirements allowing the parties to trade in safety. It then extracts a sum from the value of the exchange itself as payment for its continued support. In the case of the Mafia or other criminal enterprise, it might be complicity in their criminal activities, while for the quasi-governmental Islamic entities it might be tacit acceptance of their social and religious goals.

Here again is that saddlepoint solution where the supply of needed services is maximized while minimizing costs. Governments facilitate trades and make exchanges possible. In this way they facilitate personal and national wealth creation. Yet governments are not self-supporting. They are a *net cost* to the economy, creating no wealth themselves. They are like chemical catalysts that make the energy conversion reactions in our body possible by reducing the heat and pressure required for them. Catalysts must be made and maintained from available energy stores but they add nothing to the energy stocks directly.

So how large must a government be? It must be large enough to facilitate all transactions but no larger. If too small, transactions will be ineffectively regulated. This can be very costly. In fact, it can be shown that this is a general result for an facilitative service that is not internally self-supporting.

It is no good to ask suppliers to regulate their own industries. The history of the appearance and spread of 'mad cow' disease in Great Britain and elsewhere will convince most thoughtful people that, at least with respect to current moral education possibilities, third party governance of all exchanges is still necessary. The same is true of markets for medicine, finance, mining and resource extraction, waste management, etc. If large sums of money are at stake, strong laws must be used for the purpose. However, if government becomes too large its costs will begin to exceed its benefits. Governments, by definition, regulate things; if they get too large there might be too much market regulation and this could be the form excessive costs will take. Other costs would include a reduction in the volume of transactions since at the margin some exchanges would not be able to make enough in the form of mutual benefits to be justified in the presence of the additional transaction costs imposed by the regulations.

If the need to trade is pre-existent in man, trading has nonetheless required some sort of outside facilitation from the very beginning. This argument is a settled reality in a practical sense. All important markets operating in advanced nations are now closely regulated to protect users from exploitation and other untoward outcomes.

Now the realities of incipient globalization impinge every market. From what has just been argued it is obvious that *global trade can never fulfil its potential for increasing per capita human wealth and well being until true third party governance and facilitation in world trade exists.* In the meantime such trade will take place more like political trade, with vast opportunities for exploitation. Characteristically, such trade benefits strong players and disadvantages weak ones almost without exception. This is the typical nature of trade in political arenas for both *inter*governmental and *intra*governmental exchanges where powerful parties manipulate results to achieve desired ends.[7] The reasons include powerful vested interests not having to take a price discovered in market exchanges as given and having the power to demand that a different price prevail. The strong trader is called the price-maker and the weak one is called the price-taker. In short, market outcomes will always favour a powerful trader who can control the market and the relative power of the trader is the sole determinant of outcomes.[8]

Market power, the ability to influence price, exists in practically all markets where goods with a brand name are sold and also for commodities where supply is by the few, such as for oil, diamonds, etc. But price requires a formal definition. We need to know what it is, where it comes from and what influence it plays beyond where it acts directly. Furthermore, we must be able to relate price to this sense of value for material things but also for spiritual things.

Price Discovery and Relative Value

The definition of price has three parts.

1) Price is the relative value of a good or service exchanged.

2) It is discovered by resolving the forces of supply and demand.

3) It provides information so that scarce resources can be used to produce goods and services of the highest possible value.

I have used this definition for a number of years in college lectures and have not found any defects in it thus far, as long as we understand that it covers price discovery and formation where no market power exists, as just defined as the ability to influence price. Clearly, where such power does exist, price is not discovered but rather manipulated or set for the benefit of some interested party. This area of market power soon leads us into an extremely complex market analysis existing very much on the border of what is presently known and settled in economics and where a lot of fundamental questions have still to be researched. So the definition covers markets where such power does not exist. Even where market power does exist, however, parties are often very restricted as to price-setting in an effort to maximize their returns because the law of demand cannot in any case be repealed.[9] If the unit price is too high people will buy fewer units and this could hurt seller returns.[10]

The first point made by the definition is that price is the relative value of what is exchanged. Absolute values are assumed to be unknown and it is understood that assigned value results from various things such as relative scarcity, needfulness, tastes and preferences, etc. Also involved is whether the item is used to make something else or is directly consumed as a final good. This is just as true for non-material as for material goods.

Second, price is discovered, not set, ordinarily. This means that traders are price-takers and they discover underlying value by resolving supply and demand forces, what is actually wanted, by whom and how willing suppliers are to offer it. All this depends on what else can be supplied using those same resources, or what else can be bought using available trading channels, and what all those relative values would be at any particular time. This refers to the opportunity cost of resources – what you give up in terms of foregone benefits to do what you are doing now, as discussed in an earlier chapter.

Do people actually calculate all present and future prices without making systematic errors? Of course not. Were this true, how is it possible that crimes are committed by those who know they will be caught? How would speculative bubbles be possible? And why would people ever 'waste time', engage in frivolous activities or do things that feel good now but will cause great loss later on? Market decisions are much too complex for agent omniscience to be assumed. However, over a broad range of situations common sense and experience sufficiently inform market actors and guide their decisions somewhat, so that what is wanted in a market is what is obtainable and supplied over time.[11] People reveal their preferences by buying or not buying things but always in the limited context of what the current choices are. In this way their preferences are said to be revealed.

Third, the discovery of price as value becomes information essential for use by producers so they may supply what demanders really want and/or need. In other words, the price becomes translated into a myriad of other prices for all the things that go into making that good. If a car is sold then every resource and product comprising that car also receives a price. So the plastic in the dashboard, for instance, is also priced. Suppliers of dashboards can now decide whether they should continue making them or whether more profit could be made from making wastebaskets or other kitchen products from that same plastic. These countably infinite calculations are made almost continuously and it is this decision process which amazed early scientists when they first realized what was happening and how miraculously all the different markets seemed to be able to coordinate themselves using nothing more than posted prices.[12]

All markets ration in this manner according to the rules under which they operate as dictated by social institutions. In this case the rules state that *prices* declare value. There are many other ways that value might be discovered or declared, such as government fiat (it simply decides what things will sell for) or by altering the declared value of the resources used. For example, under the plan of the Soviet Union, prices were simply set by government planners and did not reflect the value of the good or of the resources used in making it. We saw in the Introduction the mischief that this practice can lead to, the incorrect signals it sends throughout the economy, etc. But now consider what artificially low prices mean in consumer markets, where supply is not allowed to adjust because there is no resulting price signal. Since the price is too low suppliers will not get a return they can live with and will not supply very much to the market. On the other hand, consumers see the low price and respond by demanding a great deal.

So there is a shortage of the good supplied; many more units are wanted for purchase than the market will supply at that price. The result in the Soviet Union was what eventually came to be regarded as a symbol of Soviet Communism: long lines of people waiting to buy things. Thus instead of price rationing sales of a good, time waiting in line performed the rationing function. If you could wait for it you eventually got a chance to buy it, otherwise not. But there is more to this. Some people could be paid to wait in line for you. Also, important people didn't need to wait; they just bribed the clerk to set aside some of the good for them. It was 'sold out' but actually not.

A further result of the time rationing system is that anyone waiting in line is not working at his or her job. This hurts production. If this situation exists on a large scale then national production will be depressed. However, if price does the rationing there is a strong incentive to work more and harder, assuming such increased effort is rewarded with higher pay,[13] pay that can now be used to acquire more of what you want from the consumer market. This system stimulates production and increases national output.

Generally, economists are most happy with seeing price discovered forthrightly, where all resources are priced according to costs based on relative scarcity, etc. If it is then decided to aid certain disadvantaged market agents to obtain that good, this should be done directly by increasing the purchasing power of those agents through some means. This way, at least the market mechanism discovers underlying value and this information can be used to discover what things cost. Involved parties then have incentives to respond accordingly. For example, many Americans have health insurance paid through their employment so they might not worry how much medical services cost them. But all can still see what is happening to medical service prices and how they are inflating astronomically. An investigation might then be carried out that could reveal the forces behind these price gains, to see who is profiting and by how much, or if there are outside forces involved and if something can be done to change things. All this would be impossible were the government to simply set a price.

The healthcare delivery sector is an example of where markets do not coordinate to produce efficacious results when everyone just pursues their own selfish interests. Contrary to the 'invisible hand' mantra, in America it is clear that medical costs are being driven not by technology or new discoveries in the healing sciences but mostly by litigation costs, the enormous settlements that have broken the budgets of hospitals, insurance companies and doctors alike. It is getting so bad that no one can afford personal medical insurance, doctors cannot afford to insure themselves against professional liability and hospitals have been forced to sharply curtail emergency room, obstetrics and other services or have had to shut their doors altogether. Clearly, we must ponder the external aspects of all these suits and judgements and ask how long the healthcare system can be expected to survive under this increasing burden of litigation. The impingement of the legal market into the healthcare market is therefore far from efficaciously coordinated, to the clear loss of price discovery efficiency and the setting aside of society's broader interests.

There are many reasons why market coordination may not operate efficiently. One is that information may not flow between markets or not be generated at all because the real price of things is not discovered or publicly announced. Perhaps it is because deals have been made in secret or the things themselves may not have prices *per se*. External effects or the prices of public goods are difficult to discover because there is no one-to-one relationship between a unit of benefit and a unit of cost.

Another situation exists where the price of a good does not reflect its full cost because some of the costs are being pushed over to another market. Two examples. Sugar is produced either from sugarcane in the subtropics and tropics or from sugar beets in the temperate zones. Florida grows sugarcane. In order to increase harvests nitrogen is added to the soil. But owing to the lightness of the soil the added nitrogen washes away after a rain, ending up in the Everglades and surrounding waters, resulting in algae blooms and other harmful developments. Sugar is expensive in the United States because foreign sugar is not allowed to be sold in its markets, since that would depress the price below what American farmers need to maintain themselves in the business.

But who cares about a few cane farmers in Florida? Can they be powerful enough to keep the price paid for sugar by all Americans twice as high as the world price? But the cane farmers don't have to worry because the corn farmers – of which there are many and who are rich and powerful – will support the high sugar price. That is because the substitute for sugar, at least in liquid form, is made from corn, high fructose corn syrup or HFCS. If the American sugar programme is eliminated then sugar costs less than HFCS and a very big corn market is gone. That is why Everglades cleanup costs are pushed onto one group by another group living elsewhere.

The other example of this shifting is when one generational cohort runs up debt on its current account that will be paid, not by them, but by generations yet unborn or matured, in the form of higher taxes, a reduced standard of living or both.

Such harmful mischief is the result of amoral pricing in transactions from a set of tastes and preferences uninformed by the divine Word for mankind. In the presence of divine teachings, preference sets link present generational well-being to the well-being of those yet unborn or the benefits for one group to the benefits and costs of another group of the same time period.

Market coordination fails if external benefits and costs are not known, where public goods issues exist or where information fails to flow to all interested parties. Otherwise, the discovery and posting of prices and their continual incorporation in valuing things *ad infinitum* does indeed coordinate markets, with results from one exchange enabling other exchanges to continue the process, covering all values in an economy over time.

The evident seamlessness of this continual process of market coordination through price discovery has led some economists to search for a way to construct models of an entire national economy. It seems simple enough, requiring only a comprehensive list of all items of the economy in the model. But there are many difficulties. First, prices can be 'sticky', economists say. In markets like real estate, natural resources and some others, prices tend to rise but not fall, or fall very slowly. In equity markets, in contrast, prices tend to fall rapidly but rise more slowly. Price movements are thus asymmetrical. How is this asymmetry to be reflected in the model? Second, as soon as you say, 'Go!' prices begin changing all over in a dynamic process. Equilibrium, a sort of economic stasis where prices settle in the absence of external shocks, rarely if ever occurs because there is almost never a time when some new piece of relevant information is not influencing prices.

All these things stand in the way of general equilibrium analysis, not to mention undermining the conviction held by many economists of a common theoretical foundation explaining both micro market activity and macro market coordination. Some feel that macroeconomic phenomena can be modelled as random events or as chaotic bifurcations and that models purporting to explain why macroeconomies do what they do must be capable of predicting behaviour *at least* as well as the conventional wisdom, or null hypothesis, that market actions are random or chaotic events.[14]

***

So far supply has been discussed more than demand, production more than consumption. Consumption will be treated in detail in the next few chapters but here we are looking carefully at costs and benefits of being in a market exchange as a supplier. Most will agree that, besides having the willingness to buy, there is not much risk involved in being a consumer as compared to the much larger risks in being a supplier, at least before the sale and purchase. It costs you nothing to window shop but it costs the suppliers a great deal, starting with the window rental or purchase and adding all the things in it. If s/he has been wrong in guessing what you want or has been wrong in judging costs and selling prices, personal financial ruin will be the likely result, along with wasted resources used in the production of things no one wants. So this is a much higher stakes game for the supplier than for the demander. Certainly, consumers lose in purchases, get cheated, etc. But this is one financial event among many and it usually does not mean that the consumer will be ruined financially. For the supplier, there is a greater chance that capital limitations have restricted supplies to selling just a few well chosen products, increasing the risks for total loss.

What to supply the market is a matter of finding out what consumers want, then whether you as a supplier are able and willing to bring it forth. Markets are clearly demand-driven. Eventually, if you try to give consumers what they don't want they will turn away as soon as they get the chance. Just ask American and British automobile manufacturers. Therefore, consumer tastes and preferences are supreme in determining what things scarce resources will be used to make. Also, the divine message targets tastes and preferences and attempts to establish institutions that foster the formation and maintenance of truly spiritual preference sets.

5
Spirituality as Economically Rational Behaviour

This chapter very briefly defines economic rationality as understood within the paradigm that dominates most current economic modelling. The purpose is to show the extent to which *homo economicus* is actually assumed to be a rather forward-looking fellow, capable of sacrificing current wants unstintingly for his own future needs and the future needs of society.[1] Whether s/he will act in this manner is completely dependent upon his or her taste and preference set, which in turn is the result of influences experienced during the formative years. The role of divine speech as a potential influence can therefore hardly be overemphasized.

A 'spiritual' person is one who understands not only the relative value of things but also their absolute value, taking into account their total discounted value of all actions summed up at the 'cash-out' time. Thus if 'spiritual' is defined to mean 'forward-looking' behaviour or the ability to comprehend future results of present behaviour and so avoid doing anything now that will hurt future prospects, then *homo economicus* is clearly spiritual. He is assumed by economics to comprehend all present and future prices omnisciently and never to make systematic errors in judgement. But there are two problems with this conception: 1) the existence of a person with such a characteristic is impossible and relaxing the assumption of price omniscience, even a little, vitiates many central results supporting standard theories of how the world works, and 2) this assumption is insufficient to explain learning from past mistakes and, therefore, how resources are turned into finished goods and services of higher value, that is, how wealth is created.

Both these problems are rooted in the static nature of *homo economicus* as received without alteration from practitioners of an earlier era in the codification of economic science before dynamic, intertemporal mathematical techniques were utilized to the extent they are today. The solution that allows a relaxing of the omniscience-of-all-current-and-future-prices assumption without vitiating standard economic results informing public policies is to build into our models the recognition that economic activity takes place over time, either in discrete stages or continuously, and that if this knowledge is applied to the models, relaxing the assumed omniscience of economic man will not fatally affect them or the economic theory employed to explain various other individual and group behaviours.[2] Doing this makes *homo economicus* wise and spiritual.

Rational behaviour as it is defined here does not require that we can predict the future but only to learn from the past in forming present plans. We attempt to provide for our future welfare by learning to act positively now. As social people we care for those around us and provide for the unborn, as this will also enable us to live better now and in future, because, as we grow older and must retire, our offspring must take our places and will need at least as much social and economic capacity – if not more – than we had. Formal modelling and testing using economic dynamics confirms this approach. It provides a mathematical confirmation of the need to develop and maintain personal utility functions – measure of our likes and dislikes – that are linked to different time periods (intertemporal) and to other individuals and groups in society (interpersonal). Doing this avoids a life that would otherwise be, as Thomas Hobbes characterized it in 1651, 'solitary, poor, nasty, brutish and short'.[3]

This statement was employed to argue in favour of a paternal central authority to govern the people. Here it is employed the same way but in this instance the governance comes from adherence to a divine standard, which develops within individuals a common set of assumptions about how life works. In Hobbes's time little was expected from individuals beyond fealty to the royal sovereign and the need for a strong – even unlimited – central authority was generally assumed. Today western liberal democracy expects more of its citizens. But this expectation is based on the assumption of wisdom ruling individual choices, generating intertemporally consistent and interpersonally cooperative choices. As Benjamin Franklin is reported to have responded when asked what kind of government the American 'Founding Fathers' had come up with, 'A republic, madam – if you can keep it.'[4]

The conclusion is that economics sees society as being composed of spiritually rational agents and predicts ultimate extinction for any society in which the generality of its members are not spiritual, that is, where they are myopic and selfish. This fact is not generally recognized or acknowledged in economics. What is obvious to most spiritually-minded individuals is that the source of such attitudinal behaviour is rooted in the dialogues of the world's religions. Placed therein is the structure and logic justifying interpersonal investments and actions that delay gratification. The tracing of this source of what enables societies to continue to exist over time from modern economics to ancient dialogues spoken by Prophets to groups of often hostile listeners in deserts of the Levant, the Middle East and the Magreb is quite straightforward.

Economics identifies certain decision attributes as essential in defining what it considers to be economically rational behaviour. These are merely characteristics based on elementary logic, with only a few extensions, and they protect economics from becoming a science of irrational behaviour, which is, after all, what psychology and psychiatry are concerned with. The axioms are derived from number theory. Using these axioms assures decision theory practitioners that the defined *solution space* contains some form of answer to the problem being analysed, either unique or not. Or s/he can declare that there is no solution to the problem as constructed (or, more accurately, constrained).[5]

The following is a list of the most useful preference axioms that are the basis of all economic models of human behaviour. They are discussed here in order to appreciate how human preferences become translated into, at times, complex and influential models, which form the basis of life-transforming public policies.

Rational behavioural definitions are concerned entirely with tastes and preferences of individuals and groups. This is an acknowledgment of the reality that what people want is what people will ultimately get. Thus the key to changing behaviour is in changing personal tastes and preferences. That is precisely the task of every Manifestation of God ever sent to mankind.

Axiom 1: *Preferences are complete*. You decide either that you like apples more than pears or pears more than apples or you decide that they are the same for you. Not being able to decide is ruled out. Of course, you can change your mind later but *within the market period* – which is the time in which the decision and its outcome occur – you must decide and stick to your decision.

Axiom 2: *Preferences are reflexive*. If you cannot tell the difference between the qualities or attributes of two different goods then you must accept that they are essentially the same. Included in this is the non-importance of irrelevant differences. If you are colour blind the blue car is the same as the red car in your mind.

Look at the results of applying this axiom to whether a claimant to the office of divine Messenger is the return of the earlier Prophet. The earlier accredited Prophet will most likely have used a different language, have come from a different city, been known by a different name and have come from a different family and tribe than the current claimant. But the essence of what makes the earlier person an accredited Prophet and what makes the present claimant a Prophet is the nature of the message. This is a confirmable evidence of prophethood, that the message guides people and educates them spiritually and morally with surpassing authority.[6] Therefore, if the only difference between the earlier Prophet and the new claimant consists in these irrelevancies, then, according to the axiom of reflexivity, the claimant must also be a Prophet whose message must be accorded the same level of acceptance from the people. Rejecting one Prophet while accepting the other over irrelevant differences is impossible and says more about the irrationality of the hearers than about the nature of the questioned message or Messenger. Yet the historical record repeatedly shows that people acted in just such an irrational manner in accepting the earlier message and rejecting the latter one and that their preferences were not reflexive. Perhaps the explanation for this behaviour can be found in axiom 4 below.

Axiom 3: *Preferences are transitive*. If you prefer apples to pears and pears to prunes then you must prefer apples to prunes. This is the internal consistency requirement. A spiritual application of this principle can be represented in the trivial example that if you like order better than chaos and chaos better than systematic exploitation then you like order better than systematic exploitation. And this narrowing of your expressed preferences requires certain actions and conformity on your part. It means that you must be in favour of rules and regulations governing public and private spaces and that you will therefore pay for their formulation and enforcement. This rules out chaos. But further, you take responsibility to monitor the system so that it does not become a source of arbitrary or systematic oppression and the presence of rules and the rulers does not become worse than their absence.

Axiom 4: *Preferences are continuous*. In a technical sense, this assures that no black holes exist in our solution space. It also means that all things can be related to some other thing by comparison. 'Things are known by their opposites,' 'Abdu'l-Bahá states.[7] But does this mean that spiritual things can be compared to material things? The Prophets in their dialogues and the philosophers in their expositions both agree that this is generally impossible. Jesus' statement, 'That which is born of the flesh is flesh; and that which is born of the Spirit is spirit'[8] and Bahá'u'lláh's statement that 'Never shall mortal eye recognize the everlasting Beauty'[9] would seem to confirm this.[10] This principle is elucidated further by 'Abdu'l-Bahá:

> . . . know ye that the world of existence is a single world, although its stations are various and distinct. For example, the mineral life occupieth its own plane, but a mineral entity is without any awareness at all of the vegetable kingdom, and indeed, with its inner tongue denieth that there is any such kingdom. In the same way, a vegetable entity knoweth nothing of the animal world, remaining completely heedless and ignorant thereof, for the stage of the animal is higher than that of the vegetable, and the vegetable is veiled from the animal world and inwardly denieth the existence of that world – all this while animal, vegetable and mineral dwell together in the one world. In the same way the animal remaineth totally unaware of that power of the human mind which graspeth universal ideas and layeth bare the secrets of creation . . .
>
> In the same way the denizens of this earth are completely unaware of the world of the Kingdom and deny the existence thereof . . . Yet the mineral and vegetable, the animal and man, are all living here together in this world of existence.[11]

According to this, the reason for the discontinuity between our conceptions and the reality of the next world is based on our not having the native capacity or equipment for doing so. A dog, say, is incapable of comprehending why the sun is hidden or how a livingroom table begins as an idea in someone's head. Further, there is no way to explain these things to it. In the same way we humans are incapable of doing any more than understanding allusions to the next world's unsearchable forms. This theme is repeated many times in all religious writings and in the dialogues of the Prophets.

Therefore axiom 4 cannot bridge death. However, what axiom 4 cannot encompass, mathematics is capable of at least expressing. In the discussion of the next axiom, below, two methods of building mathematically compliant models are suggested.

Axiom 5: *Preferences exhibit non-satiation.* This means that more is always better in the absence of any fixed inputs. 'For self-love is kneaded into the very clay of man . . .'[12]

Volumes could be devoted to explaining the spiritual significance of this axiom. On one level it is a confirmation of 'Abdu'l-Bahá's statement that no thing can possibly be imagined by the human mind such that a better thing superior to it cannot also be imagined. Is that a possible reason why the Prophets repeatedly warn us not to become attached to material things, because in time we will think of something superior to them? How many romances have come crashing to earth when one tires of the physical allures of the other? 'They all look good when they're new,' the old men at the sawmill used to tell each other. They applied this generally – to cars, horses, the opposite sex, fishing rods and shotguns, etc. It seems they were right: while outer beauty withers, inner beauty does not age and is subject to enhancement or diminution instant by instant, according to personal will.

On another level it means that satisfaction is without limit. This result can guide us into endeavours where full scope for this process can be realized. The glory days of a superb athlete are numbered, as are the days of a fashion model, crime boss, president, artist or salaried or hourly paid employee. But the days of one involved with the discovery and analysis of new ideas or of reaching the exalted heights of understanding in spiritual realms need not be so limited. Voltaire never missed a good opportunity to extract humour from a situation, no matter how grim. Even on his deathbed his wit was undiminished. It is reported that on his deathbed, when asked by a visiting priest to renounce the devil, he replied, 'Is this any time to make enemies?'

The axiom that preferences are continuous does, however, allow us to compare the messages of the Prophets for similarities. This axiom guarantees that such comparisons can be made and that their similarities would indicate the presence of an underlying reality that, even if not directly observable, confirms the essential oneness of the messages and the Messengers.

If we believe, as explained by the Prophets, that this life is mere preparation for the next and that our life here is to develop inner capacities and strengths, then learning new things, taking on new responsibilities, accepting reverses as part of a complete life and achievements – clearly these are without limit as they transcend the artificial boundary of physical death. A proper model of such possibilities would be the *sum of the sum* of all discrete possibilities with respect to utility maximization, where the inner sum maximizes opportunities over the present life and the outer sum maximizes possibilities over the next life, a spiritual life wherein this life is nested and completely contained.[13]

Axiom 6: *Preferences are strictly convex.* This is how we would express the principle of *moderation in all things*. Technically, it requires that all the points on a chord stretched between two points within this set are themselves entirely within the set. This guarantees that most points are within the mass of the set and not located at its extreme points. Balanced, moderate bundles of goods are preferred to extreme valued bundles and tend to more easily maximize satisfaction.

Not only does this axiom prevent us from buying the car that nobody wants, the funny blouse or tie, etc., it also keeps us distant from all forms of fanaticism. 'Abdu'l-Bahá informs us that all affection and love is centripetal, tending towards the centre and proximate to reality, while all forms of hate tend towards remoteness and oblivion. This would mean that hate is an extreme position and by nature immoderate, centrifugal. Over time it would make us unhappy and we would not even understand why.

This axiom of strictly convex preference sets (moderation in all things) underpins the work of rational analysis in general and in science in particular. It creates a safe haven for spiritual inquiry by casting out fanatical and bigoted ideologies. While new ideologies are forever being formed, this preference axiom acts to protect rational analysis from ideological thinking, at least eventually. What a tool this is in protecting our thinking from the inroads of ideology and fanaticism, for by its nature fanaticism rejects objective thinking and critical analysis. The fanatical mind is incapable of correctly judging the merits of any message because all things are seen through the narrow spectrum of ideology and it is the sworn enemy of whatever refuses to be accommodated on its Procrustean bed.

***

We have now covered most of what is needed from economic science to understand and appreciate the linkages that exist between economics and spiritual laws as revealed by the Prophets and elucidated by philosophers. Specific elements will be discussed in greater detail in the following pages. In closing, and to emphasize the convolutions followed by science when it does not allow itself to be continually tested from external sources, look again at the effects of rational inquiry being subsumed by powerful ideologies that blind scientists to the implications of their ideologically-addled proposals.

In the 19th century Charles Darwin discovered that biological life was a struggle, a 'survival of the fittest'. Weaker individuals were eliminated and replaced by stronger ones in a never ceasing competition for existence itself. The myth goes that social scientists seemed to have been attracted to this theory and observation, appearing to apply it to economic life, particularly to the life of industrialized Great Britain, America and parts of Europe.

Even an element in Protestantism made common cause with the new theories, stating that it was the plan of God that the successful be successful and that giving aid to the poor and economically unsuccessful was tantamount to playing God and was interfering with the divine process. No, let them fail, as this is what has been destined for them by the All-Knowing Creator. Interfering with this divine process of 'natural selection' can only increase their pain and gives them time to leave offspring doomed to become even worse off than were their parents. Granted, it is difficult to watch their suffering, especially of the children. But we must be resolute, and once placing our hands on the plough, we must never turn back until the victory is won.

Appalling as these sentiments may sound to us now, they were adopted and declaimed by sensitive and educated people within and without the church and universities in 19th-century America, England and beyond. They offered justification and religious comfort to those capitalists and others espousing *laissez faire* social and economic policies and their refusal to aid the weak and helpless. But how much in agreement they seem to the sentiments contained in the following words, spoken a century and a half later, and in Moscow, not England or New York.

> Let us discuss what is the essence . . . An example was drawn that you must think of humanity as one great body, but one that requires constant surgery. Need I remind you that surgery cannot be performed without cutting membranes, without destroying tissues, without the spilling of blood? . . . Thus we must destroy whatever is superfluous. These are unpleasant acts, granted, but we do not find any of this immoral.

This is from Lazar Moiseyevich Kaganovich, as quoted by his nephew, Stuart Kahan, in his biography of his uncle, *The Wolf of the Kremlin*.[14] This Kaganovich was Stalin's henchman, called the 'architect of fear'. He was responsible for some major surgery on the body of mankind over a 30 year period, eliminating about 26 million people deemed 'superfluous'. See how little difference there is between the two sentiments, the one from newly industrialized 19th-century England and the other from newly industrialized 20th-century Soviet Russia.[15]

The Harvard paleontologist Stephan Jay Gould informs us that the actual direction of causation of what has come to be known as *Social Darwinism* was reversed. It was Darwin who was so won over by the assertions of the social scientists and others that life is a never-ending struggle for survival, and that by this means we progress, that he became convinced that the same forces must also work in nature. After following the current philosophical and religious debates concerning the poor, he modelled biological processes with this as the mechanism for the purposeful process of biological evolution and developed it in his seminal works *The Origin of Species* (1859) and *The Descent of Man* (1871). With respect to the dangerous presence of ideologies in science, which can poison scientific research and render it less than useless, the eminent economist Joseph A. Schumpeter in his address to the American Economic Association stated in 1948:

> . . . some of the sociological, psychological, anthropological, biological waters that wash our [economics'] shores are so vitiated by ideological bias that, beholding the state of things in parts of those fields, the economist might sometimes derive solace by comparison. Had we time we could everywhere observe the same phenomenon: that ideologies crystallize, that they become creeds which for the time being are impervious to argument; that they find defenders whose very souls go into the fight for them.[16]

From this we learn of the adamantine grip ideology often has on science and intellectual inquiry. However, Schumpeter reassures us with these words: 'no economic ideology lasts for ever and that, with a likelihood that approximates certainty, we eventually grow out of each.'[17]

Because economics is invoked as justification for policies on the left and the right and everywhere in between and because it is imagined to hold such magical promise in social engineering, we can only hope that its gross misuse may have given way to more introspection in policy design. There is no economic solution to the economic problem because the problem is not economic but social and philosophical, and in the limit, religious.

6

An Economic Analysis of Some Spiritual Themes

Beginning with the Economics of Regulation

We now complete the circle. The last chapter discussed some of the traces of spirituality in economics sourced from divine teachings; now we use economics to analyse spiritual themes. The economics of regulation would not seem to be good source material for that purpose but it turns out to be rich in spiritual implications.

As mentioned in the last chapter, economic man, *homo economicus*, is more spiritual than economic science itself realizes. He may not be capable of present and future price omniscience but the assumption that he acts wisely in economic and social situations in avoiding systematic errors has apparently always been assumed for him. This wisdom can only come with experience and therefore some kind of learning from mistakes and by example must be assumed for him as an individual. Learning from mistakes means that economic decisions are carried out dynamically, over time. Since the teachings of the Prophets take centuries for their inner significance to unfold, we must develop the meaning of spiritual themes and build the analysis within the structure of economic dynamics for the present analysis to be more than a trivial exercise of just translating religious topics into economic jargon.

This chapter begins with a look at the need for regulation in economic activities. It is the social science affirmation of the divine message that humans must live within such restraints as can guard the dignity of their station and protect them from their own selves. What are the implications of the need for omnipresent regulation? If a thing has market value or can be exchanged somehow then this would make it a candidate for regulation. But what doesn't? Bahá'u'lláh has not said much directly about technical economics in general or how its activities are to be regulated.[1] And with our definition of what constitutes such activity, His advice for many decisions is to follow what has been revealed in the noble Qur'án, and if not found there, to await a judgement from the Universal House of Justice in the fullness of time.

Some years ago I was talking with Dr Larry Libby, then Professor and Department Head of Food and Resource Economics at the University of Florida. He challenged me to come up with any act or thought, however inconsequential, that did not have economic implications. When we met again in a couple of days, he asked me how I had done. I replied that I hadn't come up with any. Whatever I thought of had economic implications.

I was surprised. Certainly, I thought, just praying alone in the dark lacked economic content. Actually, it had economic content on several counts.

1) There is the time used, our most basic resource. What else could it be used for right now? Is this its best use compared to all other current alternatives? This introduces the inescapable calculus of opportunity costs and demands that anything we do must be judged against this stern disciplinarian. 'Abdu'l-Bahá, in referring to children, exhorts, 'Let them not jest and trifle . . .'[2] As for adults, He says, 'Ye must . . . put forth a mighty effort, striving by night and day and resting not for a moment, to acquire an abundant share of all the sciences and arts . . .'[3] We also know that work is worship.[4] Similar statements exhorting our highest efforts in spiritual battles can be found in every revealed religious text. The only differences are in the details of the particular activities extolled, which change with the varying requirements of society through the ages.

2) Prayer, if it makes us more capable of concentrating on performing useful work, can result in increased output. This is well understood in industrial engineering: correctly timed and constructed work breaks yield an increased total output per worker. As prayer can clear the head and refresh the spirit, it generates greater concentration and thoughts free of worries and anxieties that sap our strength and energy.

3) The two principles of the opportunity cost of any time used and supplication to the divine Kingdom are combined in these words of 'Abdu'l-Bahá: 'Know that nothing will benefit thee in this life save supplication and invocation unto God, service in His vineyard, and, with a heart full of love, to be in constant servitude unto Him.'[5]

Now, if private prayer has non-trivial economic content, what about anything else we might engage in? This is not to suggest that prayer as a process or what is derived from it is trivial, only that its resource needs are low in material terms. But the opportunity cost of time used is always a part of any such decision. (Makes you a little scared to watch TV now, doesn't it?) This is especially true for us today, according to Bahá'u'lláh in the Book of Certitude:

> One righteous work performed in this Day, equalleth all the virtuous acts which for myriads of centuries men have practised – nay, We ask forgiveness of God for such a comparison! For verily the reward which such a deed deserveth is immensely beyond and above the estimate of men.[6]

One reason this could be so is shown by our earlier analogy of the spaceship on the launch pad. A new era, comprising numerous ages, was established and initiated by the appearance of Bahá'u'lláh, according to 'Abdu'l-Bahá. 'As to the cycle of the Blessed Beauty – the times of the Greatest Name – this is not limited to a thousand or two thousand years . . .'[7] There is also this statement: 'Wherefore, every day of the cycle of the Blessed Beauty is in reality equal to one year, and every year of it is equal to a thousand years.'[8] Bahá'u'lláh taught for 40 years, so even using this minimal value perhaps more than millions of years will pass before the appearance of another *universal* Manifestation, even while the next lesser Manifestation is expected after a thousand years. As you can imagine, even the tiniest alteration in the cycle at this earliest stage or a change in any of its initial conditions will drastically affect the direction of this time-vector and its ability to achieve its full and ultimate potential.[9] Our deeds comprise these initial conditions – the steering mechanism for its launch – and therefore profoundly affect our potential capability to achieve what we must as a race, those goals for growth and spiritualization that the Ancient of Days has set for us. In fact, this result can be shown mathematically using Optimal Control Theory and the calculus of variations.

Individual human development is no different (hence all the emphasis laid upon child rearing) from the initiation of epochs and stages or from the stages in the development of mankind from infancy to full adulthood. As spiritualized and enlightened individuals populate all social institutions there is a virtuous circle of self-sustaining gains that accelerate human development and righteousness. Because of the value of the resources of time and volition assigned for us and the leveraging of the associated spiritual gains and losses from their proper or improper utilization afforded by the opportunities of this day, the need to regulate all our actions would seem to be pre-existent. Bahá'u'lláh confirms this in the Most Holy Book.

> Regard men as a flock of sheep that need a shepherd for their protection. This, verily, is the truth, the certain truth. We approve of liberty in certain circumstances, and refuse to sanction it in others. We, verily, are the All-Knowing.
>
> Say: True liberty consisteth in man's submission unto My commandments, little as ye know it. Were men to observe that which We have sent down unto them from the Heaven of Revelation, they would, of a certainty, attain unto perfect liberty . . . Say: The liberty that profiteth you is to be found nowhere except in complete servitude unto God, the Eternal Truth.[10]

This makes clear that our lives are blanketed with a set of regulations covering every act or thought we might have. These regulations and constraints reference the existence of spiritual laws, just as the regulation to wear a seatbelt or to use caution with fire reference physical laws. We wear a seatbelt because we are aware of what will happen to us if we hit a tree at 100 kph (65 mph). Nothing will prevent us from continuing into the steering wheel, the windscreen and the dashboard if we don't. In the same way, we allow our actions and thoughts to be constrained and regulated because we know the result of being unregulated. Again, 'For self-love is kneaded into the very clay of man . . .'[11]

Actually, we act in reference to some body of regulation constantly. While young there are familial regulations or, if we rebel and escape these at an early age, the regulation of the gang (more strict and rigid) will be imposed; eventually the jail or correctional facility may be our new environment (even more strict and rigid). Freedom is a fable. It is not necessary for us to discuss how the result of past actions actually define us as to character or potential and future possibilities for action and thought.

In an economic sense, regulations comprise the constraints defining a solution space where actions occur. Without these constraints life itself, even physical life, is impossible and, like division by zero, 'undefined'. Thus existence itself on any plane requires constraints.

The following examples show how judiciously applied constraints and regulations revived systems by limiting corruption (a form of erosion of constraint that increases transaction costs to such a degree they become harmful or make some transactions impossible) and establishing transactional lifelines.

New York City and Freedom through Regulation

It is hard for people to realize just how bad things had got in the city of New York, just how far city life had sunk, since the end of the Second World War.

By 1973 Brooklyn and the other hard-working boroughs had lost most of the well-paying blue-collar jobs, leaving poorly paid service jobs as the only alternative for low skilled wage earners. There was the front page embarrassment of Mayor Abe Beame appealing to the federal government for a loan so the city could meet its municipal payroll, and the front page result in the *New York Post*, 'Washington to New York: Drop Dead'. New York had become the cliché of urban decay and neglect. Once it had been the city with some of the choicest homes on the planet but by 1975 it was more often the home of people who had no choice.

The Bronx's middle class, having moved there a generation before from Lower East Side tenement houses in Manhattan, now left for Florida, New Jersey, Westchester County, Connecticut or Long Island, leaving behind the poor and all those without the means to escape the worsening conditions. As its tax base shrank, Bronx schools declined, apartment houses were abandoned and gangs increasingly ruled all public space. TV news now showed South Bronx apartment houses in flames, torched for the insurance money because no one could stand to live there anymore, or pictures of another bloodied street in East New York or Bushwick, with the NYPD clotted around the body of some child caught in the crossfire of a drug gang dispute. And who could forget the shame of the rape and murder of Kitty Genovese on a neighbourhood street, carried out over a two-hour period by a lone assailant in plain view of people watching from the relative safety of their apartments. The assailant himself was shocked that over two hundred New Yorkers listened and watched from behind window curtains and not one called the police or went out to help her. Everywhere drugs, stolen goods and guns were available for open and uninterrupted sale on street corners. The city administration, increasingly starved for cash, simply gave up on many things, declaring that there was nothing to do, that it was part of a larger movement in the world that must run its course. The city of New York was considered ungovernable, as crimes were increasing in number and severity at an alarming rate. The subways, used by about two million people daily, were fast becoming human sewers, dangerous and smelly, covered in graffiti and strewn with human waste and even cadavers on occasion. Gangs terrorized commuters, aggressive panhandlers accosted riders, and the homeless had taken up semipermanent residence in the cars, platforms and deep, vast recesses of the largest subway network in the world. Arresting criminals seemed to do nothing to stop the acceleration in the sad decline in service and safety.

All that changed with the public safety improvements of the early 1990s. One of the most remarkable manifestations of this increase in civil order was that New Yorkers began to reassert themselves, not just in meeting rooms but in the streets, parks, buses and subways, breaking up robberies, threatening would-be assailants and 'encouraging' each other to 'curb' their dogs. This was unheard of just a decade before. As Rudy Giuliani would later say on becoming mayor in 1994, everything begins with public safety. But, out of public view, things were already showing signs of change.

In 1990 a new Transit Police Commissioner was appointed, William J. Bratton. In consultation and cooperation with Deputy Police Commissioner Jack Maple, who devised the computer tracking system COMPSTAT, they quickly applied the promising new theory of criminal behaviour. No longer would the Transit Police address serious crimes only; from now on people were to be arrested for even minor offences like fare-beating (jumping the subway turnstiles without paying the fare), graffiti painting, spitting and littering, etc., and they were to be aggressively prosecuted. These were called 'quality of life' crimes which had not received any attention from self-respecting law officers who saw their role as protecting the public from more serious offences. Very soon, not only did the incidence of these crimes fall – which was expected – but the incidence of serious and violent crimes in the subway system also fell – which was not expected, at least not by the public or the police officers themselves.

It turned out that addressing minor quality of life crimes and reducing them made for a more *orderly* environment. The order in the environment discouraged all crimes, including serious felonies, and so these too began to decline.

This is called the 'Fixing Broken Windows' theory. It explained in part the phenomenal reduction in New York's crime statistics. The crime reduction was so dramatic that New York became famous by 1999 as the safest large city in the world and remains so today (2006). Mayors from all over come to New York to study its crime fighting system, then go back to their own cities to apply its principles.

The theory that orderly environments induce public safety while chaotic ones induce crime was the result of years of research and study and some controlled experimentation.[12] Time and again, when the physical environment was 'cleaned up' and made orderly, crime rates would fall. New York subways are now practically free of any graffiti, spitting, radio playing, match lighting and gangs and are used daily by over five million riders.

But that is not all. Because the relationship between increased orderliness and decreased crime is not linear, what happened was that there seemed to be no change in the beginning, then suddenly criminal behaviour plummeted, as though orderliness had to reach some threshold before it could affect behaviour.[13] As the subways became a more orderly environment and as crime rates fell, the number of riders increased. And this, the presence of so many salaried office workers, teachers, mothers and their school-bound children, made doing crime even less likely and drove down crime incidents in the subway system even further.

As to the economic impact of all this 'orderliness', the gross domestic product of the city of New York is now far greater than that of the continent of Australia (OK, so that's mostly empty desert. But Greater New York is only a couple of hundred square miles and Manhattan is just two miles across and 15 miles long!) and has shown its greatest increase over the last ten years. It is reflected in the constantly increasing real estate values and the astronomical rents that are willingly paid as more people from the world over move to New York. With safer streets nightlife returned, as did the practicality of working the night shift. The city stopped losing population (and tax base) to the suburbs and was in 2006 greater than 8,200,000, where it had been just after World War II and just before its long and sad decline.

The point is that orderliness itself was in many essential ways responsible for the reduction in crime. And this is in contrast – and I emphasize this – to just arresting more criminals, which was not working either to deter crime or to reduce its severity. Unfortunately, New York and other urban and rural school systems have not learned the obvious lessons from New York City's crime reduction experiment. Reducing chaos and disorderliness in the state schools among our children, such as requiring appropriate dress and attire and instituting other manifestations of public civility, would be expected to have the same salutary effect on the learning environment – increasing grades and work effort, reducing gang activity and other risky youth behaviours – as reducing chaos and maintaining an orderly environment has had on street crime.

So much for violent street crime. What about organized crime or white collar crime in New York? This had also become a serious problem, as symbolized by making Mafia crime boss John Gotti, head of the Gambino crime family, into a celebrity. Again, increased arrests were insufficient either to deter this or to reduce the seriousness of offences. In his recent book *Gotham Unbound: How New York was Liberated from the Grip of Organized Crime*, James Jacobs explains that what was needed to reduce or eliminate organized crime from the city was a thorough application of licensing procedures and other ways to regulate the marketplace. These, rather than arrests, were responsible for eliminating organized crime from the garment industry, the Fulton fish market, trash collection (the cartage trade), building construction and labour at convention centres and smuggling and looting in New

York Port Authority facilities like JFK airport, the largest transshipment airport in the United States.

Regulation in Labour Unions

Whatever we may think about them, under conditions of clear lawlessness and market oppression of workers, often by colluding employers backed by ruthless and naked violent force, labour unions historically have been the sole hope of the working poor. Throughout history those renting out their labour have almost never done as well as those with capital to rent – be it financial, intellectual or some other kind, and this situation has only got worse in the United States and elsewhere over the last decades. Indeed, economics itself states that when market distortions already exist and there is no hope of eliminating them, then the next best thing to do is to introduce an opposing distortion that can balance the previous one. Unions introduce monopsony power – single buyer power – into the market where monopoly power – single seller power – exists in order to counterbalance wage and price distortions and thereby win some of the economic rents for its worker-members. Today we witness that with the weakening of labour unions, goods prices have indeed fallen but wages have fallen even more, and the middle class has been reduced, with those in the executive and well-educated ranks becoming rich and their employees losing out. Refer to any set of national labour statistics or those showing share percentages of a nation's GDP for each cohort to verify this fact.

As with every hierarchical structure, unions are open to corruption. Unions are neither more nor less corrupt than other organizations in economic space.[14] Sadly, governments in the West have generally been sanguine towards evidence of union corruption, as if to say, 'We told you so',[15] while being far more lenient towards corruption and greed among corporate and government executives, including union executives, who may be looting union dues and pension funds or making 'sweetheart no-strike deals' with management for cash payoffs. It might take the union 'rank and file' itself to bring this management to heel using legal suits and public disclosures of wrongdoing before the government takes action to reform the union for the good of its members.

For example, regulatory changes were responsible for cleaning up the largest labour union in the United States, the International Brotherhood of Teamsters (IBT) or Teamsters union. A grass roots effort, led by the Teamsters for a Democratic Union (TDU), to take it back from the corrupt bosses who had come to control it, finally generated federal support in 1990. The IBT leadership was turned out, some ending up in federal prison for various charges of extortion, money laundering, murder and other corrupt practices. The Teamsters was ordered to be overseen by the federal trusteeship of Judge William Webster, who later became director of the FBI, until new regulations guaranteeing universal suffrage rights to all members and other structural changes could be erected.[16] It was a great victory for long-suffering labourers whose own union had been exploiting them and selling them out. While an industrial sector free of the need for unions is envisioned for mankind, they will be with us until the need to protect workers from unscrupulous employers is either eliminated or given over to another authority, such as governmental control, in order to assure economic justice for all societal members.

The New Russia Strangled at Birth

It is too bad that many Anglo-American economists have failed to realize the extent to which free markets depend on regulation and control for their very existence and certainly for the relative efficiency of their outcomes. Many have not and in 1990, just after the collapse of the Soviet Union, these were called in to give direction and advice to the new Russian and other CIS states as to how they could transition from centrally controlled autocracies to fully functioning market economies. Since these economists had not appreciated how social institutions underpin markets, providing the transferable property rights and rules and regulations essential for exchanges, the result of their 'advice' was predictable and disastrous. The economies were taken over by small and powerful oligarchies of mobsters and party bosses, who looted their nations for selfish gain and left citizens with nothing to eat. Even after the rise in oil income (Russia is the second largest oil producer in the world) it is little better today. In fact, the new Russian government is returning to its centralizing ways, re-nationalizing large swathes of resource markets, just when foreign direct investment is needed to overcome decades of under-investment and neglect.

Why this complete collapse, in spite of their having solicited the advice of some of the best economic minds in the western world? Because, after a lifetime of professional work, these mostly American economists were joined at the hip to the ideology of Anglo-American capitalism, witless of its complete reliance on a six-hundred-year-old tradition of property law and contract jurisprudence underwriting it. With their intellects thus swaddled, they were incapable of ever considering the systems of regulation and control outside market operations that make them work and so would not hear any talk of transitional alternative paths or even that capitalism itself takes many differentiated forms.

In an environment of complete chaos and lawlessness, the old Soviet bosses with their unrivalled international and financial market connections and control of the government apparatus rose to the throne of economic power and the weak populous was incapable of dislodging them. Auctions were suggested by western economists, wherein the resource firms, factories and other concerns of the old soviet would be auctioned off to the populous who were given scrip shares for that purpose. In the event, a few well-connected individuals swindled the population in sham auctions and rigged bidding schemes where a shadowy bidder would somehow 'win' the auction. In a few months the resources of the largest nation on earth were in the grasp of a handful of individuals, shutting the population out. In a few years the Russian GDP was less than that of Denmark. It has bounced back somewhat since then but that is not the point. Where should it have been by 2007, were it to have assumed the growth path possible before being crippled by national looting on a vast scale?

A scathing portrait of the events of these days is presented in *Globalization and Its Discontents* by Joseph Stiglitz, winner of the 2001 Nobel Prize for Economics and past president of the World Bank. Another, more detailed analysis can be found in the compelling *The Piratization of Russia: Russian Reformation Goes Awry* by Marshall Goldman. As things now stand, with the oligarchs in 'legal' possession of most Russian property and resources not nationalized by the government, a seizure and redistribution would be required to allow ordinary citizens to win anything for themselves from honest effort, so perverted has the system become. Russia is as unfavourable to workers today as it was before 1917. Such state-orchestrated seizures are now taking place, at least in the primary resource market, as evidenced by the jailing of the wealthiest of oligarchs, the owner of Yukos Oil, Michael Khodorkovsky, for tax evasion and money laundering. But how different things would have been if the public auctions of Soviet assets had been fair and had thus generated a true profit-sharing spirit in the population?

Order in the Schools

It is beyond the scope of this book to analyse the application of religious teachings, especially the newly revealed teachings contained in the Revelation of Bahá'u'lláh and their elucidation by 'Abdu'l-Bahá. But statements regarding the need for order and regulation in all aspects of life are found in every divinely revealed book, constituting the pillars of the faith in God, that authority rests with God, and to Him all matters return for judgement. They also instruct us that by the proper application of necessary constraints true freedom can be experienced. And, as in the discussion of New York City's crime reduction through increasing orderliness, this same procedure finds application in improving public education. Further, some space must be given to the salutary effect of properly applied constraints on the lives of maturing children and the realization of their future potential outside of the classroom. 'Abdu'l-Bahá, the chosen interpreter of the Revelation of Bahá'u'lláh, is adamant that children, left entirely to their own devices, become increasingly worse off and savage. 'It followeth that the children's school must be a place of utmost discipline and order . . .'[17] We also read in the noble Qur'án: 'And human inner selves are swayed by greed.'[18]

It can be shown that if a situation of indiscipline is allowed to continue for too long children may become incapable of learning in a structured environment.[19] But structured learning environments are the very places where most training and education take place. If children become incapable of functioning within that environment most learning opportunities are beyond their reach and they will most likely face a life of economic and social oblivion. Optimizing learning potential in the child is rather the same as optimization for any other dynamic multi-staged problem. Inputs must be of the proper amount and timed perfectly for the 'system' to reach its full potential. And, like the rocket aimed towards some remote goal in the heavens, initial conditions are all-important for its success.[20]

Sections 94 to 125 of *Selections from the Writings of 'Abdu'l-Bahá* are devoted to the education and training of children and related themes. They make clear the necessity of providing a healthy and encouraging structure in the life of a child. The practical and economic effect of accomplishing this is the following.

Beyond having complete faith in the words and admonitions of the teacher, in order to learn a sense of regret must be constructed in the individual, an ability to learn from mistakes and to regard the future as a reality. Previously we learned that the subjective rate of time preference and the subjective planning horizon determine how the future is valued and of what length that future is, respectively. If child rearing is such that lessons do not occur within the child's subjective planning horizon and experience has not begun the process of reducing the subjective rate of time preference so that patience is sufficient to see a thing to its completion, then rewards and punishments will not be seen as being connected to anything the child might have done. Rather, they are experienced as random events having nothing to do with personal actions. Under this scenario learning is impossible. In this sense orderliness does not mean just physical neatness but also intemporal orderliness, so that the consequences of previous actions are seen as being their direct result and the relationship between actions and their consequences is made as strong and as sure as possible. Otherwise, events following upon actions will seem like random happenings, with no sense or understanding as to their relationship to previous actions or of being their direct and inevitable outcome. Thus, intertemporal orderliness is essential for learning to take place.

Regarding those children who suffer intertemporal chaos, experience has shown that when they begin school their behaviour requires constant intervention. These children are unable to perform in a structured group learning environment. They require all the attention while the best students most hungry for knowledge, those who come from environments that cemented in their minds the functional relationship between actions and results, who are orderly and well-mannered, get no attention at all. Thus the class moves forward only as fast as the worst prepared student allows; and if that student is incapable of learning in a classroom setting, little indeed will that class be able to learn. Good students become bored and lose hope, perhaps even dropping out of school altogether.

This situation soon degenerates into a self-sustaining cycle. Ill-prepared children cannot learn in structured environments and if forced to attend will cause the degradation of the system itself. This leads to children becoming mature adults without the capacity to become financially viable and thus being consigned to social and economic stagnation. Society loses their production and their taxes. With fewer taxes and shrinking budgets, public expenditures must be cut back, including expenditures on schools, training programmes and whatever remedial youth programmes that have thus far escaped the public's budget-balancing axe. Also being lost are expenditures for public safety, streetlights, libraries, community outreach programmes. There is a general reduction in community and social capital available for raising the next generation and maturing them into useful, conscientious adults. The social fabric Balkanizes as those with sufficient family capital live in gated communities and see their children on to successful adulthood while poor families, vexed and frustrated, witness the dying of hope in their children's young breasts and its replacement by shallow and materialistic attachments. These deprived children witness ever fewer among their own ranks that 'make it' and can serve as positive examples to others.

Thus the essential need for establishing structure early in the child's life, lest the life enterprise fails before it has had a chance to even start.[21] 'Abdu'l-

Bahá states that of all possible things, parents can have no excuse to give before the Throne of the Creator if they fail to educate or properly train their children, as the consequences are lifelong and mostly irremediable past a certain age.[22] Indeed *self-discipline and the ability to self-invest can be regarded as the greatest gift parents can bestow on their children* after the recognition of the cause of God in the person of His Manifestation, since with this practically all difficulties in life can be overcome and without it almost nothing the child might aspire to is possible of accomplishment. It would be like a beautiful bird watching as its community takes wing in full flight to far-off and wondrous places while its own crippled wings force it to look on with broken heart from its prison of earth as they all disappear over the horizon. Self-discipline, the greatest of personal possessions, is the result of conscientious and systematic training. It is learned behaviour and learning is learned behaviour also.

***

If regulations and constraints are responsible for all these good things, are they direct creators of wealth in that case? Actually, no; constraints do not create wealth but only facilitate wealth creation. As explained previously when discussing the proper size of government, wealth is created only by productive enterprises operating through time. Again, this is like the analogy of the catalysts that operate in our body to reduce the heat and pressure necessary for the conversion of the energy we need to live. The catalysts do not enter the equation directly but only facilitate the final result and make it possible; and constraints do not create wealth but only facilitate its creation. They do this by making transactions possible. They are the catalysts of transactions and wealth creation through investment.

This chapter began with the observation that imagining a non-economic action is theoretically impossible. Time's opportunity cost was employed to act as the economic and financial floor under any decision made. Then we added other valuable resources and argued that the goodness of decisions to do one thing rather than another with available resources is a basic and inescapable way of evaluating how we live. The words of Bahá'u'lláh, 'Bring thyself to account each day ere thou art summoned to a reckoning . . .'[23] strongly encourage this by setting an unknown time limit on our lives and therefore on our ability to freely use the resources that have been given to us. But it is not just the omnipresence of this calculus that gives decisions their economic quality.

Whenever resources of value are used for something there will be some kind of result. They will have been used up to some extent and so we must ask what their use has achieved. The point is that this process forms a transaction, it is an exchange process. Exchanges exist in markets and markets have rules and regulations governing what can transpire within them, what is fair, etc. This is just as true for a soul praying to its Creator as for a person buying a head of cabbage in the market. We need to understand, therefore, what is possible for us when we transact in whatever market we choose. Each has specified rules defining this. Our praying at the midnight hour as the rest of the house sleeps is an exchange. We use resources (time, alertness) to generate an exchange of our humility, our concentration, sincerity and volition and receive – what?

Religions all exhort us to eschew materialistic cravings, to develop our spiritual attributes and to approach the threshold of God in prayer, asking for things that will help us to accomplish what is worthy of accomplishment. 'The source of all evil is for man to turn away from his Lord and set his heart on things ungodly',[24] and 'approach Me not with lifeless hearts, defiled with worldly desires and cravings'.[25] Also, 'And wish not for the things in which Allah has made some of you excel others.'[26] Also, 'Say: Short is the enjoyment of this world. The hereafter is better for you.'[27] Numerous other passages from the divine teachings support this theme. Thus prayer should beg for those things that will better enable us to fulfil our duties, make us capable of increased effort and raise our value to others. We beg for insight, concentration, poise and calm, expansiveness of spirit and energy for work ('Be not content with the ease of a passing day . . .'[28]) rather than to win the lottery or other such things. 'Thou dost wish for gold and I desire thy freedom from it . . . how can My way accord with thine?'[29] Thus prayer transactions are also constrained and regulated. Of course, we can choose to ignore these laws but that in no way nullifies them, anymore than failing to use our seatbelt nullifies physical laws if we hit a tree. (Now that you really need it, don't ask for 'credit' for all the times you used the belt when it wasn't needed; spiritual laws don't work that way either.)

Every kind of market *rations* in this way, determining results based on what is available within them and on the rules for transacting. Whenever resources are used a transaction is made. In many ways the perceived goodness of transaction results depends in the largest part on whether a gain or loss is realized. If resource use continually leads to loss then they cannot be maintained and will eventually be dissipated, perhaps by an 'unforeseen calamity'. For a transaction to be judged truly successful it must do more than just maintain resource stocks, since one resource stock has been spent and can never be replaced, namely, time. Therefore there is no stasis possible in life. 'O you who believe! Spend of that which We have provided for you, before a Day comes when there will be no bargaining, nor friendship, nor intercession.'[30] Every act must somehow further our development and the quality and quantity of our contribution, if life is to be lived thoughtfully and conscientiously.

7

The Economic Concept of Sin
and Its Spiritual Counterpart

Can a science have a concept of sin? Definitions of sin generally emphasize morality and moral judgements are not supposed to be a part of scientific methodologies. This is technically correct but, practically speaking, science makes moral judgements all the time, at very least deciding what constitutes valid material for study. Economists are generally very careful not to overtly bias their work or fall into becoming advocates for a particular cause, lest their work become tainted and looked on as probably unreliable by their peers. And there is plenty in the sphere of economics to become upset about. There are taxation issues, labour and human exploitation, globalization, corporate dominance strategies, economic growth, public investments in children, etc., etc.

Since economic science studies how people use resources in ways yielding the greatest possible returns, then anything leading to systematic waste comes pretty close to our concept of sin. Waste is 'sinful' because it does not equate value in production with value in consumption. For example, if finished goods of high value ready for human consumption (bread) were diverted to use as an intermediate input good (feed) to make another finished good (chicken), this would be a sin because of the waste involved. A society insisting on such wasteful practices runs the risk of ultimate oblivion. This was the result of market distorting price policies, keeping the price of bread artificially low, far lower than the cost of its wheat, which comprises only about four per cent of bread's total value, a great 'sin' indeed.

This same principle of price distortion and improper use of resources can be readily applied to the spiritual concept of sin. It is made easier by remembering that spiritual laws exist as physical laws do and that the Prophets' task is to inform humanity of these laws. Breaking a spiritual law is labelled a 'sin' while breaking a physical law is labelled an 'error', a 'mistake'. But the result is the same in the sense that *the law doesn't care what you do*. If the laws are understood and respected there will be one set of results and if they are violated there will be another. The laws involved are indifferent to your enterprise or to the results of your acting in one way or the other. This is your business. The divine Prophets and Messengers inform us that our actions can neither help nor harm God but affect only our own selves.

Physical laws govern material outcomes while spiritual laws govern super-material outcomes, including all our exchanges, with ourselves, with other people, with intellectual abstractions, with spiritual worlds, everything. They operate as bidden by their Creator, not by us. So we must not take it personally if our poor behaviour causes despondency; it is only the result of existing laws and not some special decree designed to make us feel pain right now.[1]

The new teaching from Bahá'u'lláh's divinely revealed lectures also illuminates many of the previous prophetic dialogues, drawing out from them what had not previously been suspected of them. The Christian concept of original sin emphasized a fall from some pre-existent grace as a direct result of wanting to know too much, you might say. Sin was conceived as breaking someone's personal rule: 'You touch dat an' I kill you!' But it now appears that sin was meant by the Prophets to mean that we are created *imperfect* and that imperfection means that we are *dependent* beings. 'Why callest thou me good? There is none good but One, that is, God,' said His Holiness Jesus.[2] Thus only the independent Being – since it relies only on its own self – is perfect and, being perfect, it is, by definition, free from error and hence sin. Thus the independent Being is perfect and free of sin and all others are dependent upon this ultimate Being.[3] As dependent they are 'sinful' in the sense of being imperfect, dynamically unstable, tending to error, chaos and dissolution, incapable of independent life.

Existing near the bottom of the hierarchical chain of causation, we are incapable of imagining its ultimate cause. But we have established that there is causation with respect to ever broader and more generalized dependencies, all dependent upon the ultimate independent Being. Sin is therefore a function of the level of dependence. Within the entire spectrum it is an absolute measure, discontinuous because it compares finite to infinite values, but within any segment it must be seen as relative to what is done and what is possible. But the absolute measure is asserted with respect to the relationship of the part to the whole. From this it is defined and attains its ultimate existence.

This has a perfect parallel in economics. Parts are judged by their contribution to the whole, each whole by its contribution to the economy today and into the future. Examining the idea of a finished good versus a capital good a little more closely results in a new insight into the nature and consequences of most types of sin. Economics characterizes entities by use. Resources are considered the raw material of production and consist of what is readily available in its undeveloped form. The oil is 'crude', meaning not yet distilled into its various grades. The grades themselves are not consumed by people; rather, they are used to produce something else, transport services or energy. This makes them intermediate goods. Now say that diesel oil is used in a field tractor in an agricultural application. The soil is the resource and the fertilizer, the diesel, the seeds, etc., are intermediate goods and are inputs to the further production process of making food for human consumption.

The tractor itself is called a capital good because it is a finished good but its use is in the production of food.[4] In this sense cars are also capital goods since they are used for transportation and it's the transportation that we are after, not the car, really. (Of course, auto manufacturers realized that if they could get us to treat cars as finished goods – those things providing enjoyment for their own sake – they would sell a lot more of them, even inducing us to abandon our perfectly utilitarian older models for some fancier new rig that might not work any better than did the old one.)

The determination of one good as a capital good, another as an intermediate good, another a finished good, is sometimes ambiguous and depends in large part on the context. Generally it combines the relationships of the good to production and of the production to its end use by humans. The automobile was mentioned but in a broad sense everything serving our needs directly or indirectly are capital goods because they enable us to continue life. Even things that merely entertain could be characterized this way if they leave us rested and ready for greater effort.[5]

So, in the broadest sense – if not in the more immediate sense – things are graded in economics by their service to human needs. The greater their service to human requirements, the greater their value, all else being equal.[6]

But which requirements exactly? If a public servant is responsible for saving thousands of lives, you would think this would be worth more than being able to hit a ball with something and get it into a hole in the ground but it isn't, at least with respect to the money each is paid. This shows the current limits of two things: our ability to value *value itself* and our ability to solve everything with the use of private markets. But it also shows something else: that humans themselves serve ends and their 'value' is more or less determined by the ends they serve.

Humans are definitely capital goods. And the different parts of humans are definitely capital goods. We use our parts to serve our larger interests and we are used in turn to serve the needs of each other. This introduces the idea of waste as sin. We are constantly challenged by the historical religious Prophets to follow our best and highest instincts, to overcome our lower self, to fight against its siren call and to force it to serve our highest and noblest aspects. If we then allow our lower sides – the means to our continued physical existence – to dictate how we shall live, then this is a sin, both economically and spiritually. It constitutes spiritual sin because it breaks the law of creation which states that life follow a purposeful path from separation to continuance, disorganization to organization, remoteness to reunion, rebelliousness to radiant acquiescence and thereby create ever more wonderful life forms. It is an economic sin because it constitutes the worst kind of waste, the waste of a human life and its perversion from striving to 'make something out of yourself' to a downward spiral of serving base and carnal desires, a loss both to the individual and to the community which loses his or her potential production.

This raises the question of whether a person has the *right* to 'retire' from being as active as possible whenever enough wealth has been amassed to allow a life of ease and consumption without the need to work. The answer in both spiritual and economic spheres is that such an action would be a grave sin. Spiritually, we have a continuing obligation to be useful to our society in some way at all times, as long as health permits, until death. Economically, a human constitutes a vast, possibly an infinitely-valued, resource, the withdrawal of which from productive activities represents a profound loss to society. In this sense economic and spiritual concepts of sin are in complete accord.

For a mature human being to willingly allow his physical nature to dictate his actions is to feed bread to pigs. As 'Abdu'l-Bahá explains, all life serves the needs of its higher forms: the mineral serves the needs of plants, animals and man; plants serve the needs of animals and man; animals serve the needs of man; and all serve the needs of God. Any reversal in this direction is destructive and is called by different names, all bad. In biology, when an animal is invaded by bacteria or a virus it is called sickness and disease, which can become fatal if not addressed. In chemistry when a metal is attacked by some agent it is called corrosion; in geology it is called erosion, in geopolitics it is called war; in crisis intervention it may be called divorce or abandonment; in jurisprudence and religion it is called corruption; in economics we have waste and in spiritual spheres it is sin. In all fields, while the name of the reversing process is different, its operation is much the same: it works to tear down the formation of higher levels of unity.

Violating spiritual laws can even lead to physical disease, and since that can result in physical extinction and since the body is the instrumental expression of the immortal and elemental soul, this is more serious than an attack just on the animal plane of life. It may bring to an end the purposeful development of the soul, so that it emerges at its birth from this temporal life less than developed to the extent it could have been, to the experiential loss of that person.

Now consider the world as a quasi-closed system. The coincidence of needs – or more accurately, a tautology of needs – of everyone serving everyone else in some way requires that it be supported from the outside somehow so it does not run out of itself, like microbial life on a petrie dish. Whenever a civilization, for example, turns away from the spiritual principles underpinning its reason for being, it soon becomes moribund within and attacked from without. Just as in economics, therefore, spiritual sin seems to be involved with this use of a higher valued entity for a lower valued aim – getting means and ends mixed up, in other words.

In a fundamental way humans must in the end serve needs outside and above themselves. To do so reinvigorates the human system and, by introducing spiritual and intellectual material from outside, assures its survival. Therefore, when humans choose to use their God-given resources for ends that do not serve humanity's primary needs, it is a spiritual sin because it threatens the individual's development and an economic sin because it threatens the existence of the community. Demand rises for otherwise low valued goods and falls for intrinsically high valued goods. This generates market distortions of producer and consumer prices.

Social Planning and Sin

Along with the development of rational economic man, economics has also looked at collective rational decision-making and arrived at criteria for judging certain actions as good or bad, beneficial or sinful in the way it is meant spiritually, as just explained. For example, when is it acceptable for the state forcibly to seize a person's private property for some collective good? This is not the same as asking if the ends justify the means (which answer is, they do not). What is being asked here is, what are the appropriate rules – if any – for such action to be undertaken? Two sets of rules have emerged.

The first set uses the idea of 'do no harm'. A move that redistributes property rights or commonly held wealth is acceptable as long as at least one party is made better off and no party is made worse off (Pareto criterion). So making someone worse off, no matter what the reason, is a sin and must be avoided. In this sense economics uses the term identically to its spiritual use since calling a redistribution that makes someone worse off a sin is clearly a social judgement and not a scientific statement of natural law or a mathematically derivable theorem. Even if mathematically derivable, it is a value judgement to declare that whatever increases overall wealth is 'good' and what can do so without making any party suffer a diminution of privately held value is 'better still'.

This criterion of goodness in collective rule faced serious challenges in America and elsewhere when privately held land was needed[7] by a growing and expanding nation for public works projects such as flooding from dam construction, railroads, the interstate highway system, airport construction, etc. If strictly followed the present criterion would disallow all of these projects, no matter how much wealth they would add to society in general, because some people would clearly lose substantially. What was needed was another criterion that allowed losers to be compensated in some straightforward manner from the potential or realized winnings accruing from the proposed public work.

The second set of rules governing correct collective actions developed in consequence of the restrictions and impracticality of the previous set. Its advance was to incorporate the idea of 'fair compensation'. It stated that a social move that made someone worse off was justified and acceptable as long as the economic gains from the move were sufficient to compensate all persons for the associated losses, the Kaldor-Hicks criterion. This is the criterion used to decide the efficacy of all public works and other collective projects today. Businessmen and politicians loved this formulation for two reasons: 1) it provided a simple way to proceed with public works promising substantial economic gains for the community, even where some parties would suffer losses and 2) there is no stipulation that such compensation *actually be paid out* to the losing parties, only that the gains from the project be sufficient to do so.

The complete acceptance of the compensation principle opened economics up to the criticism of being disingenuous and corrupt, which we already know is a sin. A move is undertaken that makes people worse off because the collective winnings are sufficient to fully compensate for all losses. Then it happens that no compensation is ever in fact paid. Thus an economic principle has been used to deceive the public and rob the helpless. This would not have been the first time, nor the last, when scientific results were manipulated and distorted to achieve narrow political results. Recall 'scientific management' devised by Frederick W. Taylor, later called

'Taylorism' and associated with worker exploitation, although a careful reading of the principles show they were intended to achieve a better and more humane workplace.

In response, economists have argued that the science should not be held accountable for the misdeeds of society. The criterion is sound and fair; its misuse by the greedy and shortsighted is not to be blamed on science. This is correct. 'Abdu'l-Bahá states that a lighted lamp in the hands of a child will result in setting both the house and the child on fire and is not the fault of the lamp.[8] Light is good; its misuse results in damage, as is true for any potent force.

There is another problem with the compensation criterion. If a social action is possible where winners can compensate losers from project gains, then it is also possible for potential losers to *bribe* potential winners into not undertaking the project in the first place, thereby preventing society from achieving possible economic gains. This happens and is called the *reversibility paradox*. Powerful parties can block needed social changes if they would disadvantage their own private interests. For example, the American Minerals and Mining Law of 1872 allows people to obtain large tracts of public land at far below market prices if the land is to be used for mining. This law has outlived its usefulness. Today firms acquire valuable real estate with this law for pennies on the dollar, set up a sham mine then develop the property for non-mining and far more lucrative uses. But while its misuse is a matter of record and common knowledge, and while environmentalists and other interested parties working for the social good have repeatedly tried to get the law nullified, mining and other corporate interests have always been able to control enough votes in government to defeat all such efforts, even though they are a distinct minority and their operations are inimical to the common welfare.

In fact, nowhere is this practice of compensation reversal more in evidence than on the debating floors and the committee rooms of parliaments and senates the world over. Just as the commodity trading pits offer a close approximation to free market operations, so do legislative operations offer some of the purest examples of the compensation principle, and its possible reversal, to be seen. Laws, bills, amendments are swapped among lawmakers in an effort to acquire as much as possible for the home district, no matter how harmful it ultimately is for the nation. The point is that the compensation reversal (or, as it is more accurately referred to, the reversibility paradox) is not a violation of the criterion; it is just an unforeseen result of its application. *Why* unforeseen? Isn't it assumed by economics that market agents are utility maximizers and isn't it further assumed that businesses are profit maximizers? Sometimes it is puzzling[9] how these assumptions are invoked for one set of outcomes and not considered to operate for others. So here we have a situation where economics has bravely established a criterion for right and wrong, and it is followed, but the result is often socially damaging. (Perhaps they were correct to stay out of the morality business after all.)

Business science (a branch of applied economic theory[10]) has its own version of sin closely associated and informed by corporate jurisprudence and usually involving some kind of deceit against shareholders, workers, customers, partners, investors or the surrounding environment. Deception would seem to be the cardinal sin in business and in practice it is assumed that as long as people are told the truth no further responsibility need be taken for them. They can make their own decisions. That was before corporations discovered modern advertising. But even there, standards of conduct exist, so-called 'truth in advertising' laws, such as prohibitions against 'bait-and-switch', phony 'going-out-of-business' sales, etc. Much of the jurisprudence of 20th century America dealt with business regulations, especially in food businesses. (It is reported that when asked, President Calvin Coolidge stated, 'The business of the United States *is* business.')

Cheating in any form is a spiritual sin because it is a form of deceit and, according to 'Abdu'l-Bahá, lying undermines the very foundation of civilization and where present in the individual makes spiritual growth impossible.[11] If the corporation is the ultimate expression of modern western capitalism, it must be troubling to read and hear so much about corporate malfeasance. The reason why this business model gets into a lot of high profile trouble is not immediately apparent[12] beyond observing that its structure disperses responsibility to the extent that no person feels responsible for corporate actions. Economics would require that property rights, i.e. responsibility, be clearly assigned as a way to internalize the externality of non-responsibility for corporate actions.

***

We have looked very briefly at concepts of sin in economics and spiritual constructions. Volumes could be dedicated to this subject without exhausting the discussion. Economic sin is associated with waste and spiritual sin is associated with higher levels of existence serving lower levels, the reverse of the proper and purposeful direction for all life. After analysis it is clear that economic waste accords with the spiritual idea of sin because waste in economics is often the practice of using higher valued goods for lower valued ends – bread for pigs, exactly the same concept as spiritual sin. In the next chapter we will look at learning, that is, the application of reward and punishment to influence behaviour. It will be seen how close are these two spheres, the spiritual and the economic, with respect to this concept.

8

Reward and Punishment:
Changing Behaviour

Economics shares with the spiritual dialogues of the Prophets a belief that *people respond to incentives.* This fact is built into both messages. It is an explicit assumption in economics and it is a teaching of the religious dialogues of the Prophets. 'For where your treasure is, there will your heart be also,' said Jesus.[1] 'Abdu'l-Bahá states,

> . . . it is impossible for a human being to turn aside from his own selfish advantages and sacrifice his own good for the good of the community except through true religious faith. For self-love is kneaded into the very clay of man, and it is not possible that, without any hope of substantial reward, he should neglect his own present material good. The individual, however, who puts his faith in God and believes in the words of God – because he is promised and certain of a plentiful reward in the next life, and because worldly benefits as compared to the abiding joy and glory of future planes of existence are nothing to him – will for the sake of God abandon his own peace and profit and will freely consecrate his heart and soul to the common good.[2]

He goes on to say that

> . . . even if we grant for the sake of argument that instinctive intelligence and an innate moral quality would prevent wrongdoing, it is obvious that individuals so characterized are as rare as the philosopher's stone. An assumption of this sort cannot be validated by mere words, it must be supported by the facts.[3]

And further,

> We also observe in infants the signs of aggression and lawlessness, and that if a child is deprived of a teacher's instructions his undesirable qualities increase from one moment to the next. It is therefore clear that the emergence of this natural sense of human dignity and honour is the result of education.[4]

So the point is made that *market agents respond to incentives* and that intervention is needed if humans are to become of optimal value to themselves and others. This is a finding of behavioural science, even though the science has no goal of changing behaviour but only to explain the world in its own terms. Yet it can certainly examine how various private interactions and public policies will likely affect behaviour in different ways; indeed, it has often been employed for just that purpose, so that the efficacy of a policy might be estimated before implementation. But these findings are sometimes ignored and result in puzzlement when certain otherwise predictable behaviours are observed.

For example, under the old Public Assistance programme in the United States, commonly called welfare, people were accepted into the programme based on need and that need had to be recertified every few months. Money in a savings account was not permitted beyond a nominal amount, a person could not be working; more cash was paid for more children and a person could not be married except to an invalid or a completely disabled individual. What were the results? As could be predicted, no one attempted to work or save their way out of welfare; single parents tended to have many children because this was rewarded with a larger cash payment and these children would be raised by a single parent in an atmosphere where growing up to work and make something of yourself was neither encouraged nor rewarded.[5]

Why was this system guaranteed to be a lifelong trap? Let us say that a brave soul attempted to get off welfare and some work was obtained. Because no savings were permitted, there was nothing to enable that individual to purchase useful training, such as certification programmes in healthcare, mechanics, food service, import–export, computing or office tasks, etc. – or even to obtain a driver's or chauffeur's licence – the work was low or no skill and poorly paid with no benefits. On welfare, a dollar was deducted for every dollar earned in work. There was also no childcare provision, so no place for children to go while the parent worked. But let us suppose that an arrangement had been made for a capable friend to look after the children during the work day. Eventually, the individual made enough money so that s/he no longer qualified for any welfare benefits.

What was the immediate result? The subsidized housing was lost and market rents had to be paid, probably far beyond what this worker could afford. Food stamps, which cut the cost of food, and other food programmes were lost. Also, the free medical coverage on the individual and all dependents, Medicaid, was stopped.[6] This individual thus faced 'an offer s/he couldn't refuse' with no effort required, to return to welfare and do nothing ever again. Considering that the low skill job paid little, and as mentioned there was not enough for market rents, much less medical insurance for the children, the individual faced a *150 per cent tax on every dollar earned while on welfare.* With little children to take care of, what would your choice be? That is why it became almost impossible for people to get off welfare if conditions become such that they ever had to be on it.[7]

Certainly, a different set of incentives could have been devised, one that sees financial self-subsistence as located on a continuum from complete helplessness to complete independence and covering a life career that may include any of these states at any time. For instance, savings dedicated for school or training programmes might be allowed. Having both parents live together and help to raise the children would have the effect of reducing the chances that their children would themselves need welfare, especially if it allowed at least one parent to work. For the working poor, daycare, medical insurance, food procurement and rent subsidies could be offered, smoothing the transition to full self-subsistence, at least for the maturing children.[8] (With respect to medical insurance, the United States is the only industrialized modern economy not providing universal medical coverage to all citizens. At very least, covering all children until age 21, or even 18, would vastly reduce the economic burden on the poor, working and non-working.)

Thus the reward and incentives built into any system determine results. At the other end of the earning scale, what might happen if corporate heads were rewarded with the opportunity to sell at a high price company stocks given to them at a low price, with no stipulation that they hold them for any length of time, say five years? Predictably, the head would have an incentive to drive up the price of the stock then sell the shares given – pump-and-dump, as we say. S/He wins, even if the stock subsequently plummets in value. Has the corporation been helped? Looking at the business press covering all the scandals and obscene profits made by corporate CEOs with stock options in 2000 to 2002 while their companies sank or went out of business, it would seem not. From where did such a perverse system originate? Sadly, it must be admitted, from two highly regarded economists in a series of papers dealing with the principal–agent problem. Apparently, they were too convinced of their science's stylized assumptions on agent behaviour in economic space – the kind of unquestioning belief wherein these assumptions are never questioned and are treated as received wisdom – the kind that asks, 'Now we must try to see why so many people during the Great Depression [of the 1930s] chose leisure over labour'! They are still plying their trade in two of the most exalted economics departments in the United States.

Economics is therefore challenged to investigate reward plans that yield sought-after results, 'For where your treasure is, there will your heart be also'.[9] The more complex the system to be optimized the more sophisticated the incentive plan must be. Historically, spiritual teachings have used a progressive process of revelation to do this also. Incentives have evolved from rather stark choices into seeing behaviour – personal, collective and societal – as existing in a spectrum where what the human being is capable of is part of the measure of goodness and acceptance. Bahá'u'lláh explains that

> The whole duty of man in this Day is to attain that share of the flood of grace which God poureth forth for him. Let none, therefore, consider the largeness or smallness of the receptacle. The portion of some might lie in the palm of a man's hand, the portion of others might fill a cup, and of others even a gallon measure . . .
>
> Beseech ye the one true God to grant that ye may taste the savour of such deeds as are performed in His path, and partake of the sweetness of such humility and submissiveness as are shown for His sake.[10]

This introduces several possibilities. One is that using each other as a proper standard for our own conduct may no longer be possible: '. . . inasmuch as man can never hope to attain unto the knowledge of the All-Glorious . . . unless and until he ceases to regard the words and deeds of mortal men as a standard for the true understanding and recognition of God and His Prophets'.[11] We must compare ourselves to an independent standard of conduct. At the same time, while a minimum standard of social conduct has been established for thousands of years, it recognizes what is possible for each individual and states that the goal is to out-perform ourselves continually.

When the social unit was the clam comprising several extended nomadic families, punishments took a corporal form. Assuming arrest and trial were swift, this worked to provide a lesson well within the subjective planning horizon of the individual, so that learning and regret would be possible. It also presented a continual example to other members of the community who would remain in close association with that individual by family and clan ties. The rise of the city-state offered more latitude for punishment and rehabilitation but also more dissociation and the possibility of escape through anonymity. The historic record will show that punishments remained harsh and often brutal.

The Prophets of these times successively offered a more comprehensive standard of personal conduct that acted to increase knowledge of human capacity and responsibility. 'Whatever verse do We abrogate or cause to be forgotten, We bring a better one, or similar to it.'[12] If a divine Prophet puts forth a new standard of conduct it implies that people are therefore capable of following it, almost by definition. 'And We task not a person except according to his capacity . . .'[13] Knowledge of our increasing abilities and the constraints in which they could best develop was thus taught to mankind sequentially. Today, with the announcement of Bahá'u'lláh, the latest claimant to the office of divine Prophet, the explanation of reward and punishment has been depersonalized. It is now explained that punishments and rewards are the result of acting in the presence of laws of existence. This is in contrast to earlier concepts that bad behaviour is punished by an angry God. While the presence of emotions is still upheld for the divine Creator, it is less the reason for what happens to us as we move through life. That is, we become poor because we are unsuccessful at making money, not because we have angered hidden powers that now seek to humiliate us.[14] We become wise from acting wisely, not by some other means. In this chapter of revelation, *the means determine the ends*, we are told, and understanding this is the key to knowing what we are able to achieve. Emotions have not disappeared and are still ascribed by humans to divinity; what has changed is our knowledge of the instrumentality of corrective procedures on our conduct.[15]

It seems that what we do is what we are. To be sure, this is a restatement of old truths from earlier prophetic dialogues. But far more is offered as explanation for how this proceeds. Superstitious connections are denied; the reward for honesty is that we become honest and are known as honest by others, and so too for other attributes. These are attained by action and nothing beyond them is to be expected. This is by law, the law of existence itself.

Bahá'u'lláh explains that some things cannot be understood unless life is lived a certain way. So one of the rewards of good conduct is understanding. This is shown by Bahá'u'lláh's words in several places. For example, when giving the requisites to comprehending the divine Word, He states, 'He must so cleanse his heart that no remnant of either love or hate may linger therein, lest that love blindly incline him to error, or that hate repel him away from the truth.'[16] Bahá'u'lláh declares that divine knowledge can only be understood by those having a 'pure heart', meaning a mind free of material conceptions and a heart uninfluenced by selfish calculations or attracted to animal pleasures. 'The understanding of His words and the comprehension of the utterances of the Birds of Heaven are in no wise dependent upon human learning. They depend solely upon purity of heart, chastity of soul, and freedom of spirit.'[17] He also established a code of conduct which, if strictly adhered to, would offer the prerequisites for true understanding.

This process of reward as knowledge, and understanding through correct living, enjoys a long tradition. About 500 BCE Pythagoras, who is credited with giving us the word 'philosophy', established a school in Italy (at that time part of Magna Græcia) and taught using a cryptic and parable-based method. Its purpose was to keep essential knowledge away from all but true initiates, those who had passed through a long and rigorous aesthetic discipline in Pythagoras' school. He believed that to make his teachings available to the common people risked their misunderstanding and ridicule or their trivialization or sale.[18] This did not begin with Pythagoras. The idea of establishing correct living as the way to true wisdom is, of course, ancient. Pythagoras himself is known to have travelled throughout the ancient world in search of knowledge. Each time he entered another school years of rigid discipline would be required of him before he was accepted to learn its secrets.[19]

We still carry on a semblance of this tradition in the trappings of academe. They are on display at graduation ceremonies in colleges and universities, with long black robes emphasizing to the common herd the sad burdens of knowledge, the vestigial hood of coded colours identifying the new initiate with a certain guild (and its secret elongated pocket to stash a slice of sausage to see you through those cold nights of solitary study!), all designed to produce the impression of belonging to a secret society aloof from the grunting and idleness, the crassness and blind followings of the ordinary people.

In economics, knowledge for *homo economicus* is assumed to result from human capital formation. Its possession bestows wealth and economic success upon the possessor. Knowledge of prices implies knowledge of the whole economic condition, according to what prices represent. If it is understood that a price contains the posted value of everything in the good in question (that is, that markets are efficient), then knowing this value also reveals the value of all its components, its labour, raw materials, marketing costs, transportation costs, packaging and advertising, etc. Acting appropriately upon this knowledge is supposed to yield profits, or at least protect from loss.

Assuming market equilibrium, however, this last statement is vitiated at least in part. All agents are assumed to have this knowledge. If this is so, then in equilibrium there is no advantage for anyone and all receive the same result, called the *market return*. If, however, equilibrium is not normal and markets are in constant flux in response to unbalanced forces experienced dynamically, then knowledge of prices is advantageous; and this is the typical experience in the economy.[20]

Ignorance is costly. Ignorance might be bliss but bliss is costly if based on ignorance. As a research science with the expressed goal of explaining the world in its own terms, economics is a branch of philosophy and logic, as are all other research sciences. It accumulates and analyses knowledge for its own sake. It has applied branches that attempt to achieve some tangible result in finance, public policy, agriculture, trade, etc. but even here pure research is carried out for its own sake.[21]

Thus knowledge is its own reward and is attainable only by dedication and personal sacrifice. But is it also its own punishment? That is, can knowledge (or more accurately its possession) both reward *and* punish? In economics the more you know the more you can profit or the less you can lose. In the spiritual realm it is true that a situation may arise where you learn some truth too late to take advantage of it in a practical way (in this world, at least), by changing behaviour, for example. But this is not a loss caused by knowledge but from having been previously ignorant of the reality. 'Yes, I did pay $50 for the gold Rolex but, honestly judge, I didn't know the watch was stolen' is an example of this situation. Having engaged in risky behaviour like sex outside of wedlock that resulted in contracting HIV-AIDS is another. The situation here is in not having appreciated what was known or suspected about the consequences of a behaviour pattern. This has spiritual connotations. Living forces us to decide on lines of behaviour where the marginal value (the immediate consequence) is far different from the absolute value (the future or final consequence). 'All decisions are made at the margin', according to economics. The object of economic dynamics is to clearly display these prices and their true underlying value by optimizing outcomes through time and identifying the optimal growth path, thereby allowing the individual to choose that set of goods and services having the greatest intertemporal value.

We know already that such a process can only yield benefits insofar as the agent's subjective planning horizon is sufficiently long and his or her subjective rate of time preference is sufficiently low. This is possible where social institutions have nurtured these two conditions in the individual.

Finally, according to 'Abdu'l-Bahá, as quoted at the beginning of this chapter, future rewards, tangible or intangible, must be offered to induce abandoning otherwise enjoyable behaviour in the present. Delayed gratification resulting in a rich and full life that avoids the marginality trap[22] is a spiritual process that requires practical methods for its realization. Economics provides the essential metrics for translating spiritual aspirations into practical reality.

***

As mentioned earlier, economics has been striving for a kind of unified theory encompassing both individual and collective actions. The result of building a theory about the macroeconomy based on individual market behaviour or individual actions has been less than satisfactory. The difficulty might be that the orientation of these two worlds has been not on the individual but on the market, and that therefore economics has been futilely attempting to combine in one theory macro and micro markets and their actors. There is a sort of dichotomy between the actions of individuals operating rationally in the abstract and the observation of real people acting with collective rationality in particular markets such as insurance, markets, equities and food and making decisions on how many children to have, and in other ways where individual will and volition is subsumed beneath that of the group. How could rational people continuously commit systematic and ruinous errors as we observe? Even in microeconomics what an individual will do in a given market at a given time is still largely not deterministic but a matter for statistical analysis. Only few scenarios really assure that market agents will act according to plan (that is, theory). The reason for this might be the continued association of behaviour models to the static roots of classical economics, while the real world is decidedly dynamic and time itself is a variable in events.

A possible solution to this difficulty is to abandon the concentration on individuals in *markets* and turn attention to individuals in *time*. This would not mean setting aside all our findings regarding market activities or exchanges but would require a broader application of the concept of the transaction to include super-material as well as material transactions. This is already done to some extent in economics. The real change is in reworking results to accord with dynamic analysis and modifying utility maximization and marginality to include rewards based on the subjective planning horizon and the subjective rate of time preference of the collective body as well as the individual. *Dynamic modelling allows for learning and regret.* It can explain the presence of systematic errors and what happens when people will not, or cannot, learn under a particular set of circumstances. How can we speak of sin if the agent cannot learn from experience because its lessons play out over a time period transcending the subjective planning horizon s/he is able to encompass?

Changing the Subjective Rate of Time Preference and the Subjective Planning Horizon

We reside in the nexus of powerful social forces that fundamentally influence our personality, behaviour and the potential level of our spiritual, emotional and intellectual maturation. Some of the obvious institutional sources of these influences are represented by the following list of capital forms.

Family Capital

This is the sum of learned interpersonal and inter-emotional relationships that model for us how we must act in society and express ourselves to ourselves (self-image), to others and to our Creator, if we have and maintain such a relationship. It also informs us as to how much responsibility we should assume for the world around us. Family capital also comprises the all-important sum of intellectual schooling, training and native ability passed on intergenerationally from parents and other caregivers to children.

It includes the catalogue of material sources for learning and the ability to develop curiosity in a constructive developmental way. This includes the presence in the home of a dictionary, books for children and older people, representations of art and science and technology, a computer or calculator, paper and writing tools, drawing, colouring and painting implements, etc.

It also includes the study and work habits of the family members, since this establishes what is possible and normally expected of the individual growing up and once grown. How many are working? How is free time used? Does anyone study a musical instrument, go to museums or take science trips? Are parents college educated? And so on.

Community Capital

This comprises the community environment and the extent to which learning and work is the norm. Outside the door of the home, how many people within the immediate vicinity of the home are employed, are preparing for work or are retired from work? Is the physical environment well maintained so that it looks as if the community cares about its inhabitants? Also included in community capital, besides the opportunities for paid employment, are the available venues for personal development and recreation including museums, art galleries, science fairs, music concerts, sports arenas, research parks, playgrounds, etc. Other entities of note would be family support and intervention service centres, including counselling for teens and children, elderly daycare enrichment programmes, etc.

National Social Capital

By this is meant the available stock of goods and services for each citizen's use, including roads and highways, information and communication infrastructure, national defence and other public goods. It also includes the set of expectations inherent in being a citizen of this particular nation, meaning available economic support services such as unemployment and retirement benefits, medical services, public safety and order; and individual duties, such as taxation, civil or military duty, voting, jury duty, etc.

An important element of national capital is attitudinal. Is the nation perceived as basically honest or corrupt. Is there a sense that it strives to be just over time or that the powerful and well situated derive far more benefits and pay far less than the ordinary citizen? This is attitudinal since reality and perceptions often differ. Such attitudes can either promote self-development, active citizenship and social responsibility or discourage these tendencies. Further, what is the national creed? How much weight does it give to economic and commercial freedom and how much to spiritual, intellectual and non-commercial pursuits, and must there be a trade-off between commercial and non-commercial activities?[23] How are criminals treated, especially juveniles? Is the criminal justice system perceived as punitive or rehabilitative, lax or firm?

Academic Capital

This refers to the availability of schools of a quality sufficient to prepare students for the world they will face, according to the mandates of society. Such preparation must begin with instruction in the process of learning in a structured, mostly group environment. It may also include specific subjects like civics and language development, social development and subjects related to becoming financially and economically viable. It must also prepare the student for further education. Ancillary goals met by schools could also include family planning, etc. if this is no longer performed by the families themselves or where social upheavals have caused a breakdown of family units.

Spiritual Capital

This underpins all else. It can be shown that every moral teaching is derived from the verses of God revealed by a Prophet, somewhere and at some time. This is discussed more thoroughly elsewhere.

These sources are some of the essential elements that make up the totality of our human capital. The primary influence is from family capital; if this is sufficient the individual will have the best chance of developing to full potential, even to the extent of overcoming whatever may be lacking in the other sources of capital from outside the family.

Arguably, there are three bequests to the individual from family that are more important than all others. After the first, recognition of the cause of God through the divine Messenger for this day, the second, already mentioned, is self-discipline. With this most of life's difficulties and challenges can be overcome and without it even an otherwise bright and good-natured person has no chance of accomplishing very much.

The third is the ability to learn from life itself and is the subject of this chapter. In the presence of a comprehensive training programme, dynamically measured and phased in, the concept of *future value* is inculcated in the individual. With the future conceived of as a concrete reality, it is possible to delay gratification and to regard absolute values rather than just local marginal values. *This, and this alone*, allows the individual to avoid the marginality or network trap, to learn from mistakes and achieve personal success in life.[24] This is clear since, if the future is not real, then present actions are perceived as having no effect upon possible future states. Only where a solid link has been built between present actions and their effects on future states is it possible to alter behaviour. Actions are carried out in the present; if these are seen as determining the goodness of future possibilities then they can be analysed for the purpose of seeing how their alteration could enhance future conditions. Otherwise there is simply no reason to abandon any behaviour that gives immediate satisfaction, no matter how deleterious it is towards future conditions, since it is not understood that any such negative consequences will actually occur. The four year old cannot understand the connection between going into the street and being harmed as a result because the faculty needed has not yet developed. But if certain measures by caregivers are not taken conscientiously and systematically, this faculty may never develop to a degree necessary for learning from life's lessons. And as the four year old must be restrained by its caregiver from running into the street, so the 24 year old must be restrained by the state if s/he is incapable of self-governance.

***

It has now been argued that the ability to learn from life, avoid its many dangers and obtain overall success is dependent on regarding the future as being determined by present actions. It has also been argued that this is *learned behaviour* undertaken while the individual is very young and requiring systematic continuance thereafter. We are now at the point of considering what other social institutions intersect the individual's developing personality and consciousness, which either promote this process or degrade it. This necessarily brings into play the other capital forms mentioned above. Important to this discussion is not so much their obvious tangible values but rather their indirect values.

For example, with respect to community capital, consider the influence of a local branch of the municipality's lending library. This has the obvious benefit of increasing opportunities for learning and stimulating recreation. Now imagine that it has been closed for some reason while the building remains. Months turn into years and it still is not reopened. The property shows the effects of neglect and vandalism. What message is this sending to school-aged children and other patrons? The message could be that the town does not care for the children and other patrons of the neighbourhood. If the neighbourhood is predominantly of an ethnicity different from the town managers, another, more ugly, message is also being sent.

Children and others respond to what they perceive as purposeful neglect by the municipality in various ways. The least common is to contact the town powers to see what is going on. The most common is probably to harbour and maintain civic-based resentments, leading to antisocial behaviour. This would include doing poorly in school, since it is others who want this work from the student, possibly more than the student wants it from herself at that age. And since it is work, and hard, victimization will certainly do as an excuse to take the student off task. Thus a library's presence may not be as important as its absence, even if the neighbourhood seldom actually patronizes it.

Many other such examples of indirect influences from social institutions and sources of capital can be found. One was referred to in an endnote above. What is the effect of permitting aggressive advertising targeting children and adolescents? This asks, what is the effect of treating children and teens as proper subjects for having their tastes and preferences altered in line with corporate demands for a docile and consumerist populace? Whatever else such systematic targeting of advertisements may do or be responsible for (and the list is controversial and long), it cannot be said to diminish the desire for instant gratification or to increase temperance, modesty or self-sacrificial behaviour. It has also never been shown to lead one to eschew conspicuous and wasteful consumption, to regard future states as dependent on present actions ('*Just do it!*') or to develop critical analysis of direct or implied message content. And once the hyperbolic superlatives and qualitative nature has been seen to be mostly untrue, it may teach a diminished regard for the truth and for accurate speech. In sum, none of these things strengthen the perception that present actions determine future results. They therefore militate against developing the ability to learn from life's lessons and messages. To the extent that they erode the ability to analyse messages critically, they degrade the individual's ability to learn from anything.

Alteration of the Subjective Rate of Time Preference and the Subjective Planning Horizon through Prophetic Instruction

When analysed, the spiritual dialogues of the Prophets and founders of the world's major religions are shown to promote the development and maintenance of those characteristics that strengthen understanding of how present actions create future states. In fact, the main thrust of their message is precisely this. They detail how to optimize the time path leading to the best possible future state, one providing true happiness and bliss and not just its appearance or outward semblance. In other words, these dialogues and teachings show us how to *maximize total value, under the integral, from time zero to infinity (the subjective planning horizon), where value is the exponential (raised to the power of the quantity of minus theta (the subjective rate of time preference) times the real discount rate) multiplied by the quantity of utility with respect to consumption in time, all with respect to the time derivative and subject to various state and control constraints.* They constantly call mankind to self-restraint and temperance, modesty and seriousness of purpose, socially responsible and active behaviour, hard work, chastity and patience. They also exhort agents to turn away from all forms of materialism and consumerism, hedonism and selfishness. In fact, their personal appeal is to a life characterized by these words of Shoghi Effendi, religious historian, oriental scholar and Guardian of the Bahá'í Faith.

> Such a chaste and holy life, with its implications of modesty, purity, temperance, decency, and clean-mindedness, involves no less than the exercise of moderation in all that pertains to dress, language, amusements, and all artistic and literary avocations. It demands daily vigilance in the control of one's carnal desires and corrupt inclinations. It calls for the abandonment of a frivolous conduct, with its excessive attachment to trivial and often misdirected pleasures. It requires total abstinence from all alcoholic drinks, from opium, and from similar, habit-forming drugs. It condemns the prostitution of art and literature, the practices of nudism and of companionate

marriage, infidelity in marital relationships, and all manner of promiscuity, of easy familiarity, and of sexual vices. It can tolerate no compromise with the theories, the standards, the habits, and the excesses of a decadent age.[25]

To the extent that these words characterize the messages of the Prophets directed towards modifying personal behaviour, it is clear that such a message would absolutely reduce the importance of *purely marginal current results in favour of globally optimal absolute results.* We must now find evidence of specific teachings from the Prophets that enable people to follow the above directions.

Without the requisite consciousness of the link between current actions and future states, behaving in such variance with prevailing social standards of conduct would be well nigh impossible. From where would come the motivation to eschew current gratification in favour of a more desirable future state? Even if otherwise convinced that current actions determine future states in this life, what about the next, for which direct evidence is impossible to obtain? This was discussed above where 'Abdu'l-Bahá was quoted as saying that those dwelling in lower states of life are constitutionally incapable of comprehending the reality obtaining in higher levels. It was also asserted previously, quoting 'Abdu'l-Bahá, that delaying current gratification, *per se*, is impossible without the belief in the certainty of a future reward for so doing, whether for future states within this life or beyond it. As just argued, proper training of children and youth within the family and beyond can create the needed link. We therefore need evidence from prophetic teachings that current actions are characterized as having variable effects on our future state, both within this life and beyond it. It turns out that we do not need to look far for the sought after evidence. Consider these verses from the Qur'án that give evidence that the Prophets promise great rewards for anyone, regardless of family background, race, intellectual, mental or physical endowments or of any other material consideration.

Everyone shall taste of death, and only on the Day of Resurrection shall you be paid your wages in full. And whoever is removed from the Fire and admitted to Paradise, he indeed is successful. The life of this world is only the enjoyment of a deception.[26]

You shall certainly be tried and tested in your wealth and properties, and in your personal selves; and you shall certainly hear much that shall grieve you from those who received the Scripture before you, and from those who ascribe

> partners to God. But if you persevere patiently and become of those who are righteous, then, verily, that will be a determining factor in all affairs . . .[27]

> Except those who show patience and act righteously, for these will be forgiveness and a great reward.[28]

> And strain not your eyes in longing for the things We have bestowed for enjoyment to various groups of them, the splendour of the life of this world, that We may test them thereby. But the provision from your Lord in the Hereafter is better, and more lasting.[29]

> And those who kept their duty to their Lord will be led into Paradise in groups, till when they reach it, and its gates will be opened and its keepers will say,'Peace, to you! Well done! Enter herein in peace secure![30]

> We will certainly show them Our signs in the universe and in their own selves, until it becomes manifest to them that this is the truth. Is it not sufficient in regard to your Lord that He is a witness over all things?[31]

And finally,

> You received your good things in the life of the world, and you took your pleasure therein. Now, this Day you shall be recompensed with the torment of humiliation, because you were arrogant in the land without right, and because you used to rebel against God's command.[32]

All these verses refer to future states dependent on current behaviour. From the Gospels of Jesus come the following verses.

> Children, how hard is it for them, that trust in riches to enter into the kingdom of God! It is easier for a camel to go through the eye of a needle, than for a rich man to enter into the Kingdom of God.[33]

> But seek ye first the kingdom of God, and his righteousness; and all these things [good things of this world] shall be added unto you.[34]

> And every one that hath forsaken houses, or brethren, or sisters, or father, or mother, or wife, or children, or lands, for my name's sake, shall receive an hundredfold, and shall inherit everlasting life. But many that are first shall be last; and the last shall be first.[35]

In terms of interpersonal behaviour there is this 'Golden Rule' standard. Jesus explains in Matthew[36] that an invisible judge, a king, will, on a certain day divide mankind into two large groups, goats (unruly, ego-centred and unteachable) and sheep (personally self-effacing, group-centred and teachable). The sheep will be told that they did good works for the king, even though they were unaware of it, because whenever they treated each other well they were treating the king well, as these opportunities were really disguised opportunities to worship the king. 'Then the King shall say unto them on the right hand [the sheep], Come, ye blessed of my Father, inherit the kingdom prepared for you from the foundation of the world.'[37] But the goats shall be directed to enter everlasting fire.[38] The structure of this lesson provides both carrot and stick to induce the alteration of individual behaviour. It certainly relates present actions to future states. And as far as the certainty of the next world, the Qur'án asks, 'Do you think that We had created you for sport or without serious intent, and that you would not be returned to Our presence?'[39]

Bahá'u'lláh states that after death,

> Thou shalt, after thy departure, discover what We have revealed unto thee, and shalt find all thy doings recorded in the Book wherein the works of all them that dwell on earth, be they greater or less than the weight of an atom, are noted down.[40]

He also has revealed that,

> It is clear and evident that all men shall, after their physical death, estimate the worth of their deeds, and realize all that their hands have wrought . . . They that are the followers of the one true God shall, the moment they depart out of this life, experience such joy and gladness as would be impossible to describe, while they that live in error shall be seized with such fear and trembling, and shall be filled with such consternation, as nothing can exceed.[41]

However, what is truly meant by the terms 'followers' and 'living in error' is not completely known. Finally, Bahá'u'lláh gives this promise:

> O My servants! Sorrow not if, in these days and on this earthly plane, things contrary to your wishes have been ordained and manifested by God, for days of blissful joy, of heavenly delight, are assuredly in store for you. Worlds, holy and spiritually glorious, will be unveiled to your eyes. You are destined by Him, in this world and hereafter, to partake of their benefits, to

> share in their joys, and to obtain a portion of their sustaining grace. To each and every one of them you will, no doubt, attain.[42]

Thus a future state is confirmed, in this life and beyond it, that is related to current deeds and actions. Future payments, duly discounted, are declared for various behaviours in the present, as well as encouragement for overcoming the inertia of social indifference and even the hostility of others towards your efforts. Only a few verses have been used, and probably not the best of those that could have been chosen, since the central theme of these prophetic dialogues is concerned with revolutionizing personal behaviour. With these lessons or, indeed, with the lessons found in any of the prophetic dialogues, the subjective planning horizon (SPH) is extended to include a world of permanence beyond this contingent one, represented in mathematics by the symbol for infinity. The subjective rate of time preference (SRTP) is diminished by exhortations for patience, temperance and perseverance in the face of difficulties.

We recall from earlier chapters that the *marginal* value of a thing is its value relative to what has happened just previously during this market period and that all economic decisions are made 'at the margin'. For example, we might be willing to pay a great deal for a small glass of water if we are very thirsty, that is, if we have had no water for a long time and this water is therefore extremely valuable to life itself. On the other hand, if we have just got up from a good meal and finished our after-dinner coffee or tea, then the value of an additional glass of water is likely to be very small.

The holy Prophets exhort us to look at *total values* rather than just *marginal* ones because over an entire lifetime it is the total value of our choices that determine our character and our fate. Left to our own devices, we choose marginal values but this could be a trap: most things of real value in life have start-up costs and only later do they show their real and significant value, while many harmful things start by giving us momentary satisfaction but may have significant long-term costs. Don't we refer to people who act by calculating total benefits and costs 'wise', while people who just look at marginal benefits and costs are 'foolish'?

Note that nowhere does it say that life is *fair* in the sense we might imagine it to be, that 'good' people will live in materially prosperous security and peace, that 'bad' people will live in poverty and loss. There is little in the way of worldly riches promised for good behaviour. 'Is the reward for goodness other than goodness in return?'[43] the Qur'án asks. Bahá'u'lláh states, 'Know, therefore, O questioning seeker, that earthly sovereignty is of no worth, nor will it ever be, in the eyes of God and His chosen Ones.'[44] It seems clear that those who advance financially beyond most others just have the knack for this. There is a talent involved here, just as for other endeavours; some have it and some don't; and in a 'winner-take-all' competitive society, the winners win big and the losers are forgotten. Any association of material success with moral behaviour or religious conviction is spurious.

Philosophers also have the ability to give humans a broader perspective, beyond narrow marginality, and the ability to seek global solutions to the problems of life. But their work, if the logic of the creativeness of prophetic speech is adhered to, is derivative and lacks the authority of the prophetic dialogues beyond what is contained in their logic and reasoning. Even so, by focusing analysis on a particular aspect of life (work, truth, knowing, existence, etc.), much material is available. Bahá'u'lláh discusses the merits of philosophy in the Tablet of Wisdom:

> The essence and the fundamentals of philosophy have emanated from the Prophets. That the people differ concerning the inner meanings and mysteries thereof is to be attributed to the divergence of their views and minds.
>
> . . . Verily the philosophers have not denied the Ancient of Days [an honorific title for divinity]. Most of them passed away deploring their failure to fathom His mystery, even as some of them have testified.[45]

***

Economics has been termed a branch of philosophy (Schumpeter) and of logic (Keynes). It should be no surprise, therefore, that economics is well capable of absorbing the prophetic dialogues underpinning the world's religious systems, since the prophetic dialogues are rationally and logically constructed and are supreme examples of scientific reasoning. Until now, the religious systems nominally associated with their respective holy books – presently experiencing their nadir in terms of vision, energy and creative influence – display static models of behaviour, even as they once offered the world dynamic and revolutionary models that shook the *status quo* to its roots, overthrew systems that had existed for centuries or so influenced them as to cause their metamorphosis into systems capable of responding to the needs of a mankind fitfully growing into maturation. Now under threat from the increasing light of the Bahá'í Revelation, they have become reactionary ideologies, incapable of introspection or rejuvenation from within. But this is fated, after all.

Bahá'u'lláh's dialogues, overarchingly comprehensive in their sweep and the subjects treated, are thus far unburdened with ideological accretions from centuries of human use and misuse. The social models contained therein are clearly dynamic and a challenge to the static models of which social sciences are currently composed.

Since the 1920s economics has seriously begun developing dynamic models of behaviour. These initially dealt with questions of aggregate savings and consumption in the presence and absence of various levels of investment and taxation. Later on other constraints and variables were added. At first these models could not be expressed in closed form and the calculus of variations (the calculus that solves problems involving time as a specified variable, i.e. dynamic models) had difficulty handling certain terminal conditions. In the 1950s the Russian mathematician Pontryagin found a way to apply a method of internalizing external constraints. This was already in common use in non-dynamical optimization models (and called the Lagrangian or Lagrange multiplier). This has made it possible for many more models to be analysed. It has pushed economic dynamics onto centre stage and is making economics well prepared to analyse and model many of the assertions and constructions embodied in the dialogues of Bahá'u'lláh.

While this transformation of economic science into a more dynamic analysis is occurring, its progress is uneven and fundamental revisions of existing models are still not getting into the economic principles classes where all the ontological questions about the world and economic science are usually answered. As this occurs, however, economics will become even more able to receive and investigate the teachings of the latest claimant to prophetic office, Bahá'u'lláh.

9

Competition:
Spiritual and Economic Concepts

> . . . man is endowed with two natures: the one tendeth towards moral sublimity and intellectual perfection, while the other turneth to bestial degradation and carnal imperfections.[1]

With these words it becomes clear that we shall never be rid of competition. There is a mortal struggle between our higher and lower natures for control of our life. Day by day the game is played and the winner will not be declared until our last breath has gone out of us:

> How often hath a sinner, at the hour of death, attained to the essence of faith . . . And how often hath a devout believer, at the hour of his soul's ascension, been so changed as to fall into the nethermost fire.[2]

We have, however, this statement of 'Abdu'l-Bahá:

> The obstacle to human happiness is racial or religious prejudice, the competitive struggle for existence and inhumanity toward each other.[3]

Most have erroneously taken the words 'the competitive struggle for existence' spoken by a perfect spiritual authority and the appointed interpreter of the Bahá'í writings, to mean that competition is strictly bad and should be eliminated. Indeed, these sentiments have been extended to include markets themselves. What 'Abdu'l-Bahá criticizes, however, is *the need to compete for the requirements of material life itself,* for such necessities as food, education, shelter, healthcare and the right to work, to contribute to society and to raise a family. But He has not condemned the competition forced upon all of us to strive to better ourselves in all possible ways, to produce, to work hard, to educate our children not to trifle and to apply themselves to important tasks and to be financially successful, lest we and our offspring be consigned to economic – and therefore social – oblivion brought upon us by our lack of effort.

In today's world this struggle forces us to market our very selves in a winner-take-all competition with others where the winner obtains life's necessities and the loser starves in poverty. Some would call this chattel slavery, where the only measure of a person's varied attributes is in the price the market assigns to them. It is this attitude and the human antagonisms that it engenders that 'Abdu'l-Bahá condemns.

This attitude is becoming a common experience in many societies. Artists lacking commercial success are mocked and ridiculed, while commercially successful ones are lionized. Teachers who dedicate their lives to educating the next generation and preparing them for the world are paid little and are often respected less, while basketball players and others in the entertainment industry have become multi-millionaires. More and more financial success is the only imprimatur worthy of consideration. It is as if this alone certifies one's true worth and value. It is against this kind of naked crassness that 'Abdu'l-Bahá's words are mainly directed. Market valuation of humans limited to their commercial productive capability places the very young and very old, the weak, the less strong, those less bright, even those with yellow teeth and disfigurements, at a disadvantage, restricting the future for children and stripping the old and weak of dignity.[4] It also ignores all those essential human characteristics and talents so needful to society that the market is unable to price. In our interpersonal relationships competition for material advantages can become destructive to community life. 'And those who hoard up gold and silver and spend them not in the way of Allah, announce to them a painful torment.'[5] Bahá'u'lláh warns us not to seek an advantage over others for personal gain or for selfish motives. All the Prophets declare that we are to prefer our neighbours before our own selves. Here is but one expression of this teaching of the *golden rule*.

> O Son of Dust! Verily I say unto thee: Of all men the most negligent is he that disputeth idly and seeketh to advance himself over his brother. Say, O brethren! Let deeds, not words be your adorning.[6]

A true believer 'should not wish for others that which he doth not wish for himself . . .'[7] Competition should never lead us to vaunt ourselves over others: 'Vaunt not thyself over the poor . . .'[8]

Thus, just as for other attributes and conditions, like anger or pride, everything depends upon how competition is employed and to what use it is put. Competing to 'do good', to be helpful to others, to defeat our lower self and even with what we accomplished yesterday is divinely approved and encouraged, while the sort of competition that piles up material benefits for ourselves leaving others with less is denounced. *There is thus no evidence that competition* per se *is regarded as bad by the divine Prophets, their appointed interpreters or derivative philosophers; indeed, quite the opposite seems to be true.*

Competition arises between prophetic teachings and purely materialistic teachings for the hearts and minds of our children. Since the days of Abraham history notes that Prophets have also encouraged parents to raise children to compete in possessing a good character, memorizing divine writings, in giving talks promoting religion and in other character-forming activities. None has suggested that we should avoid this competition. Contests where children are pitted against each other to attain a prize, say for the best work in school, is not criticized. 'Abdu'l-Bahá, in referring to the education and training of children, states:

> Among the greatest of all services that can possibly be rendered by man to Almighty God is the education and training of children, young plants of the Abhá Paradise, so that these children, fostered by grace in the way of salvation, growing like pearls of divine bounty in the shell of education, will one day bejewel the crown of abiding glory.[9]

> Ye must therefore put forth a mighty effort, striving by night and day and resting not for a moment, to acquire an abundant share of all the sciences and arts, that the Divine Image, which shineth out from the Sun of Truth, may illumine the mirror of the hearts of men.
>
> It is the longing desire of 'Abdu'l-Bahá to see each one of you accounted as the foremost professor in the academies, and in the school of inner significances, each one becoming a leader in wisdom.[10]

The quality of our individual and collective future rests upon our winning more than a tentative victory over what currently exists in life, if we accept the logic of when Prophets appear among us. Historically, their announcement is timed to coincide with a period of decline in civilizations. The prophetic dialogue appears in sharp contrast to notions, in vogue at the time, that uphold the *status quo*. Its creative energy reinvigorates thinking, redirects social sciences and revolutionizes approaches to interpersonal and intergenerational transactions. Even a cursory look at the historical record demonstrates this and it is argued in an earlier chapter of the present book. A struggle is commenced between the *status quo* and the new prophetic message, one in which no intellectual safety is afforded, where the prize is the peoples' hearts and where the competition has even resulted in war.

There can be no question that the Prophet sees Himself (if we can speak in these terms) as speaking in open opposition to the standards of the age. In whatever way the avowed religionists of the community have expected the 'return' and the 'resurrection' to be fulfilled in terms of confirming the goodness of current religious practices, the Prophets have consistently refused to do this. Indeed, each and every Prophet has denounced the religious practices and beliefs cherished by the people they met. From the Qur'án we have these words:

> And if the truth had been in accordance with their desires, verily, the heavens and the earth, and whosoever is therein, would have been corrupted.[11]

The Prophets even denounce the actions and beliefs of the unborn descendants of their own new adherents, saying that they will treat the Prophet appearing in the future as the present generation is treating Him.

> And the Messenger will say, 'O My Lord! Verily, My people deserted this Qur'án. . . .'[12]

The following is evidence that the Prophet and His message are in direct and unremitting opposition to current social and religious standards. The purpose of relating this here is to show the extent to which competition is a spiritual process.

Jesus indicated that following Him was to follow God Himself (since Jesus was God's appointed representative among the people of that era) and to follow what currently existed was to prefer man's teachings to God's:

> And he said unto them, Full well ye reject the commandment of God, that ye may keep your own tradition.[13]

This theme is reinforced often in the Qur'án:

> They said: 'Have you come to us to turn us away from that which our fathers followed . . .?'[14]

> And when it is said to them: 'Come to what God has revealed and unto the

> Messenger.' They say: 'Enough for us is that which we found our fathers following,' even though their fathers had no knowledge whatsoever, nor any guidance.[15]

Finally, Bahá'u'lláh explains that were the promised Return to do nothing more than to affirm what the people currently believe, declaring them to be the true worshippers of God and the manifestations of His Will in the world, why would anyone oppose Him? But the new Prophet has always denounced the people's conceptions, overturned the *status quo* and established a novel standard of truth and faith, of service and value. After citing various religious prophecies from the past that pertain to conditions expected for today, Bahá'u'lláh states,

> Behold, how, notwithstanding these and similar traditions [prophecies], they idly contend that the laws formerly revealed, must in no wise be altered. And yet, is not the object of every Revelation to effect a transformation in the whole character of mankind, a transformation that shall manifest itself both outwardly and inwardly, that shall affect both its inner life and external conditions? For if the character of mankind be not changed, the futility of God's universal Manifestation would be apparent . . . And should the Essence of Truth reveal that which is contrary to their inclinations and desires, they will straightway denounce Him as an infidel, and will protest, saying: 'This is contrary to the sayings of the Imáms [apostles] of the Faith and of the resplendent lights. No such thing hath been provided by our inviolable law.' Even so in this day such worthless statements have been and are being made by these poor mortals.[16]

This is a clear statement that the prophetic message will be in disagreement with standards of thought currently held by the people. Over time the power of the message asserts itself and effects a change in the structure of society. Thus in this competition it always eventually prevails, even while at its emergence its light appears to be completely eclipsed by local oppression and by the self-satisfied indifference of the wider world. This could be the meaning of the Qur'ánic verse, 'And, verily, our host shall conquer',[17] since obviously the literal meaning has never yet occurred.

This also suggests a possible meaning of another well-known verse from the Qur'án whose literal meaning is otherwise nonsensical:[18] 'Swift is He in reckoning.'[19] As argued previously, we are informed that our spiritual status in this world and in the next is dependent on our endeavours and the ability to overcome our lower natures. In this we are constantly comparing ourselves with how we were a short time ago or with the accomplishments of others in the Faith. This too is competition; it is how characters are honed and perfected and is a dynamic process. Adults are encouraged by the Prophets to compete in acquiring spiritual attributes, since these are considered the fountain of all good human qualities.

> O people of the world! Follow not the promptings of the self, for it summoneth insistently to wickedness and lust; follow, rather, Him Who is the Possessor of all created things, Who biddeth you to show forth piety, and manifest the fear of God. He, verily, is independent of all His creatures.[20]

In this light competition is seen as an essential characteristic of a well-balanced personality and an indispensable tool for overcoming barriers to personal and social growth and development.

***

An aspect of competition that makes some people uncomfortable is that it is often a *zero-sum game*: if someone wins, then someone else must lose. This can be hard for the very young and others to accept, in sporting contests, for example. Why must we expose children to losing? Isn't it perverse to insist on children's participation in such contests in the belief that they will prepare the children for the pitiless contests of the marketplace in which they will soon be thrown? Are sports clichés, sayings like, 'Winning isn't everything, *it's the only thing!*' (attributed to Vince Lombardi, legendary coach of the Green Bay Packers football team) to be their stay and guide?

First, all are scored or graded and all such grades are relative. Second, sports contests are not what is primarily intended. Third, it is not certain that your child will lose; s/he might win, after all. But contests will reveal the various strengths and weaknesses of the individual on some basic level, including likes and dislikes, the ability to work comfortably under pressure or on several things at once, the way one deals with distractions, etc., information useful for career decisions later. In any case, inculcating the desire to constantly strive to out-perform one's 'personal best' allows one to gain an insight into his or her strengths and weaknesses and to seek a natural speciality that takes full advantages of whatever talents exist and minimizes whatever personal weaknesses there may be.

The only way to really know what you are good at is by experiencing different things, trying different work. Most likely, the individual will fail at everything he tries until he finds what work best suits him, because few, after finding it, continue experimenting. So it is expected that, for most of us in the working world, there will be a string of failures before our first success is realized. That is life. What can make this process more palatable is understanding its nature beforehand and experiencing a few losses where the cost of failure is slight. In this way the importance is shifted to the *process* of work and effort rather than on whether success is actually attained sooner, later or not at all.

Niche Competition

Specialization also leads to a kind of structured competition that actually is not competition at all in the sense ordinarily understood but is rather a type of cooperation made possible by specialization. Niche competition is when you have something I want and I have something you want. By exchanging we are both made better off (mutual benefits accrue). We specialize in the supply of what is easy for us to make and is demanded by others. Thus specialization, by taking advantage of our strengths, makes us all rich. It allows for exchanges between all individuals in society and to added wealth for every societal member.[21] If one is good at gathering food while another is good at making clothing, and they cooperate, their wealth will increase in two ways. The first way is called the *pure exchange* gain. Since the food expert has a surplus of food but a shortage of clothing and the clothing expert has a surplus of clothes but a shortage of food, by trading, that is, cooperating in mutually beneficent trade, both are made better off.

The second cooperative exchange gain is the *specialization gain*. Now that the food gatherer is freed of the burden of making his own clothing and the clothier is freed from the burden of gathering food, each can specialize on the production of what each does best. This leads to more food and more clothing for both or more leisure time for both. These gains are usually covered in elementary trade theory books as being gains from trade but a little reflection shows them to be really gains from cooperation, and the willingness to exchange comes out of that. 'Abdu'l-Bahá says

> . . . the community needs financier, farmer, merchant and labourer just as an army must be composed of commander, officers and privates. All cannot be commanders; all cannot be officers or privates. Each in his station in the social fabric must be competent – each in his function according to ability but with justness of opportunity for all.
>
> . . . Difference of capacity in human individuals is fundamental. It is impossible for all to be alike, all to be equal, all to be wise. Bahá'u'lláh has

> revealed principles and laws that will accomplish the adjustment of varying human capacities. He has said that whatsoever is possible of accomplishment in human government will be effected through these principles.[22]

Thus the idea of specialization of individuals for the collective gain of the community is enshrined in the principles of Bahá'u'lláh and of those of all the Prophets.

This is an example of local utility maximization, where all are made better off and none is made worse off, using a simplistic model. Is it too simplistic to be useful in the real world? Certainly not: such gains occur constantly in intercorporate trade and international trade. The reason for these gains is often attributed to the wonder of competition and the 'invisible hand'. But competition has nothing to do with it; cooperation is what yielded these gains. Then where does competition fit in? In getting us to the point where we can specialize and transform the value of our labour into something others want. The exchange itself is not competition because each person only makes one thing that is wanted by someone else. After World War II the United States became wealthy and confident. The world, destroyed by the war, supplied America with raw materials and America supplied the world with finished goods. No one really competed with the US in manufactured goods until the mid-1960s. After that America faced direct competition from Japan and Europe and the competition has only become more intense since then. For example, America dominated consumer electronics until the mid-1960s but ten years later American electronic brand names had all but disappeared.[23] What had happened was that the US no longer just 'swapped' its goods for someone else's as others started making the same goods the Americans did and started directly competing with the US for customers. For the first time in over a generation American products were compared against others for quality, innovation, features and service in the marketplace and the comparison began to lead to more sales for the others and fewer sales for the US. This is true market competition.

In the short run, that is, using a static analysis, competition is a zero-sum game; several products are offered, one is purchased. The risks of failure can be frightful: the producer has already spent money getting something to market and must gamble that enough units will be sold to pay back what has been spent. The same is true for a person taking four years of pre-medicine studies and trying to enter medical school in competition with others. *Failure is normal* hence the rise of large corporations making many similar products which *spreads the risk* of failure and increases the chance for success. In fact, the rise of the corporation can be partially explained just as adequately by the need to manage risk rather than as the result of exploiting scale economies.

In the long run, however, that is, using a more dynamic analysis, the result of competition is a positive-sum game. Over time goods improve, successful suppliers are rewarded and unsuccessful suppliers find something else to do.[24]

In this context there are no assurances from the prophetic messages which guarantee success in business or anything else for sincere believers and adherents. Whether you are successful at some endeavour is conditioned by ability and timing (what is happening around you at the time). This result flows from other statements in the prophetic dialogues indicating that *results depend upon means* and that a thing must be related to its purpose. Evidence must be related to what is being proved and ability must be related to what is being attempted. Kindness to animals and small children does not translate into mathematical prowess or skill in engineering. Numerous acts of pious worship and humble service will not make you a successful playwright if you cannot write interesting dialogue or develop characters convincingly.[25] As Bahá'u'lláh states in *Words of Wisdom*, 'True reliance is for the servant to pursue his profession and calling in this world, to hold fast unto the Lord, to seek naught but His grace, inasmuch as in His hands is the destiny of all his servants.'[26] And in the Qur'án we read, 'And stretch not your necks in seeing what we have endowed some of our servants over others . . .'

***

Being an organic part of our inner struggles and a perfecting influence in all things, competition is essential for the creation of new things and the improvement of existing ones. Market competition, however, often displays a brutality and ruthlessness in human actions upsetting to many (and invigorating to some). In this pitiless arena there are real benefits for the winners and punishing costs for the losers. It is in this application that 'Abdu'l-Bahá's words characterizing competition as an obstacle to human happiness would seem to apply most strongly. In addition, there are obvious limitations to the entire notion of competing for everything, especially as it pertains to resources held in common, whether natural, intellectual, spiritual or of some other kind. When bidding for the common resources and wealth of the world, for example, direct and unfettered competition can be ruinous to the resource stock. It turns out that with all acting rationally a publicly accessible resource will become totally depleted.

The Tragedy of the Commons

The seas are considered a free resource by the nations of the world and the fish in them are no one's property. Therefore no one has the recognized authority to regulate offshore fishing activity. Nations depending on specific fishing grounds for their fishing have reacted to this situation by unilaterally declaring those grounds off-limits to other nations. At present the George's Bank fishing grounds off the coast of North America is practically depleted, according to Canadian officials. In 1997 that government used gunboats to seize a Spanish trawler fishing the George's Bank and arrested its captain and crew, bringing them back to Canada for prosecution.

Over-fishing is an example of a phenomenon called the *tragedy of the commons*, a principle enunciated by Garrett Hardin in a talk he gave in 1968 and subsequently printed in the journal *Science* that same year. While the immediate subject was population growth, the general themes developed and their universal application has led to the use of the principle in myriad applications and explanations. It predicts that with no party having responsibility and power to regulate the amount of a resource accessible to all that is utilized, it will become depleted inexorably.

However, there is a further prediction that can be made, which is not part of Hardin's thesis: As the depletion of the resource becomes evident there is added competition to utilize it even faster, thus accelerating its demise. Each user is afraid that if he or she waits for the resource to restore itself others will not wait and there will be nothing left. The cause of this relates to increased enterprise leverage and the need to cover increasing fixed costs.

This last prediction explains a lot of otherwise puzzling behaviour. For example, it explains why a natural resource is depleted at increasing rates when it has become obvious to all users that it needs time to restore itself.

The tragedy of the commons is linked to the fallacy of composition. This is the idea that what is good for some to do might be disastrous when all act in the same way. Individual thrift is praiseworthy but when all act the same way, saving all their disposal income, people working to produce things will lose their jobs and income, forcing them to spend their savings until nothing is left. Trading and buying within moderation is essential and makes us all better off over time. 'The beginning of magnanimity is when man expendeth his wealth on himself, on his family and on the poor among his brethren in the Faith.'[27] Resources are public goods, and spending and saving decisions, though private (internal), have public (external) consequences.

It also explains why poor parents usually have more children than they can adequately take proper care of while rich parents usually have fewer children. In the case of the poor having large families, people think, 'Maybe a few of our children will survive and live to take care of us in our old age; and if we refrain from having many children, others will not and their claim on resources will be greater than our own, thus increasing their chance for survival and reducing our own.'

But following this policy reduces the capital bequeathed to the next generation, inexorably drawing down society's capital base. By having offspring for resource purposes, benefits flow from children to parents in a regressive process that impoverishes all over time.

The rich, on the other hand, treat children as an investment in the future. They therefore have few children since they are seen as an investment expense rather than as a parental resource. Thus benefits flow from parents to children, assuring that each subsequent generation is better off than the last.

The end result of both these practices is to concentrate the wealth of the wealthy and the poverty of the poor and to consign the world's toiling masses to economic oblivion.

Why do elected officials tend to spend general revenues at a rate faster than they can be collected as tax revenues? Again, the answer comes from a deadly combination of competition and the fallacy of composition, the main result of the tragedy of the commons.

Each public elected official is acutely aware that s/he is responsible to those who elected him or her and that re-election depends on the ability to get as much of those general revenues spent in his or her home district as possible. Failure to do this will result in being turned out of office. Thus public deficits grow and public monies are used for increasingly myopic ends.[28]

The complications resulting from the *publicness* of the above decisions stem from their characteristics, as mentioned in an earlier chapter and offered below as review. *Rivalry* in consumption means that a good is diminished with each use. A candy bar or a sheet of paper, a gallon of gas or diesel, is rival because if I use it then there is less for anyone else. So also for the paper usage or the fuel. Light from a light source or a radio transmission, on the other hand, is not diminished by usage. Whether one book or a hundred books are under a light, or whether ten radios or 100,000 radios tune in makes no difference to the amount of light or the strength of the radio signal. The light or the signal is independent of how many users are benefiting. Such a good is called *non-rival* in consumption.

Exclusionarity in consumption means that persons can be excluded from using the good or service. My car is exclusive since I own it and, furthermore, while I use it no one else can. The same holds for most of what is termed *private property*. For other goods, however, there is just no way to exclude use. The fisheries problem discussed above is an example of non-exclusionarity, as is any commonly accessible resource. Some manufactured goods are also non-exclusionary, such as national defence, roads and highways and the laws of the land.

Goods that are both non-rival and non-exclusionary in consumption are public goods. Their significance to economics and spirituality lies in their obvious importance for the common good and the difficulty in seeing to their provision. Public goods, if they are not some form of natural resource but rather a produced good like national defence or the public transportation system, are supplied by private firms and parties but their supply is paid for with public funds, from tax revenues, in other words.

The problem with natural resources is that they are public goods only at low utilization levels. At higher use levels they are *congested goods*, becoming rival even while retaining their non-exclusionarity. This is the tragedy of the commons Hardin addressed in 1968. Since then some things have improved, at least locally. The air and water is now cleaner in the United States. But the Sahara is still spreading south as locals strip brush from the land for fuel; water is disappearing and is expected to become in the early decades of this century what oil had become in the final decades of the last. More species of fish have been completely fished out. Unregulated commercial fishing is stripping the seas of fish at a rate faster than they can replace their numbers and this will certainly become a major concern to coastal nations that rely on fish for their major source of dietary protein.

Such situations await the application of international laws to regulate the fishing of the seas of the world. Recall what a market needs to survive. It needs transferable property rights, acceptable regulations and standards and mutually beneficial exchanges. Then the true value of the fish taken can be established and the forces of demand and supply can force the establishment of a price for fish. Until international ownership and stewardship is established, the condition of the international fishing grounds of the world will only get worse and may lead to international altercations and even war.

Once property rights have been established and there is an acceptable body of rules that all sides agree to abide by, then competition will assure that only the best fishermen of the world will be involved in the harvest. This will lead to lower prices for fish for all consumers over time and a sustainable harvest for current and future generations. The true value of this resource to the peoples of the world should, however, *not* be found by simply resolving the forces of supply and demand, since this result would not take into consideration future requirements. Setting aside for the time being the disparities between national wealth, if the price becomes too high either because demand has increased or because fishing costs are rising, consumers may not be able to shift from their consumption of fish to other dietary sources of protein and oils in the short run. Nations requiring fish as their first and best source of food must be given priority. Is this act of fairness and international morality non-economic or unscientific? Not at all.

Assume nothing is done to limit the catch of nations for whom other dietary sources of animal protein and oils are available and as a result the fish supply collapses. Will the populations with fish as their main source of oils and animal protein radiantly acquiesce to this situation? Or rather, will they take recourse in armed conflict or acts of terror against those who are actually, or who are perceived to be, responsible? It is naive to think that as customers are observed buying fewer fish as the price rises, fishermen will reduce their catch in order to cut their costs and maintain their productive investments. Evidence and theory exist that show that fishermen, with dedicated and expensive harvesting equipment to pay for, face a barrier to exit and are thus impelled to harvest as much as possible and for as long as possible, no matter the danger to future supplies. Again, third party authoritative regulation alone allows fish stocks to increase over time. In this way a dynamic balance is established and maintained between supply and demand which protects fish stocks over time.

The same principles hold true for the depletion of the Ogallala Aquifer, a vast underground system of lakes which supplies the water for many American western states. Since it is owned by no individual state, each is free to pump out as much as it wants. Moreover, if any one state realized that this vast underground lake is being emptied faster than it can be recharged, it might respond by pumping it out even faster than before, in order to assure that it got all it could before the lake went dry or receded so far into the depths of the earth that it was regarded as practically inaccessible. After all, if it did not do so, it would only be depriving itself, for other states using this same resource would not be expected to act any differently.

Federalism is supposed to address and adjudicate such problems. But aquifers are not considered the territory of any one state or region. Like clean air polluted by one state then breathed by people in another, there is still a long way to go before the American government establishes regulations and enforcement policies, including compensation, for such situations.

Recall 'Abdu'l-Bahá stating that the federalist system of the United States is a model of world government, *with the understanding that the representatives think of themselves as citizens of the world.*[29] The same holds true for its working within the United States. Unless the representatives think of themselves as responsible for the commonwealth of all Americans the system breaks down and each tries to outdo the others in hogging as much of the resources as can be acquired by whatever means for the home district.

The solution is to establish an institution of federal ownership for the Ogallala Aquifer which would regulate its performance over time and protect the aquifer from depletion. Water would be sold to users at its actual value, not a cheaper, false value. As water stocks fall and the pumping cost to users rises, its price would rise and its use would be reduced wherever possible, perhaps by planting less water-intensive crops or reducing the size of golf courses and charging more for private consumption.[30]

The Great Lakes which border the United States and Canada experience high levels of pollution since neither side wants to incur all the costs of cutting pollution if the other side will respond by simply increasing the levels of dumping its own pollution into the lakes. The same solution of third party ownership must be applied. In this case the third party is a world federal entity. Under such a system the cost of cutting pollution would be added into the selling price of the products being manufactured and sold that generate the pollution. If it is decided that the good is essential and would become too expensive for those most in need of it, the international federal body, using internationally levied tax revenues, could subsidize producers who would then be required to pass the savings onto customers in the form of lowered prices.

One economist, Ronald Coase, developed a theoretical approach, which calls for the auction of property rights and the mutual negotiation of rights impingements.[31] If my radio is disturbing you, maybe you could offer to pay me to keep the volume down. The difficulty with this application of the compensation principle is that it would encourage extortion. Knowing you do not like loud music, why shouldn't I just raise the volume to extort a payment from you? (This is the reversibility paradox referred to earlier.) This problem is solved by the government declaring certain obnoxious behaviours illegal by statute and assigning responsibility for regulating that behaviour to its originator. As intimated in the fishing example, this is an economic solution when we consider the costs of all the alternatives. (In this and many other cases, since transactions costs do exist, the main result of the Coase Theorem – that the end result would be the same whether using civic codes or market mechanisms – becomes a theoretical artefact.)

The *full-costing* method, that is, making the product sales price reflect all the costs of manufacture, including the costs of whatever pollution was associated in production, solves many of the problems inherent in the presence of externalities and public and quasi-public goods. Manufacturers cut costs through cutting pollution by favouring more advanced manufacturing technology that does not pollute in the first place. The technology is paid for by the reduction in pollution costs to the company and soon is showing profit increases for the firm. The radio is turned down so this bit of obnoxious and chaotic behaviour does not lead to even worse problems, murder, for instance.

Full costing also means internalizing costs that were external before, making public costs part of private accounting balances. We set aside considerations of national wealth in discussing the world fisheries problem and imposed a solution using international authoritative fiat. When national wealth and influence is included, the result is that some nations can afford to supply their citizens with enough fish to eat and some cannot. If fish becomes very scarce and remains desirable to consumers, its value – and thus its price – will rise ever higher. This will mean that some people will not be able to afford those prices and must do without. This is acceptable, as long as there are alternatives that they can afford. But what if they are a small nation very reliant on fish because the expense of obtaining food other than fish is higher still? Perhaps this nation has few resources and is located far away from central markets.

The only possibility for raising the standard of living of the people of that nation is for it to unite with other nations in a federalist structure. How would this yield a higher standard of living? It does this by internalizing certain markets so that *they no longer compete* but cooperate instead. Rather than citizens of each economy being limited to the opportunities obtainable only within their home market, they now experience a greater variety of opportunities for employment, reducing shortages and surpluses within the home employment markets that once existed when each was separate.

The federal system also allows the pooling of finance and capital, enabling the separate states to acquire a share in expensive but needful systems, such as health, education, information, agriculture and manufacture. This is an application of the 'unity in diversity' principle in economics. It allows every citizen involved to gain from providing for lower cost exchanges and from specialization of resources and markets. Today this can happen in unexpected ways because of the reformulation of society now occurring. If another prophetic message has been announced then what has happened at such times in the past will be repeated. A description of the reorganization to be expected is offered by these words of Bahá'u'lláh:

> Those words, sharp as the sword of God have separated the faithful from the infidel, and severed father from son . . . How many fathers have turned away from their sons; how many lovers have shunned their beloved! So mercilessly trenchant was this wondrous sword of God that it cleft asunder every relationship! On the other hand, consider the welding power of His Word. Observe, how those in whose midst the Satan of self had for years sown the seeds of malice and hate became so fused and blended through their allegiance to this wondrous and transcendent Revelation that it seemed as if they had sprung from the same loins.'[32]

This is a description of what took place as a result of the appearance of His Holiness Muhammad. Apparently the same process occurs with the appearance of each major Prophet, those producing a body of teachings responsible for the establishment of one of the major world religions. Another appearance would produce the same results, which would have the economic effect of realigning current international relationships and even in reformulating the basis of those relationships. This may allow the establishment of a truly federalist international system.

***

Competition is an inseparable part of life. For the most part, even in constituent, the idea of a winner or a loser in competition is often indeterminate, appearing between polar extremes on a continuous experiential spectrum. Market competition, where similar products directly compete for customers, is but one of its aspects. In the short run there are indeed winners and losers in market competition of this work, with winners winning big and the losers getting badly mauled. In the long run trading increases wealth for all and even losers, if they survive on some level, can be made better off.

The worst aspects of competition seem to be on display in the world's labour markets. Today labour markets are decidedly a zero-sum game in the short run and even over longer periods, concentrating wealth and poverty and leading to other social pathologies. While generations of families can do so, individual workers cannot operate in the long run; they survive or die only in the short run, where losing can mean swift descent into financial destitution. 'In the long run, we're all dead,' said the economist Keynes. At present European labour markets are far more forgiving and humane compared to all others, especially in comparison to what prevails in the United States. The costs of their system of unemployment and transitional retraining programmes, combined with the other social benefits offered as a right of citizenship, are seen in several ways while the benefits generating net gains to society are often hidden and are more subtle. Goods are priced slightly higher than they are in America because minimizing labour costs is not the priority it is in the US. Unemployment rates in Europe are generally higher than in the US, though not always, since people are not forced to work at *anything available* just to eat. You do not see as many unemployed middle managers in Europe pumping gasoline or working for tips in restaurants as you do in America, for instance.

Different ways of measuring and comparing living standards exist, with the two main ones represented by North America and Europe. Rather than basing the standard of living on having the greatest quantity of high quality goods available at the lowest possible cost (the American standard), Europe opted for a standard emphasizing universal basic income, even if this results in slightly higher prices, prices that can in any case be afforded since each person is guaranteed a minimum level of spending power. The rationale for this standard, in contrast to the 'personal lottery', find-a-job/keep-a-job, standard of the US, is intimated by the writings of Bahá'u'lláh and 'Abdu'l-Bahá, in which softening this particular and personally experienced obstacle to human happiness, the competitive struggle for existence, is greatly encouraged.

The benefits of more generous unemployment insurance compensation flow from human capital retention and enhancement. In the United States unemployment insurance never covers more than 60 per cent of existing salary and is terminated after just six months. This poses difficulties as we move from a society using mostly unspecialized and untrained labour to one where labour is highly trained and specialized because, while leading to greater pay for work, it also increases the likelihood that if a position were lost it may take a long time for that worker to find another suitable position. If an engineer, for instance, does not find a job within six months in the United States, then s/he is forced to work in a different and usually less valued employment in order to obtain any income at all.

But this increases the likelihood that the worker may never work in that speciality again, especially if it is a highly technical one where new developments occur continuously. The worker has not been able to keep up with changes because s/he has had to work outside of the profession, possibly doing more menial work, and had neither the time nor the energy to remain competitive and up-to-date in his or her professional speciality. This is a gross waste and write-off of expensive and valuable human capital.

Now look at the European example of unemployment insurance paying as much as 80 per cent of employed compensation for up to two years, if necessary. Rather than being forced into menial work after six months the European worker can remain sifting through the best job offers and keeping fully informed and up-to-date on the important skill changes in his or her profession until re-employed. Thus human capital is retained and the training and experience of a lifetime are not wasted by forced abandonment and lower-level work.

Today practically all jobs of any content require high levels of training and education. Enlightened economic competition requires that workers be given time to adjust to market changes and the destruction of old technologies and their replacement by new ones. This is a complex problem faced by all societies. Short-run market structures will fail to address such complexities. But these have been fully addressed by the divine teachings of the holy books, which emphasize collective action along with strengthened individual responsibility for maintaining human existence with dignity for all its elements. Competition here means finding the best solution to such problems.

***

In this chapter we have enlarged our concept of competition to include the competing ideas and beliefs that face each person, the hourly struggle to overcome our lower selves and the kind of horse-trading that constantly goes on in the chambers of parliaments and other deliberative bodies; and the necessity for humane collective actions to guarantee a dignified existence for all society's members. Next we look at investment from an individual spiritual standpoint and discuss its economic implications.

10

Societal Transformation

From Individual and Collective Investments

Part I

The Investment Process

Reading the divine message in any of God's holy books reveals that the prescription for a good life in all the worlds of God is to learn patience and to delay our need for gratification. Everything about the character of the holy Word suggests that humans are to develop a sense of future values, future costs and benefits and approach the decisions of life in a total-cost/total-benefit framework. It is total costs and total benefits we must keep focused upon while marginal valuations – the change in something's worth for a change in the quantity or units already used – should be used only if our marginal calculus includes what happens to us in the future. Our marginal valuations must be cognizant of not only possible future states for ourselves but also for anyone else likely to be affected by our decisions.

The way to accomplish this is to train humans so that tastes and preferences are linked to other times and to other people in our world. That is, our satisfaction should be derived not just from our own present and current increases but from the satisfaction of knowing that others are similarly benefiting. As parents, this comes naturally, most of the time. Our own happiness and satisfaction increase as our children gain victories over the challenges of life and they decrease when they fail. We also willingly set aside some capital as a bequest to be used by our children in order to support their development into mature and capable societal members. The Messengers of God have enjoined us to develop this same satisfaction linkage to everyone, keeping in mind, of course, that we have direct and inescapable responsibilities towards the welfare of our own children beyond those for others. But this is a minimum standard, after all. Further, we cherish the value of future states as much as present states.

Why is this so important? Because it protects us from personally and socially short-sighted and destructive behaviour, behaviour which, if allowed, would threaten our existence and the existence of society itself. What we are constantly encouraged to do by the Messengers of God is to *invest*, in ourselves, our futures and the future of society.

Investment can be defined as *dedicating capital for the exclusive purpose of increasing its future value*. This can vary in the specifics but, using the earlier result that the object of all economic activity is individual utility maximization (which still holds under the strictures of the prophetic dialogues), its ultimate goal is to increase future consumption prospects. We know that consumption also takes many forms, only one of which is material, so this increase can maximize utility over time in many different ways.[1]

The purpose of individual investment, therefore, would seem to be motivated by the desire to increase happiness somehow or to decrease unhappiness – from poverty, for example. This may be true but not very instructive. This chapter will test earlier claims made for utility as a prime mover of personal actions by revisiting the concepts of the subjective planning horizon (SPH) and the subjective rate of time preference (SRTP). We will take the results from the chapter on behaviour modification utilizing these two concepts and apply them to the problem of investment, one of the most central problems for human beings and one addressed repeatedly in prophetic divine speech. Economics, while not making our decisions any easier, has at least framed the problem in an understandable fashion.

With respect to market operations the investment problem is that, in spite of neoclassical economic assumptions about human behaviour in economic space, most people do not have enough knowledge about the future or its requirements to know what to do today to prepare for it. So even if we want to increase our total happiness over time, we make a lot of mistakes, even when we know what we want and how to get it.

Most of the time we do not know these things. So we follow general lines or principles and hope that within their scope and reach success will be found. Additionally, the workplace is changing rapidly. Whereas in previous generations a worker might have expected to change jobs at least five times in his or her working life, now it is expected that s/he will likely need to change careers that often, not to mention jobs within these career paths. Also, far more responsibility for preparation is being placed on the worker and less on management. For example, over the past 30 years the labour market has changed in developed nations. Low skilled work or skilled jobs where on-the-job training was the way to learn have all but disappeared.

Jobs paying a middle or even lower-middle class salary or wage require that the worker know what is required to do the job before his or her first day at work. This training must be purchased in many cases at personal expense, which has had the effect of placing everyone on the level of a supplier or producer because *the risk of costly investments must be made before any income is received*. The first income stream must be used to pay the indebtedness incurred to become a skilled worker.

In such a system of *radical entrepreneurial capitalism* everyone is a corporation of one, and since nine out of ten businesses fail in the first year, how much personal security can there be in that? This is socially regressive. Too much of the risk burden, which had been shouldered by large and diversified corporations, is now a private cost to the individual even while the benefits of success and the damage from failure are both private and public and accrue mostly to the employer. Governments are beginning to become cognizant of this reality and the associated costs to communities when people have failed to invest in themselves and are not prepared for the new globalized, internationally competitive workplace.

It is in the interests of society to increase the number of economically and socially viable individuals and thereby decrease the number of dependent ones.[2] Self-investments can benefit everyone over time and alone will transform not only the individual but society as a whole. Let these words, delivered to the avowed followers of Bahá'u'lláh from the appointed Guardian of the Bahá'í Faith, act as a guide to personal – and thereby social – transformation:

> Not by force of numbers, not by a mere exposition of a set of new and noble principles, not by an organized campaign of teaching – no matter how worldwide and elaborate in its character – not even by the staunchness of our faith or the exaltation of our enthusiasm, can we ultimately hope to vindicate in the eyes of a critical and sceptical age the supreme claim of the Abhá Revelation. One thing and only one thing will unfailingly and alone secure the undoubted triumph of this sacred Cause, namely, the extent to which our own inner life and private character mirror forth in their manifold aspects the splendour of those eternal principles proclaimed by Bahá'u'lláh.[3]

Without discussing the goal itself, these words indicate that social transformation is dependent upon personal transformation. It has already been established that personal transformation is a complex process involving the personal investment of time and treasure and the sacrifice of current wants for a better future.

Let us examine whether successful personal investment of this broadly-defined type is responsible for the transformation of societies. It would seem to be a truism requiring no evidence but its aspects are manifold. Two such aspects will be examined now: one involves societal changes resulting from the presence of the earliest and most influential followers of a new prophetic message and the other is an economic analysis of the conditional states of mature individuals and their effect on society.

It is a matter of historical record that the twelve Apostles of Jesus of Nazareth dispersed throughout the Roman Empire and surrounding regions after the death of their Prophet. Within a few centuries that region of the world openly and officially declared allegiance to the Christian cause. Tribal Europe also fell under its sway. The result for Europe was the establishment of a cultural centralism that subsumed tribal and ethnic creeds to an extent unimaginable previous to the rise of Christendom. Within the dominions of the Holy Roman Church and of Byzantium interstate war was largely checked. Literacy spread among a population tutored by monks who invited any promising male to enter the monasterial fold for a lifetime of dedicated study and scholarship where varying ideas could be more or less freely debated within their number and study abroad was possible. Natural science and philosophy developed and culture, previously centred only around constant intertribal and inter-ethnic warfare, developed considerably.[4] All these developments claimed association to the Christian religion. Since the original twelve Apostles of Christ were the ones to spread the new teachings of Jesus (and, by extension, Judaism as well), it is demonstrated that the personal transformation of those twelve individuals from what they were before their portentous association with Jesus to what they subsequently became was solely responsible for the social transformation of Europe. This is not to say that the nominal religion of Christ and its structural and sacerdotal manifestations were in line with Christ's teachings but only that the subsequent developments in Europe, for better or worse, are traceable to the teachings and example of these original twelve people.

As to what resulted in later centuries, we have this reference from 'Abdu'l-Bahá in *The Secret of Divine Civilization*:

> Those European intellectuals who are well-informed as to the facts of Europe's past, and are characterized by truthfulness and a sense of justice, unanimously acknowledge that in every particular the basic elements of their civilization are derived from Islám.[5]

Elsewhere He explains how previously Moses transformed the Israelites, allowing them to found a culturally, artistically and intellectually influential civilization.

This argument extends a previous one made to demonstrate that the presence of the Prophet Muhammad was responsible for the transformation of Peninsular Arabia and later of the Middle East, the Maghreb and most of the Levant. Clearly, if no life had been transformed by His words, how could society at large have been transformed, even to the extent of a single town, much less to the extent of an entire region?

Using a more deconstructed argument, *individuals comprise the instrumentality of social purpose and form the societal institutions responsible for transmitting the collective will.* As people change, the collective will changes and the societal institutions they staff change. Individual transformation, therefore, causes and is solely responsible for societal transformation.[6]

The other aspect of personal transformation we will look at is how society is affected by the presence of different terminal (final) conditional levels of personal maturity among its members. The mature terminal states of individual development determine the complexion of society. If members cannot support themselves then their support must come from others who produce even more than they personally need. All societies have such members. Each of us was once dependent and will again become dependent on others for our material and social support if we live long enough. But if society, through lack of planning and provision, allows too many dependent people it could diminish aggregate wealth. There is even a term for this situation, the *dependency index*: how many non-producers must be supported by the producing sector on a per capita basis. Certain sub-Saharan African states have many non-producers being supported by a few workers – and the HIV/AIDS pandemic is just making this situation worse. It also works for companies. Some companies have just a few retired workers being supported by a very large cohort of current workers while some older industrial companies have hundreds or even thousands of retired workers being supported. This raises costs and makes it even harder for the company to compete. Addressing this problem is a constant challenge to governments. One solution is to ensure that each generation has more and more valuable human capital than the last, so that even with a shrinking workforce and a growing retired or dependent population the money is still sufficient to support all of society's members adequately.

***

The formation of viable human capital can be thought of as a production process, whereby society takes a child-cohort and uses its standing resources to develop finished human capital in the form of rational social agents capable of sustaining and expanding society's possibilities from one generation to the next. In fact, if society wishes to avoid the pitfall of squandering all its resources in a vain attempt to attain economic and social rationality for every one of its citizens, some form of bench marking would be needed. This is done, and nations are deemed successful in this endeavour if some acceptable percentage of the citizenry achieves success. It is an application of the *law of diminishing returns*. The fixed resource (required for the law to work) is the total natural talent of the child-cohort. At some point it is not sensible to push development further. Costs will eventually grow without bound and eat up all available resources, with very few additional gains to show for it. Humans differ, obviously; not all can be economically or financially successful. (This is just one of the measures of success for the human condition, an important but narrow one.[7])

It has been argued that if rational beings are to be produced certain inputs must be made available at specific times during this process for success to be achieved. (In this sense human capital formation is very much a 'just-in-time' production process!) This depends on an investment flow to have been made in the past so that necessary inputs are available when needed.

Let there be three, mutually exclusive states or possible outcomes for individual development in terms of the individual ability to create wealth and consume goods and services over time.[8]

The optimal of the three states is the development of an individual capable of creating enough wealth for all personal needs, to support all dependents and to make additions to collective wealth stores. The minimal acceptable state is a person capable of self-support, even if incapable of supporting others or adding to public wealth stores. Finally, the third state is an individual incapable even of supporting himself or herself, who must therefore rely on the wealth of what others have created to meet his or her own irreducible needs.

In the first case the person is a net gain to society and in the second at least s/he represents no direct costs, even while unable to shoulder the entire burden of citizenship. In the third case, however, the individual represents a net loss to society, at least financially. This dependency will be an ongoing problem for society, depending, more or less, on what form it takes. In one form, others assume responsibility for the person and essentially adopt him or her; this can also include publicly available support programmes. The other form of dependence is where the individual actively appropriates the accumulated wealth formed by others through criminal pursuits. If passive dependence is not obtainable or does not provide acceptable subjective minimum consumption, then criminality is the only path to economic sustenance.

Clearly, societies benefit from investing in or promoting the investment in the individual in order to minimize the number of dependent individuals and increase the number of those capable of supporting themselves and others.[9] But it is often difficult to identify specific investments in children intended to increase the number of such individuals. We have already looked at the principles of rational personality formation. Whatever the programme's specifics, it must be capable of reducing individual subjective rates of time preference and increasing subjective planning horizons. We have also discussed how the prophetic message and its derivatives perform this function by increasing future values, promoting total or absolute value assessment over marginal valuations and by increasing the planning horizon to consciously include states of existence after death. We also saw that in order for future states to be fully apprehended and exploited, the agent must be certain that current actions result in specific future states.

Thus investments in human capacity must produce people who are able to appreciate the effects of their actions and the dynamic worth of those actions, to themselves, to others and to society at large. This must be the fundamental result of socially sustaining investment. From this all else can follow. The reason this is true is that in the end societies need people to be self-investors and then pass on this tendency to the next generation. None of the many investment schemes devised to increase national income or personal income are possible without the affected and participating agents being able to appreciate their own actions and to apprehend what leads to increases or decreases of wealth over time.

Recall that wealth is the production of some good of greater value than the sum total of the value of the resources composing it. For example, put solid graphite into a small wooden cylinder or shaft and end up with a writing implement capable of representing and recording communication, something impossible for its component parts. Or construct a bicycle, automobile, diesel train or rocket ship from parts and achieve transportation, something impossible by the collection of disassembled parts making up any of those entities respectively. Wealth requires investment, here expressed as the setting aside of available capital used for other purposes, for the exclusive use of forming future wealth. This is no different from its earlier definition. And investment is impossible without a sufficiently long planning horizon or a low subjective rate of time preference (personal degree of patience). These conditions are only possible if social, cultural, family, religious, intellectual and other capital forms existed *before* their need in forming and maturing human capital.

This closes the circle of social existence, of sustenance, growth and social reformation essential for the continuance and improvement of human life over time. We have ended at the beginning point of establishing the need for self-investment. Since self-investment, like all other forms, requires the setting aside of capital, be it time or other available resources, investment is, practically by definition, sacrifice in the spiritual sense. We also argued above that one or a few transcendentally influential people are capable of reforming a society. Over time such influence is formally channelled and provided to society through specialized institutions constructed for that purpose. These direct the flow of this influence into the institutions of the family, the school, the workplace and other social constructions and thereby change the lives of new and unborn generations by affecting their tastes and preferences, the economic term used to describe 'character'.

We now have all we need to understand the transformation of society. Now assume that a new prophetic message has been revealed to society as has happened in the past. We may expect that what happened to past societies will again happen but this time, owing to advances in communication and the internationalization of all commerce and information, the entire world would be affected.

Since we now understand in broad terms the mechanics of social transformation, several lines of analysis are open. One is to use this information to decide if evidence exists that would indicate that a Prophet has indeed reappeared with a divine message, and if so, by tracing social transformational changes back through time, decide approximately when this might have occurred. Thus we could position ourselves to take full advantage of the sweeping changes we know will be rapidly occurring and avoid being entrapped by the falling debris of a crumbling social edifice. We could adapt, in other words, to the changes likely to occur in our lives and plan our futures accordingly.

If such changes are inevitable and, however chaotic they appear to us 'on the ground', are purposeful and result directly from the influence of this new divine dialogue, then we might decide to actively participate in the realization of its stated goals. The result of this would be to transform ourselves by personal investments and transform society by influencing by our presence one of its institutions and thereby alter the tastes and preferences, the character of newly emerging individuals and of those still impressionable enough to have their characters altered.

The Transformation of Society via Individual Character Alteration

Character transformation is not ruled out in economics, even using the most restricted set of neoclassical economic principles. Certain very influential academic practitioners have indeed declared that *tastes are fixed* for the life of the agent and that they are a 'given', that is, they are exogenously supplied to the market arena and are not considered malleable, at least to market influences.[10] If by this is meant that market activities do not alter tastes, then this is consistent with the assumption that market activities cannot change behaviour, which must be argued on its own merits. But if by this is meant that agent tastes cannot change by any means and are assumed fixed for the lifetime of that agent, then this assumption is inconsistent and violates economic first principles which state that *in the long run no inputs are considered fixed.* Certainly technology is expected to change in the long run and there is no justification for assuming a priori that while all else can change, tastes and preferences must remain fixed. We might ask, given that all things change over time, *by what process would such fixity be maintained?* Rather, we observe that tastes change radically over time both collectively and individually. Obviously, were this not to happen and were people to assume that it did not happen, then advertising would be abandoned as well as the sponsorship of all other socializing influences requiring the expenditure of resources.

But this is not the case: Actually, after declaring that tastes are exogenous to market forces, it was rather silly to assume any particular thing about them since neoclassical economics rules out treating all but strictly market actions. The definition of *long run* is that all inputs or factors can change. Tastes and preferences are an input (or argument) to the demand function. Tastes and preferences therefore change in the long run.[11]

It is therefore clear from arguments made above and from economic first principles that tastes and preferences can and do change over time. Those elements exerting the greatest influence in this have been discussed, with the most influential being the family. Within the family, logic and the writings of 'Abdu'l-Bahá indicate that the mother is the first and greatest influence in the life of the individual. It was further argued that initial influences are difficult to change once a certain period of time has passed, i.e. tastes are at least quasi-fixed after puberty has passed, reflecting the difficulty of changing certain fundamental things in a person's character after maturity.

Foremost of the elements of consciousness needing development in the individual is a utility function that chooses what is intertemporally consistent and interpersonally constructive. Intertemporal consistency refers to choosing today those behaviours that will enhance future states of being. Choosing interpersonally constructive actions means preferring actions that help others as well as oneself, in other words, to feel happy in the knowledge that others are also well off or to be afraid of doing something that will burden others.

Utility functions linked intertemporally and interpersonally are a matter of character and personality, tastes and preferences. These are formed in the nexus of the emerging individual and social institutions. A society whose members have intertemporally and interpersonally linked utility functions will maximize available choices in such a way so as to advance society in the present and in the future. This, of course, is the goal of any spiritual message.

One thing more should be mentioned before discussing how social change is a function of individual change. This is to note that the functional relationship is almost certainly *nonlinear*. That is, for a little change in the individual there might be extraordinary changes in society as a result. The reason for this is what was briefly discussed earlier about how little changes seem to have no effect then, suddenly, there is a profound change in the system in question. Malcolm Gladwell characterized this as the phenomenon of the 'tipping point'. Social changes act in a manner similar to epidemics or the spread of infectious agents through a population.[12] This means that it is not necessary for a large percentage of people acting in society to effect its transformation; a much smaller number could succeed. Because transformed individuals populate and work within the social institutions that form the tastes of the next generation, transformations can occur suddenly.

Sacrifice as Investing

Now view what we have discussed from another perspective. In the language of spiritual science, sacrificing means becoming that to which you completely give yourself over. But this is just common sense. If we pursue a life of accumulating artworks we become art connoisseurs; if we spend our time at work we become workers, if it is hours with Latin or mathematics we become knowledgeable in these things, etc. We therefore take on the attributes of that for which we sacrifice. Further, we receive in proportion to what and how much we give up. This is just saying that the greater the investment, the greater the payoff, all else being equal. The words are a little different but the concept is identical. Even the idea of what is being sacrificed or invested is identical, that is, resources at the disposal of the agent, time, concentration, leisure, money perhaps, etc.[13]

The process of sacrifice is also a birth–death process.[14] In non-economic speech, in order to become something new we must give up or die to what we are now. Then the new can be established in us. There are basically two choices for capital use – consumption or investment (savings can be a form of investment or future consumption). Since consumption has a larger ordinary marginal value than investment, it takes a good reason not to use it in consumption to make you happier right now. Successfully navigating this decision determines if investment will ever take place and it is based entirely upon the ability to visualize the greater importance of total value relative to marginal value. The ability to do this does not change much. Each time it is faced the values are about the same, so if you cannot decide to forgo consumption today in favour of investment, it will not be any easier tomorrow or at any other opportunity. This is why people who can quit smoking have probably done so already and those who have not yet done so probably never will, until it is too late. Some can become someone else, some cannot.[15] *Those who can regard total value as greater than marginal value can change behaviour* and their present life for another.

Compound Benefits

It was argued above that the rate of societal change is not necessarily a linear relationship proportional to the increasing number of transformed individuals. One reason besides the 'tipping point' mentioned above is that the individual benefits of personal transformation, from sacrifice and investing, are compounded through time. Intellectual and moral capital act just as financial capital. The size of their base will increase by some measurable amount each market period. The way such gains are represented is as a *rate of interest* that the base earns. For example, if you put $100 into an interest-bearing account for one market period – a compounding period – you could withdraw $110 thereafter. But if the money plus the earned interest payment is left, there will be not $120 but $121 at the end of the second term because the added $10 also earns interest of one dollar. This is compounding.

Consider taking a series of mathematics classes with the goal of learning calculus techniques for research work. If you had the ability to solve an array of difficult real-world problems from biology and weather forecasting to financial economics, crude oil reservoir management and industrial engineering, you would see a gradual increase in your computing power, a straight line on a slow rise. This would continue for years. But after taking a two-semester sequence of differential and integral calculus your computational prowess would shoot up. The number of important problems you could then handle would just about double in amount. Most of the interesting problems of living things and dynamic systems (like weather and economic growth) require calculus techniques to be understood. This sudden gain in computational ability is an example of intellectual compounding.[16]

As a new life is taken up and time and treasure is dedicated to investing in the future, and the patterns of the old life give way to the new, the process of personal transformation accelerates. There is also no reason to think that the principle of initial actions having an inordinate influence on the success of a dynamic enterprise is not of equal importance on a personal scale, just as it is on the collective or even global scale. This also offers an additional explanation for the nonlinearity in intellectual growth rates. A good childhood yields positive results for the adult with results far in excess of the value of the inputs taken out of context.

***

We now have explored and suggested how societal transformation results from individual transformations. We now link individuals together from different time periods and different lives using the concept of utility to show how individual preference satisfaction, properly calibrated by the divine Messenger, can lead to a socially optimal growth path and optimal state. It is not an 'invisible hand' process, which sees socially positive results flowing from the myriad private activities pursued by individuals seeking nothing more than their own gain. Rather, this process will be shown to be the result of purposeful public investments in social institutions that can produce preference functions linked interpersonally and intertemporally, as directed by the Prophets of God. Initially, the divine Messenger transforms the lives of a few key and fated individuals, who subsequently, in the fullness of time, transform the growth path of an entire civilization. Finally, the leaders of that civilization preserve the transformative process by establishing institutions that foster personal transformation in its individuals, 'Light upon light! Allah guides to His light whom He wills.'[17]

11

Societal Transformation

From Individual and Collective Investments

Part II

Trust Accounting

We have heard the argument that, as the individual goes, so goes society. We also recognized that after the release of inspiration from a new prophetic dialogue the causality does not flow only in one direction, from individual to society, but also, especially in later generations, from society and its institutions back to the individual. As individuals become transformed they serve and live in those social institutions that come to influence the tastes and preferences of the next generation. How will it ever be possible to separate individual from societal feedback influences after the divine Messenger has begun the process? We have seen pictures and images of Buddhists in Tibet and elsewhere spinning 'prayer wheels' with their hands as they pass them by. Is this so different from what the Prophets and Messengers of God do with their hands for the wheel of mankind?

All these various influences find their expression in the abstract concept of a utility function that we know outwardly as a set of tastes and preferences. It is on the hearts of humans that the eye of Bahá is fixed, we are told. That is, all in heaven and earth has been created for our edification, so that our hearts will incline towards God and His cause. Economics does not discuss the heart, only tastes and preferences – wants – and utility as the representation of the heart. So it is useful for us to spend a little time understanding how utility functions in economics as an explanatory tool.

This expression – utility – can be analysed for the presence of certain attributes without the need to refer directly to the cauldron of centrifugal wants and needs, specifically, what is desired by the individual from others and to what extent individual well-being is dependent on the presence of well-being in others.

Utility functions underlie individual preferences and, as stated in earlier chapters, are determined largely by the individual's exposure to specific societal institutions, primarily the family environment, which in turn results in the formation of various capital forms within the individual. To what extent has the family stressed the need to see the welfare of others as a source of one's own bliss and contentment? Because this is learned behaviour, left to one's own devices such interpersonally linked utility functions would never be formed. If this were not so the early years of the Prophets, during which they show exemplary generosity and selflessness, would not be noteworthy because such behaviour would not appear to be extraordinary. 'Verily, the self is inclined to evil, except when My Lord bestows His mercy.'[1] As we have seen and emphasized throughout this book, people must learn to care about the future and see that its quality depends largely on their own present actions. This means that individual utility functions must be interpersonally linked but also intertemporally linked. That is, individuals must care about the future, not just for themselves but for those not yet born.

The extent to which prophetic dialogues are responsible for transforming societies has already been noted and analysed. The effect of such a transformation on the individual is difficult to overemphasize. This statement of 'Abdu'l-Bahá reiterates this point but makes the additional claim that the philosophers of ancient times regarded the fruits of their efforts as the transformation of personal character:

> . . . Galen, the celebrated physician, although not himself a Christian, in his summary of Plato's *Republic* extolled their actions. A literal translation of his words is as follows:
>
> 'The generality of mankind are unable to grasp a sequence of logical arguments. For this reason they stand in need of symbols and parables telling of rewards and punishments in the next world. A confirmatory evidence of this is that today we observe a people called Christians, who believe devoutly in rewards and punishments in a future state. This group show forth excellent actions, similar to the actions of an individual who is a true philosopher. For example, we all see with our own eyes that they have no fear of death, and their passion for justice and fair-dealing is so great that they should be considered true philosophers.'
>
> The station of a philosopher, in that age and in the mind of Galen, was superior to any other station in the world. Consider then how the enlightening and spiritualizing power of divine religions impels the believers to such heights of perfection that a philosopher like Galen, not himself a Christian, offers such testimony.[2]

The reason for including this passage here is to focus on the aspect on which Galen also focused, that is, the importance of belief in a future life and state as a test for the goodness of present actions. The worth of any and all present actions should be measured by their ability to assure a blissful life after death. In this life what we prefer is largely determined by what we are taught to prefer. Utility functions express the way in which these preferences are translated into actions. It is in this sense that the object of all economic activity is said to be individual utility maximization.

Some may jump to the conclusion that this is an example of the phenomenon of the 'invisible hand' so often – and frequently incorrectly – invoked to explain market operations. That phenomenon, however, describes people pursuing private selfish interests which, owing to their interconnectedness and what economists have termed network externalities or network spillovers, result in rising material prosperity for the group from increased trading activity. But in the present case *people choose to act altruistically* towards each other for the purpose of gaining admittance into a blissful kingdom after death. These people have become convinced by some means or combination of arguments that what is our essence survives physical death and continues on somehow and, further, that the quality of the 'afterlife' is largely dependent on the quality of our present character, i.e. the sum total of what it is we want and what we do. 'Verily, We give life to the dead, and We record that which they send before (them), and their traces and all things We have recorded with numbers in a Clear Book.'[3]

Such people have also heard the accounts of the abuse, pain and martyrdom experienced by the Prophets and their devoted followers, have noted their willingness to suffer these things and recognized that history has judged them to be transcendentally wise. As a result, by argument, example or both, generations have decided to alter their own lives and to regard their *total utility* as of greater importance than *their marginal – or contextual – utility*. 'This is because of that which your hands have sent forward before you. And verily, God is not unjust to His servants.'[4] Note the perfect harmony of this economic calculus of utility with the description of the lives of those 'born anew' in the religious sense. It is yet further evidence that *reality is one*, even while the different parts we choose to study may seem to sharply differ. But here there would seem to be no difference even in this sense, as the same phenomenon is being described in two different ways, each internally consistent yet each in complete agreement with the other.

With a set of cultivated preferences expressed as interpersonally and intertemporally linked utility functions relating actions with their associated results, individuals can now pursue their life work and activities. The result will be a society as close to perfection as is possible to realize. Important to this process is adherence to the turnpike principle of economic growth, namely, that it is essential to identify the optimal growth path, to get on that path and to stay on it as long as possible. This is just good sense and is universally applicable.

Goal-seeking systems require that every action produce some positive result or reduce some negative result. Waste must be minimized. Any wrong or needless move will result in lost time and/or treasure which cannot then be used to attain the sought-after goal. Each life is like this, from the one-celled amoeba to the human being, to a field of ripening wheat or a rocket travelling in space. This is also true for societies and nations: 'Now that ye have refused the Most Great Peace; hold ye fast unto this, the Lesser Peace,'[5] Bahá'u'lláh says to the leaders of the world. They missed their chance and it slipped away irretrievably. So this other goal, of lesser value, but still a treasure, is offered as still possible of accomplishment. We see this principle at work in our personal lives. We reach a day when it is clear that certain things we might wish to do are no longer possible; the time for those things is past and other things must be taken up. Had we been capable of acting as needed years before, our lives would have led to another end than the one it now targets. A good start, cultivating wise preference sets and leading to utility that makes the individual and society better off, ensures that each of our individual systems achieves its greatest potential – yields the greatest happiness – possible. In economics this is called *path-dependence*. Results are strongly influenced by initial conditions, and given limited time and resources, degraded initial conditions cannot be overcome and the most great goal is unattainable, although many other great goals may still be.

What are some of the tangible gains a society will realize if its members have higher levels of morality? It should be clear that increased levels of morality in social agents will result in diminished operating costs for society as a whole. There are the obvious cost savings of reduced policing requirements and target hardening (making targets more difficult for criminals to break into or steal, for example), reductions in costs for anything where interpersonal trustworthiness is important, such as in medical costs, liability and jurisprudence burden, etc.

But added to these is the increased output from those who would otherwise be incarcerated. Output increases are also realized because children receive the best possible start in life, one that does not mutilate their hearts with abuse, oppressive vexing, neglect, indiscipline, chaos or the adoption of wasteful habits and behaviours. Some of the other examples of savings and increases in useful and constructive output are described by Shoghi Effendi and every point he makes can be seen as the logical outcome of cultivating truly beneficial preference sets in individuals who in turn populate the institutions responsible for the welfare of society. Though framed in the broadest terms, each element and beneficial attribute he describes is the result of individual actions:

> . . . economic barriers and restrictions will be completely abolished, and the inordinate distinction between classes will be obliterated. Destitution on the one hand, and gross accumulation of ownership on the other, will disappear. The enormous energy dissipated and wasted on war, whether economic or political, will be consecrated to such ends as will extend the range of human inventions and technical development, to the increase of the productivity of mankind, to the extermination of disease, to the extension of scientific research, to the raising of the standard of physical health, to the sharpening and refinement of the human brain, to the exploitation of the unused and unsuspected resources of the planet, to the prolongation of human life, and to the furtherance of any other agency that can stimulate the intellectual, the moral, and spiritual life of the entire human race.[6]

Each of these gains is the direct or indirect result of establishing sound initial conditions for children from their earliest ages. The above is a spiritual, moral and religious statement of this fact but it is just as much – and just as effectively – an economic statement of this fact as well.

We now discuss some additional benefits. We have mentioned the extent to which ethics and moral teachings, found in many sources including, increasingly, the classrooms of business schools, are all derived from the prophetic dialogues. The beginnings of a logical proof of this has been sketched out in this book and the statements of the Prophets themselves support it.

In this context Bahá'u'lláh's Tablet of Wisdom has been mentioned in a previous chapter. Here is another verse offered by this divine Messenger asserting that the source and foundation of the stabilization of all transactions is trustworthiness, a spiritual attribute:

> We will now mention unto thee Trustworthiness and the station thereof in the estimation of God, thy Lord, the Lord of the Mighty Throne. One day of days We repaired unto Our Green Island. Upon Our arrival, We beheld its streams flowing, and its trees luxuriant, and the sunlight playing in their midst. Turning Our face to the right, We beheld what the pen is powerless to describe; nor can it set forth that which the eye of the Lord of Mankind

> witnessed in that most sanctified, that most sublime, that blest, and most exalted Spot. Turning, then, to the left We gazed on one of the Beauties of the Most Sublime Paradise, standing on a pillar of light, and calling aloud, saying: 'O inmates of earth and heaven! Behold ye My beauty, and My radiance, and My revelation, and My effulgence. By God, the True One! I am Trustworthiness and the revelation thereof, and the beauty thereof. I will recompense whosoever will cleave unto Me, and recognize My rank and station, and hold fast unto My hem. I am the most great ornament of the people of Bahá, and the vesture of glory unto all who are in the kingdom of creation. *I am the supreme instrument for the prosperity of the world*, and the horizon of assurance unto all beings.' Thus have We sent down for thee that which will draw men nigh unto the Lord of creation.[7]

This indicates that human affairs are naturally dynamically unstable and, taken in their entirety, incapable of self-governance without periodic divine intervention. We have already established that transactions require a third party to supply the rules and regulations acceptable to both sides in the exchange and their necessary enforcement, as well as the transferable property rights needed to accomplish the exchange. Bahá'u'lláh, claiming the office of divine Prophet, suggests an inherent logic in the above passage: in this instance the words are supplied to the human level by a third (and transcendent) party and comprise the rules and regulations required for human exchanges.

Some Direct Gains from the Presence of Trustworthiness

Certainly, many would consider it a truism that all human affairs rely entirely on the trustworthiness of the transacting parties. If we recall that transactions rely on mutual benefits, transferable property rights and enforceable rules and regulations acceptable to both sides of the trade – and that only the mutual benefits are supplied in the form of preferences by the trading parties, with the other essentials coming from an unbiased third party – we see the direct link between trustworthiness and transaction costs in the economic sense. But this reality is not generally understood by most, who assume that other things matter more, things ancillary and derivative or concocted as a response to the lack of trustworthiness in human affairs.

Economics, however, denies this. It maintains that no transacting is possible without trustworthiness, even with third party enforcement of all accepted rules and regulations, because the idea that all eventualities can be represented contractually is a myth in practice. Therefore, if the above words represent the act of supplying the third party intervention required for human affairs, then what now follows is a technical discussion of how the resulting gains are yielded from various exchange arenas.

The Gains from Reduced Transaction Costs

Target-hardening costs and who pays them

We have seen that transactions always involve some sort of enforcement procedure, even if only as a stand-by element. The less trust the parties have in each other the more comprehensive this procedure must be. It is not without cost and the cost is borne by the traders themselves[8] but not only by them. These must be added onto the cost of the goods themselves, whose final price must reflect the costs of all inputs, including transactions costs. What happens next is determined by the nature of the good.

If the good is deemed a necessity then people just continue to buy it, even if the price is higher. (What choice is there?) The good's higher price and its needfulness leaves users a little poorer; there is less money to buy other things so the bundle of goods purchased is reduced by the higher prices of the necessary good. In contrast, if the good is deemed not a necessity then consumers are free to purchase less of it or switch to the purchase of another good entirely. The result of the former situation is that the consumer bears the burden of the transaction cost increases, while in the latter the producer bears these costs. But with the widespread corporatization of consumer goods supply, what might happen is that the supplier supplies a variety of products, no one of which is essential but which as a group are quite essential. This is the reasoning behind the multiplication of choices offered by suppliers, for many experience goods, those purchased on impulse or to 'try out', such as a new brand of spaghetti sauce or a brand of deodorant. While any particular brand or grind of coffee might therefore be non-essential, coffee is indeed essential to many consumers. If any particular good experiences a price rise owing to transaction cost increases such as increased insurance or monitoring costs, etc. the corporation can choose either not to raise its price and make up for this by charging customers more for some necessity they supply or they can spread the cost increase over all similar goods which, taken together (as for tea or bread) will be purchased. In this way, even if the good is a non-necessity the customer will pay more since some variety of that good's category will be purchased.

By expanding the transaction to include virtually all *inter*personal and *intra*personal exchanges, it is evident how much we rely on the good character of the person we deal with. Many are the people who have bought a bicycle to 'simplify' their life and to return to simple pleasures. But it is soon obvious that bike usage is anything but simple. Upon arrival at your destination the bike must be locked up. So, where to store the lock and chain on the bike until it is needed? What about in a nice pouch slung from behind the seat? Well, when the bike is locked and the owner is elsewhere that pouch will be stolen, as will the bike's wheels and seat itself, if not also locked to the bike's frame. A ten-minute ride requires another ten minutes to get the bike and all its parts secured. By the time our rider has returned home his appearance resembles that of a mechanic at the end of his or her shift, covered with grease, metallic stains and road dirt. Simple pleasures, indeed.

But, like the purchase of insurance, the bike lock adds nothing to the value of the bicycle itself. Neither do police add value to the items in a store. But if no police, no store either. All this costs tangible assets which must be supplied and which cannot therefore be used for productive, value-added purposes.

Raising the level of morality reduces these costs absolutely. Certainly the bike must be locked as before but now only to prevent opportunistic stealing, not concerted larcenous effort, which has for the most part disappeared through the effects of education and the adoption and acceptance of a superior personal utility function, one that does not threaten the quality of the life to come.

This same tendency and these same savings are experienced all through the economy and in our daily lives. Transaction costs fall and the savings – which can be immense – will be added to the value of goods in use in the form of lower prices and higher quality. Additionally, more trades will occur since the reduced transactions costs will allow more agents to participate in what had been too expensive an enterprise to consider. Increased interpersonal safety results in more people choosing to utilize public space, thereby civilizing it from the enforced chaos of morally-marginalized usage. People shop later, eat out longer and take fuller advantage of the night life. This increases the amount of time and number of people who can utilize all of society's expensive infrastructure and reduces its per capita costs. Commerce increases many fold, as do tax revenues, adding to the capacity for better schools and facilities for children and youth. See the pattern?

Reducing costs from adverse selection and the lemons problem

Consider other situations, such as the purchase of a factory or even an automobile. Economics has identified a problem with car sales, called the *lemons problem*. Assume you are in the market for a good used car. At the car lot, you recognize, of course, that the seller knows much more about the actual condition of the car than you possibly could. Even a test drive and an independent mechanical inspection cannot reveal all the things that could be wrong with it. But this is your lucky day, for you are standing on the lot of an honest car salesman whose prices truly reflect the car's value.

Of course, you do not know this and from experience your assumption is that he is not being honest. You offer about two thirds of what he is asking for the car to protect yourself and cover those repairs for which you know you will soon have to pay once the car of your dreams is actually yours. But at such a price the honest dealer facing you cannot possibly stay in business; the price s/he seeks is reasonable, after all, just covering the extra expense incurred to make sure the car sold is of good quality. In other words, s/he has already incurred the costs you anticipate and s/he must be paid for them. But you are adamant and walk away without paying what you consider to be too high a price for a used car. The result is that this honest car dealer is not a dealer for long and s/he is forced out, leaving the business to others . . . who act how, exactly? Thus it is that the used car market is ordinarily populated with less-than-honest dealers, since the honest dealers must obtain a slightly higher price for their cars and customers do not realize this and have no way of verifying it. Such a study in adverse selection can be duplicated in most markets where the seller knows far more about what is being sold than the buyer ever could. A rise in the *general level of honesty* in the marketplace eliminates most of these added costs, as the market becomes populated with honest traders. At that point, it is the dishonest traders who are run out as no one trusts their low prices and assumes something must be wrong.

However, the situation can as easily be reversed to show the costs of deceit on the part of the buyer rather than the seller, as just alluded to when the majority of traders are honest. Consider borrowing money from a bank. The banker cannot, in the end, be sure that you will pay the money back. Even collateralized loans are not free of fraud and abuse. So the banker must charge a high rate of interest to protect the bank from loss if he suspects the borrower may be 'distressed' or not easily capable of returning the money on time, as indicated by certain metrics forming the borrower's credit rating. The higher the prevailing interest rate, the greater the likelihood that the borrower will not be capable of paying back the loan, since only someone thinking unrealistically could imagine that the enterprise needing the borrowed capital would be capable of earning enough to allow for the loan to be paid back in full. This is another example of adverse selection, also greatly diminished in the presence of higher levels of morality.[9] Also note that interest rates will fall in the event, saving borrowers millions and increasing the output of the entire economy over time. Borrowed capital is a business and consumer input, like energy, food, housing, rent, etc. When its cost falls, this leaves more capital for other things.

Reducing Costs from Moral Hazard

If the banker knows the borrower's scheme has little chance of success in the current economic climate, or in any economic climate, but feels that, since all deposits are insured there is no danger if the money is lost – and the interest payments are lucrative – so grants the loan, what is this? This is a moral hazard, where the banker does not exercise due diligence in the fiduciary responsibility with which he has been entrusted. He should be more careful with what happens to the bank's money or soon the bank may end up in default.

There was a great deal of moral hazard in the United States savings and loan, or thrift bank, sector during the 1980s. Many large banks went under and their assets taken over by state and federal authorities. Since the accounts were insured to a large extent, the government had to reimburse depositors, at a cost of hundreds of billions of taxpayer dollars. In 2007 the costs have still not been fully paid off and have been added to the debt to be paid by the unborn, who had no say in the loan decision. The cost to the public from adverse selection from unqualified people being able to borrow the bank's money is generally inconsequential. But the cost to the public of actions involving moral hazard, where banks have aggressively generated high interest bearing business to customers they know cannot pay back the borrowed capital, has at times been catastrophic in its total effects. When people have real power and responsibility they can do real damage to the commonwealth of the community.

Such things are eliminated by increased morality of character. What is more important, since the work of powerful people having public responsibilities involves complex decision-making, their activities are essentially incapable of being monitored. The strength of their moral character in the presence of the strong and seeming costlessness of abandoning the public trust is the only force keeping such people from doing evil. And evil are the consequences of such high-level indiscretions. The loss of trust, the growth of cynicism and indifference on the part of the public, the loss of faith on the part of our youth – all these damages must be added to the direct costs of the corporate or public officer's corrupt practices.

Many such stories of public corruption can be cited. The events of 2002 in the United States will be remembered for their examples of corporate officers who 'pumped and dumped' the stock of their companies and cooked the official financial statements, to the bankruptcy and unemployment of thousands of workers and the looting of private retirement plans, while adding to their own personal fortunes. And let's remember the failure of Parmalat in Europe. However, current criminal law will not be too hard on the culprits.[10]

When Criminal Costs are not Addressed: The Third Russian Revolution

An estimate of the cost of criminal prevention strategies, criminal prosecution and enforcement and contract compliance would represent a very large percentage of any developed nation's GDP (gross domestic product). As for less developed nations, the *lack* of such strategies and procedures in the presence of either the same or greater levels of criminal tendencies means that such economies might not be capable of performing at all. Consider that as of 2001 the tiny nation of Denmark, with a population of roughly five million and having no natural resources, had a greater GDP than Russia, a nation of over 168 million and endowed with gold, diamonds, vast stores of energy and strategically important sources of ores and a well-educated population. This extraordinary result was mostly due to the lack of law and lawfulness in Russian business behaviour – trustworthiness, in other words – compared to what obtained in the Danish population. Numerous studies force the acceptance of this conclusion. One has been extensively discussed in these pages.

There can be no doubt whatsoever that were the Russian business and political practitioners to have raised the level of trustworthiness prevailing in their nation it would have allowed it to realize its vast potential. And the lawlessness and corruption still prevails, now in 2007. While vastly improved from its 2001 level of GDP growth, what else could possibly cause its present underperformance, compared to other nations not nearly as well endowed by natural resources or human capital? Given its educated population, with its unrivalled prowess in science and mathematics, and its enormous resources of energy, wood, strategically important metal ore deposits, diamonds, gold, water, its adequate transportation infrastructure – shouldn't it be capable of at least out-performing smaller countries? In 2006 the Russian Federation's GDP was greater than South Korea's but behind Spain's, that is, Spain had a higher GDP than Russia. On a per capita basis, Russia's GDP was only slightly better than Thailand's and just half that of Mexico.

The institutions of society that ordinarily can promote individual trustworthiness and the rule of law are completely lacking in Russia. Heretofore conformism to the ideological political standard was all that counted and there was no concept of individual incentives, initiatives or responsibility. It was as if everyone worked for a monolithic corporation, where no one had responsibility, where the goal was to be invisible and occasionally Delphic-like pronouncements altered their tone. Furthermore, the positive moral influence of religion provided by belief in an afterlife, the quality of which is dependent on the goodness of one's current actions, had been totally uprooted.

Billions of dollars were given to Russia by western agencies after the collapse of its centrally planned soviet economy in the 1990s, in a vain attempt to stave off the inevitable collapse, as markets with long and complex production flows, previously using institutionally interdependent accounting practices, were set adrift. The result was chaos in the marketplace, an explosion of nominal prices and a precipitous fall in national production levels. Without property rights established in law and universally accessible, a few powerful and ruthless 'oligarchs' stole the best of the *ancien régime's* production capacity. This they used for private aggrandizement. As for the billions of dollars loaned or granted to Russia for its benefit, almost all of it ended up in the private foreign bank accounts of those same *Mafiosi* and little ever got to the people who desperately needed it.

It seems once the mantle of soviet communism was thrown off there existed no keel to guide the ship of state and no culture beyond an abandoned ideology, imposed on the people for 70 years, to order their affairs or prioritize their economic expectations. It was fatal for the state that as it moved from a centrally planned command economy to a market economy there was no system of jurisprudence regulating transferable property rights. In its absence the transformation from communism to capitalism, and the preservation of the middle and educated classes, was simply impossible.

The Costs of Hate

Ethnic, racial and religious disputes have their root cause in the lack of mutual trustworthiness from ignorance and the worship of false ideologies. For a generation Marshall Tito's adamantine grip enforced peace between the disparate ethnic and religious groups in Yugoslavia. Soon after his death, however, the nation broke up under the centrifugal forces generated by ethnic leaders desiring a 'greater nation' for themselves, at the expense of others. This zero-sum game soon led to open armed conflict and the 'ethnic cleansing' of unwanted people. When the partisans first opened fire on their perceived enemies, observers were struck by how closely the new battle lines resembled those existing at the cessation of World War II, as if the aggrieved parties were simply re-engaging after a long interruption.

The backdrop of this social disintegration included 30 and more years of members of different ethnicities intermarrying and intermingling their families and districts, and of children being educated in ethnically integrated schools. But at its core this semblance of unification lacked real inter-ethnic trust. Each pursued its own goals and kept to its own logic, systematically uninformed of any other's. Goals were ethnically based and included the establishment of a temporal 'homeland' to be seized from existing shared territory. Each faction assiduously maintained the observances celebrating a past of glorious domination and ignominious defeat at the hands of their neighbours. As soon as Tito died, therefore, spokesmen for a greater Serbia, a greater Croatia and an independent Bosnia-Herzegovina rose to light a fire in the political consciousness of the people. Within a few years open warfare existed between the 'belligerents' and the rising prosperity that had been established was reversed. Sarajevo, a beautiful city and host of the 1972 Winter Olympics, was largely destroyed and its exquisite skating arena bombed and ruined. It seemed nothing had changed since 'Abdu'l-Bahá had observed 70 years before, 'The Balkans will remain discontented. Its restlessness will increase. The vanquished Powers will continue to agitate.'[11]

This basic lack of trust is the source of every similar standoff, in Northern Ireland, Lebanon, Turkey, the United States, Canada, Thailand, China, the Northern Gulf States and sub-Saharan Africa – every nation having minorities, be they the 'First Peoples' or the last peoples, Shí'á or Sunní, Jew or Arab, Christian or Buddhist. And now (2007), how tragic and spectacular is the example of Iraq.[12] Inserting trustworthiness into these old hatreds means more than developing the willingness to hear another point of view; it must also include abandoning the endless recitation of historical wrongs by grandmothers into the ears of tender-hearted and impressionable children. It is certainly true that every people has much of which they can be justly proud – and much to be ashamed of also.

It is beyond the scope of this book to analyse the process of transforming inter-community hatreds into cooperation and mutual respect and appreciation. Our concern here is to identify the benefits accruing to a society when these sources of destruction are eliminated. It is obvious how much blood and treasure has been wasted, how many generations have been poisoned by such hatreds and rubbed out by their interactions. Observers who have put their thoughts to paper have created some of the most eloquently tragic prose in its characterization and description, not the least of whom were the Prophets and Messengers of God themselves and their appointed servants and apostles. There is no doubt that were such activities to be rededicated to useful endeavours both the people directly involved and their respective communities would benefit. Since such disputes and wars are present today in almost every country on earth, and are proliferating and increasing in number year after year, their elimination would allow the rededication of vast human and other resources. Consider that the entire continent of Africa is enslaved by such racial, tribal, religious and national wars. It lacks the infrastructure to support international trucking and commerce, health delivery systems, information systems or even the ability to feed itself.

Manufacturing Productivity Gains and Worker Justice

Because the 20th century has been termed by some 'the American century' and because American industrial might played such a large role in many of the pivotal events of that century, it is appropriate to use industrial relations in America as a cautionary tale of things not to do. If an example of the economic consequences of trustworthiness were still needed, surely its role in worker–management relations in North American heavy manufacturing will suffice.

Data will easily show that America has been losing its manufacturing sector as a percentage of total production and GDP for about 30 years. The importance of this is not reflected by the size of its overall economy, which is larger than the next three economies combined. The US has been adding service jobs as it has been losing manufacturing jobs. Manufacturing jobs offer semi-skilled and on-the-job trained positions paying a middle class wage or salary with generous health and retirement benefits. The jobs that have replaced these lost manufacturing jobs have been mostly in the service sector and pay very little, often not even one half or one third of what a worker had been earning in manufacturing,[13] and they are usually lacking any medical or pension benefits. This has economically devastated a generation and more of skilled manufacturing workers, whose dedicated on-the-job skills have no value outside of their industrial job, now defunct. Since job tenancy in services is also less secure than in the manufacturing sector, this has led to a 'contingency workforce', where job tenancy is never guaranteed and where it is impossible to make any long term plans as a family or individual because the threat of lay-off and dismissal is the only constant even while the pay is too little for saving against periods of unemployment. It is a statistical fact that one of the major markers for being in the middle class is job tenancy. People who can hold onto a job for, on average, three to five years between lay-offs and quits are generally regarded to be middle class and enjoy higher modal earnings; while those who find that they are changing jobs from lay-offs and quits more often than once every three years usually live near or at the poverty level. So staying at one job for several years on average is of significant importance in economic security and advancement. However, over the last few decades, the number of American workers with an average job tenancy of less than three years has increased overall.

But it did not have to be that way. Those nations that have largely replaced America as suppliers of manufactured products pay their workers about what American workers receive in local spending power (purchasing power parity) and, certainly, few could fault America's use of technology in the workplace. So what happened? Why has American manufacturing shrunk so much?

While there are many contributing forces to the demise of American manufacturing prowess, including an increase in the value of the dollar against other currencies before 1985, the high cost of borrowing, increases in labour costs generally, tax laws favouring international outsourcing of labour, increasing dependency ratios of workers to retired cohorts, leading to high legacy costs per unit of production, etc. any explanation for the demise of American manufacturing must include a discussion of the adversarial climate that has always existed in the American industrial workplace. Plant and factory owners – apart from a few notable and famous exceptions – have simply refused from the beginning to pay their workers adequately for their efforts. Nor have they been willing to listen to their suggestions for increasing outputs and otherwise cutting costs, believing that engineers should engineer and workers should work. The shops were often very dangerous, the hours long, the work hard and dirty and, above all, the workers were held in arrogant contempt by the factory owners. Thus labour unions were radicalized and a generations-long battle commenced for worker rights, job safety, an end to child labour and worker exploitation, and for workers to be treated with dignity and to receive a living wage. Yet who is to say that had the owners adopted a more progressive attitude towards workers and treated them as partners in the enterprise, and the workers had reciprocated, all the animosity, the distrust and connivance that has poisoned labour–management relations to this day could not have been avoided?

Consider the examples of industrial relations in the two nations representing America's stiffest competition in manufacturing during the last decades of the 20th century, Germany and Japan. In both, industrial workers are paid on a par with American workers but the products they produce are often superior in overall quality and technological content. A full explanation of manufacturing techniques responsible for this is beyond the scope of this book. However, let this one example suffice, that of Toyota manufacturing.

In Toyota cash awards are given to the worker for practical cost-cutting and quality-improving suggestions. If the suggestion would lead to the elimination of that worker the company guarantees to get him another job in that plant at equal or increased pay. Thus the line workers, who know how things are really put together and how well ideas created by engineering are actually realized in practice, compete to come up with the best ideas and they feel more responsible for the success of the company. By being freed of the fear of losing their jobs they feel loyal to the company for providing them with the means of material life. Workers such as these will certainly out-perform those who live in fear of being terminated at any time and who know that management cares not a whit if they live or die. Evidence of this is that in 2006 Toyota America moved ahead of General Motors in car manufacturing numbers in the United States market. While Toyota was buying plants and increasing output each year, both Ford and General Motors reduced output numbers in the United States market. Toyota practises a type of 'open books' management, allowing each worker to see the extent to which his or her output affects company profits. In Germany, union representatives often sit on the board of directors of corporations and are engaged in all decision-making affecting the present and future of the company. Even janitors can tell plant visitors pay-out times for new acquisitional project costs. Workers at Toyota are given more enabling responsibility, enhancing job satisfaction and increasing the quality and character of interpersonal relations between supervisors and workers.

Another aspect of this trust is seen in the remuneration schedules for workers and managers expressed as a multiple of what the lowest paid employee in the organization earns. In the year that the chairman of Sony Corporation was paid 72 times as much as the lowest paid worker in that organization, the chairman of Disney. Inc. was paid about 36,000 *times as much* as its lowest paid worker. No wonder, then, that American workers, many of whom have no insurance, no retirement, no sick pay, no vacation or job security – while the executives are the highest paid employees in the world – regard the cultivation of industrial relations in the United States unpromising at best.

The new methods of manufacturing, which utilize greater levels of cooperation, result in such gains in productivity that those wanting to remain competitive must adopt them. Since their application was seen as impractical by industrialists in the United States, the new products available to US customers are generally not manufactured in the US unless they are made by a foreign corporation operating in the United States. While American centres for industrial science and technology are the equal to any other nation's, the one ingredient that is different for American industry when compared to Germany and Japan is in its industrial relations.[14] While exceptions are notable and not insignificant, the general picture is that the new manufacturing techniques based on cooperation have largely been foregone in the United States, adding to the expense and cost of manufacture and often making its products uncompetitive, to the loss of both worker and manager. This was the case in its largest heavy industries and manufacturing sectors, including rubber, steel, auto and auto parts, heavy equipment and construction, textiles, machining, consumer electronics, metal fabrication, photocopying, even newspaper business operations.

Some will object that one of the primary reasons for the shrinking of American manufacturing capacity is that unions became too arrogant and demanded more pay and benefits than their work justified. Let us admit this for the sake of argument, especially for steel and rubber. Yet how could they have realized that this was the case and reversed their tactics by partnering with management for mutual gains when the operating books were off-limits to union accountants? Managers during these days made no concessions, even as a gesture, that would have allowed labour to begin analysing the relative value of its own work. The interactions of Walter Reuther as head of the United Auto Workers in trying to establish industry-pooled and funded pension plans for all workers and General Motors's refusal to discuss such collective actions is emblematic of this failure. Now (2007), America's biggest car makers are facing certain decline and market share loss to Japanese manufacturers because of America's stubborn refusal to have addressed medical and retirement costs per worker while these costs were still manageable. But all collective schemes at cost-sharing were regarded as smacking of communism and corrosive to individualism. At that time there was still the ability to change the course of events, had management agreed to outside arbitration and brought in accountants to inspect their books and ledgers, labour would have had to look hard at its own practices. Worker–manager unity in the face of concerted offshore competition could have been established at that point for the sake of staving off the threatened imminent demise of their industry. But the chance was lost. The upper Midwest of the United States had always been known as 'America's foundry'; now it is known as 'America's rust belt'. Ohio, Indiana and Illinois, Southern California, the Northeast – these regions contained hundreds of towns where machine shops, factories and mills hummed day and night. In those days daytime noise and dirty smokestacks meant industrial jobs for generations of families. Now the skies are clean but the industrial noise in the valleys has been stilled.

Certainly, many jobs and factories were lost to new production techniques and changing tastes and preferences in the natural course of economic evolution through time. Many of the old mills were owned by families long retired where no new investments had been made for decades. But not all jobs were lost this way, not even the majority of them. Doesn't Great Britain also share much the same legacy as the United States? Perhaps the adversarial balance of powers of these governments is a poor model for the workplace.

It is true that after the end of the Second World War the United States helped to rebuild the industrial capacity of Europe and Japan that had been utterly destroyed during the war, giving them a new industrial base while its own was aging. With this additional aid, by 1955 these economies had recovered to full productive capacity. However, by 1970 whatever benefits had been inherited from the Marshall Plan in Europe and the MacArthur Plan in Japan had been fully replaced by their own domestic industrial programmes within Germany and Japan. After that those nations' prosperity was entirely the result of their own actions, which continued to develop and incorporate new techniques utilizing enlightened industrial relations while America did not. The experience in Germany and Japan, and in other nations during the last 25 years, and the gains those nations have made at the expense of America's shrinking market share in manufacturing, can be taken as a measure of the gains obtaining from cooperation and trustworthiness in industrial relations. Unless America adopts a new industrial workplace model it will continue to lose its heavy industry. A bi-modal economy will emerge – its early signs are already developing – with an educated class earning a good living and the non-educated class mired in poverty.

Creating Human Productivity in Schools: The Foundation Itself

As a result of becoming aware of their responsibilities towards their citizenry and wishing to advance their national character, governments the world over have instituted public education for their people. The real push was seen largely during the 20th century, as the teachings of Bahá'u'lláh, reinvigorating the spent forces in existing religious teachings and giving new direction to collective will, spread across the globe. But the need and desire for public education had been appreciated long before by most European and North American nations. Today, however, the tasks public schools are called upon to do have changed as the nations themselves have matured.

Fulfilling these responsibilities in today's changing world is an example of the application of collective trustworthiness as an essential national characteristic in the body politic.

America was one of the first nations to institute compulsory schooling for all its citizens, largely in response to the tidal wave of immigrants washing over its shores and the need to instil a basic understanding of American government and its common creed. Therefore, at one time American public schools taught the essentials of American government, civics and the English language. Teachers were largely drawn from the literate classes, the sons and daughters of professionals, and later from dedicated teacher college graduates. Skills for earning a living were learned on the job and were not the responsibility of the public school system. The majority of jobs were actually low skilled or learned as apprenticed trades. Future lawyers and doctors, scientists and musicians would proceed to college, institute or conservatory but even then most of the skills of the doctor, dentist, lawyer, teacher and research scientists would be transmitted to them in the workplace.

Thus public schools were not responsible for creating economic viability in the student; this was performed elsewhere. Since the 1960s, however, good paying industrial jobs for low skilled workers began to disappear, as discussed above. Middle class jobs were now requiring higher levels of education and training. Public schools were called upon to provide readiness for further education and to create economic viability in their graduates. This trend has only increased over time, hence the importance of good public schools under the guidance of progressive and enlightened political leadership. Under conditions where middle class jobs are only offered to the well educated and well trained, good schools from the earliest years are essential for the poor to have any chance at a better life.

The argument is often heard that European and Asian workers are far better educated than their American counterparts, especially in mathematics and statistics, so heavily used in the modern industrial workplace. This, it is argued, is the reason that they out-compete the American worker and the reason, incidentally, that American corporations are actively recruiting these workers while simultaneously discharging American nationals.

Everyone in the US knows how inadequate the public primary and secondary schools generally are today by international measures of student competency. According to available statistics (see the annual *Kids Count Data Book*, any recent year), it is the most expensive and practically the least effective public educational system in the industrialized and developed world. At one time the American school day and school calendar year was the longest in the world; now it is the shortest. South Korea and Japan have the longest school days and school years. In fact, the average South Korean student has had just about twice as much schooling as his or her American counterpart, especially in academic subjects demanded by the modern economy, mathematics and the sciences.

One reason for America's inability to modernize its public school system is the political factionalism that exists in its structure. School boards of elected individuals in each school district are responsible for school curricula and the length of the school year. Above these are the state education departments, and then the federal education authority, the Secretary of Education. In discussing the tragedy of the commons and the fallacy of composition in a previous chapter, we have seen how such a system is forced into taking a short-term view of events and is otherwise incapable of solving complex difficulties requiring mutual and broad-based cooperation and a long-term view. Even so, it is difficult for the uninitiated to comprehend the rancour, the mistrust, the sense of hopelessness that infects all interpersonal and hierarchical relations within this system. It is another example of how the lack of trustworthiness has diminished what had been a relatively successful system. The reasons for this decline are many and very complex but it is hard to think of another sector of American life that could derive a greater immediate benefit from an increase in mutual trust between teachers, administrators, school boards, politicians, students and the public than the American public school system. Many European school systems find themselves suffering similarly, especially France and the United Kingdom. Canada is in a similar situation. Other nations' school systems have simply not prospered as had been hoped, with the poor and minorities being the chief losers in the process. But in so many ways, things seem to be more extreme in the United States. Therefore the American experience with public schooling is instructive.

Years ago American schools assumed everyone could read and write and it was proved in the public schools. Now it is other nations that assume every student can learn calculus and statistics, and they prove it in their schools while Americans hold back. Because jobs require specialized training and specialized skills, education and training are more and more becoming the only practical paths to economic success, and because the poor are mostly limited to public education for their children, the social contract between citizen and state providing for a rising standard of living for hard work and study is in serious jeopardy.

In their defence, schools today are quite overwhelmed by the number of children and youth arriving for classes unable to learn or sit still and suffering from a spectrum of social pathologies that impinge on their psyches. Schools cannot be blamed for not being prepared to handle what many are calling a wholesale breakdown of the family unit, especially as there never seems to be enough money for the classroom. So chaotic have living conditions become for increasing numbers of children – so randomized the big events in a child's life experience – that they are characterized as 'experiencing too much and learning too little'.

Without systematic and appropriate learning before the child enters school, the child is incapable of correctly processing what s/he experiences when s/he arrives and the bond of trust that must exist between the child and his or her educators is diminished, be those teachers, parents, relatives or strangers.

Trust is essential for learning itself: 'Love Me, that I may love thee; if thou lovest Me not, My love can in no wise reach thee.'[15] So if children are forced by experience to become untrusting, they cannot learn. Imagine being told a set of facts you have no way of immediately verifying – which must be taken on faith, in other words – by a person you do not trust. The result is that the facts are not learned because their source is of doubtful veracity and seemingly certain irrelevance. If children learn by experience that adults cannot be trusted then adults cannot teach them anything, either by argument, which will not be believed, or by example, which will not be emulated. Children will then be educated and most strongly influenced by their peer associations, an internally-consistent closed and exclusive world, sealing them from the outside and from any more pain of deceit and treachery from adults and other outsiders.

There is no need to discuss and analyse the decrease of a sense of security in children's lives today. A few of the statistics regarding this have been noted in these pages. Worldly experiences beyond the control or even the monitoring of responsible caregivers are weakening the life-giving bond between the child and the family, essential for educational, moral and social progress. Ties may suffer even more damage where sophisticated and concerted marketing strategies to influence the tastes of young children are given free rein. It is not clear who or what is capable of raising a child if the parents' influence has been otherwise nullified but experience has shown that the state and the marketplace make poor parents indeed. How can societies be sustained, can life exist, in the absence of trustworthiness at all levels?

Since human life is a dynamic system, dynamic laws applying to such systems come into play, including the Turnpike principle and the need to time and measure properly the amount of all necessary inputs and of those 'initial conditions' we have already discussed many times. They are the inescapable calculus of the modern condition and provide instructive lessons for the dynamic process of child-rearing and maturation.

Even if various arguments indicating that children today are becoming exposed too early to the influences of a consumerist and materialistic world market can be criticized for some of their specific claims – and many of the details can be parsed – the evident truth of the overall thesis is undeniable. If we then follow these children to school and observe the high degree of chaos and lack of discipline reigning in the classrooms, little analysis is needed to realize that their ability to imbibe information and perform in a structured group learning environment is severely compromised. From this it is clear that the prospects for economic success from employing such schooling practices are not good. And this because the initial bond between the pupil and those responsible for his or her knowledge development has been decimated. It has been repeatedly demonstrated by the applied social sciences that if worldly experiences – especially traumatic ones – impinge into a young child's life, difficulties with learning and behaviour will unavoidably result. In such circumstances, circumstances becoming more common as time passes, special schooling may be needed and appropriate intervention techniques from trained and dedicated professionals required for the child to have any chance of overcoming such internal disorder and give him or her any possibility of experiencing a normal life of learning, growth, fulfilment and productivity.

But such provisions are absent for all but the very rich in most societies and especially in the United States. What is available will likely exacerbate any psychological challenges a child may already have. If it has been a while since you have been at school, say more than 20 years, step inside an urban American public school classroom, especially an inner-city classroom, to 'experience' the reality of these words.

Furthermore, 'Abdu'l-Bahá's admonitions concerning proper child-rearing and schooling, examples of which have been quoted in these pages, would not seem to support the trend today of letting children be exposed to the full impact of powerful modern media and western consumerism at every moment of their lives. In economic terms, *it is harmful to teach people sophisticated consumption techniques before they have learned sophisticated production techniques.* That is because production techniques require work and dedication to master, while consumption is a form of entertainment, a distraction from activities necessary for sustaining individual and collective life.

What are the gains expected from building trust in this context? 'Every child is potentially the light of the world – and at the same time its darkness . . .'[16] Also,

> Children are even as a branch that is fresh and green; they will grow up in whatever way ye train them. Take the utmost care to give them high ideals and goals, so that once they come of age, they will cast their beams like brilliant candles on the world, and will not be defiled by lusts and passions in the way of animals, heedless and unaware, but instead will set their hearts on achieving everlasting honour and acquiring all the excellences of humankind.[17]

The effect this result can have is shown in these words of 'Abdu'l-Bahá:

> Then will this darksome place grow luminous, and this abode of earth turn into Heaven. The very demons will change to angels then, and wolves to shepherds of the flock, and the wild-dog pack to gazelles that pasture on the planes of oneness, and ravening beasts to peaceful herds, and birds of prey, with talons sharp as knives, to songsters warbling their sweet native notes.[18]

Note that the imagery is carefully specified. Before education, training and schooling – with particular attention given to character development – individuals are 'demons', 'wolves', 'beasts' and 'birds of prey' but after proper education they are transformed into 'angels', 'shepherds', 'gazelles' and 'songsters'. The songsters are 'warbling their sweet native notes', indicating that their individuality has not become submerged but has been retained and fully developed. Whatever else trust is capable of engendering, it must include the capacity to yield this transformation. And if so, then the presence or absence of these traits is a measure of how much of it currently exists in human transactions.

The Ecology Gain from Trustworthiness

Ecological matters often involve the application of public finance economic analysis. One principle in particular seems to apply, the concept of the congested good. Recall that a congested good is one that is not changed or diminished if a low number of people use it – like a campsite in a national park or a bridge during non-rush hours – but becomes rival – congested – if too many use the good at the same time. The difficulty with managing and utilizing publicly available resources is not in their non-exclusionary but in their congested nature. Ecological stores are not inexhaustible, although, utilized at low levels, they are generally capable of self-maintenance and balance. But at higher levels these goods change from being non-rival (inexhaustible) to rival, thus congested. At that point their non-exclusionarity does indeed become a problem, one called by Garrett Hardin in 1968 the *tragedy of the commons* and referred to several times previously.

The management of the national or global environment is precisely like the operation of a cartel, for example the OPEC (Organization of Petroleum Exporting Countries) oil cartel. The cartel has a reserve of oil, with each party having a set amount of it. The world price of oil is determined, of course, by global demand and supply. The largest oil users have the biggest influence in determining world demand. Let us assume this is fixed at a particular amount in the short run, say, the next year or so. This means that the oil price will be determined by how much the cartel will supply, all else being equal. This, however, is complicated.

Before the recent increase in crude oil prices, caused mainly by increased demand from China and India, the situation for crude oil and for OPEC members was one of sustaining price, not reducing it. In this situation, as long as everybody uses just a little, the price will stay relatively high, unless demand collapses, which is not likely. However, nations like Iran and Nigeria have large and growing populations and need increased oil sales to fund expanding national budgets.[19] Their desire is to sell more oil, even if the world price falls slightly. Their attitude is that their own additional sales cannot add that much to the total amount of world oil supplies and if Saudi Arabia is so worried about it they can certainly afford to reduce their production. Now, of course, all of that has changed, as Saudi Arabia, the only country that can significantly increase production, scrambles to do so, lest the price becomes so high that energy replacements are commercialized and the vast oil reserves are never monetized.

Each nation, suspicious that its oil-soaked neighbour is cheating and overproducing, is strongly induced to cheat itself, to make as much money as possible before the price of oil falls, or falls any further. Recall that oil is a necessity, so if its price rises consumers must just pay, regardless. This makes them virtually poorer and producers richer. But it works just as well if things are reversed. When the price of oil falls, consumers will not react by suddenly buying gobs more oil. The quantity needed does not change very much with the price. That is the way with necessities. So as the price falls producers become poor and consumers save a bundle on oil costs. Therefore, for even a large per cent change in the unit price there is little change in the percentage of oil consumed. This is true for other necessities as well, even salt consumption, and even though its cost comprises a minuscule percentage of total personal expenditures.

Environmental issues are much the same. For example, over-fishing the seas or over-logging the forests follows this same pattern of behaviour. Polluting waterways and the air is also an example of this cartel mentality and, combined with the barriers to market exit for producers having dedicated and costly production resources of no economic value in any other employment, explains why the problems only get worse.

Certainly world cooperation and enforcement is needed to regulate these markets but trustworthiness is also essential. With respect to environmental elements, the price signal is often weak or non-existent, a difficulty not experienced in the operation of the oil cartel. With weak price signalling, by the time users discover there might be a problem, it may already be too late to reverse the process of environmental collapse.

Current approaches to environmental crises rely fundamentally on education to make people aware of what is happening to the world's ecosystem, how it is being degraded by our activities as humans and that we must reverse our practices if we are to avoid a collapse of life-sustaining complex biological environments. But this approach has had mixed results. For one thing, it has worked to the convenience and short-term commercial interests of governments and corporations to dispute the findings, call for more studies and sow distrust of scientists in the mind of the public. Never mind that common sense would dictate that the damage from a false positive – that we believed we should change our ways when in fact there was no actual need to have done so – is much less than from a false negative – believing there is no danger when in fact there is. It is a matter of opinion but the broad consensus of the scientific community and beyond is now that global warming is a fact in 2007, that we must trust the evidence and alter our activities. Let the null hypothesis now be that global warming is a fact, so that further studies attempt to reject this null. In the meantime we begin to change our ways.

Trustworthiness means conceding the obvious, desisting disingenuous objections and working for the world's commonwealth and welfare.

In offshore fishing, logging, water utilization, commercial-industrial farming, air pollution, whaling, it is too easy for one producer or resource harvester to cheat by over-harvesting and no individual party is much affected by the outcome, at least in the early stages of the developing crisis. Of course, this is also the result of the lack of intertemporally and interpersonally linked social utility functions but even in the absence of these, trustworthy behaviour in transactions – an unwillingness to rob the abstract and unseen world co-owners of the resource – would accomplish what even oversight or education cannot achieve: a reduction or elimination in cheating behaviour that threatens to cause environmental collapse and potentially irreversible global damage.

The Gain from Reduced Dispute Settlement Costs

There are many more examples of mutual and largely symmetrical mistrust between parties functioning in the same sectors of society – when they are placed in potentially adversarial positions, in other words. For those nation states whose formation was during the 18th century in Europe and America, adversarialism was built into their national constitutions and has its antecedents in 17th and 18th century philosophies. These viewed man as basically prone to evil and therefore in need of stabilization in his actions. It was thought that the best way to accomplish this in a democracy with universal suffrage was to construct a government of opposing forces which had to work together in action. Furthermore, it was also decided that this concept be extended into the courtroom and throughout the systems of jurisprudence because it was thought that it is often impossible to determine innocence or guilt and therefore it would be useful to have the two sides fight it out, with the winner being judged 'right' and the loser being judged 'wrong'.

Until the Revelation of Bahá'u'lláh, the teachings of God had little to say about governmental forms *per se*, only about justice. Since the dispensation of Muhammad emerged in the Middle East, where leadership is usually held by an exalted person rather than a collective body, and western democracies philosophically reject any notion of an ultimate truth against which things can be known, modern Islam is generally inimical to western-form democracy. Additionally, Bahá'u'lláh revealed that western democracy is fundamentally and structurally flawed. It is to be replaced by a different system, one based on the acceptance of an ultimate standard of right and wrong, truth and falsehood, and that this fixed point is the standard against which all in the heavens and the earth should be judged. In this principle, the dispensation of Bahá'u'lláh is in complete harmony with the teachings of Muhammad. Such a system does away with structured adversarialism in government and jurisprudence. The cost savings from operationalizing such a system could be immense and revolutionize the entire concept of government and the law.

Adversarialism raises the costs of losing, making trust more risky on all but the most trivial level. It requires and institutes a new and modern rabbinical order of lawyers to carry out all but the least important exchanges. This priesthood must, of course, be supported. This is accomplished by payment coming out of the value of the exchanges being adjudicated. As an example of this cost, the United States, comprising but three per cent of the world's population, has something like 60 per cent of all the lawyers on earth, indeed, probably of all the lawyers that have ever lived. Is this solely the result of America being a nation of laws? Probably not. More likely it is the practice of these laws of forming a zero-sum arena where someone must lose for every one who wins. The effectiveness of this structure and the thoroughness and encyclopaedic character of its results has been a magnet for any and all wishing to transact business with a minimum of risk. In effect, the United States is the residual supplier of property and corporate law for much of the world.

Even before the new system is enacted and institutionalized in the new world order, immense savings can now be realized by trustworthy behaviour becoming the normal characteristic of a population – what is expected to be one of the first manifestations of the spread of a new divine teaching from God.

With an omnipresent tendency to cheat, the need to supervise and regulate all behaviours, probable and possible, continually rises. The need to watch what everyone is doing increases. This activity is expensive. Entire economic sectors exist for no other reason. In the workplace, bosses and foremen feel they must constantly spy on workers to prevent pilfering and shirking. Workers believe that bosses will steal everyone blind if they are not constantly watched and monitored.

Taxpayers are just as convinced that government leaders are wasting the tax revenues as are the tax collectors that everyone is lying about their tax liabilities, hiding their true wealth and robbing the state of funds for running essential public programmes. Both sides of this dispute agree that it is likely that they are being charged far too much for telecom services or to go to the hospital.

The vaunted idea of the balance of powers leads directly to *adversarialism in all things*. Even criminal trials, when a person's life may be held in the balance, is concerned with winning and losing. To see this, imagine that the lawyer for the defendant and the criminal prosecutor share with the other all that is known about the facts of the case against the defendant. Then, with the combined information, they decide together whether the defendant is innocent, guilty or that the facts are indeterminate. This situation is fantasy. The job of the defence lawyer is to have the client found innocent and the goal of the prosecuting attorney is to have the accused found guilty and convicted. But this fantasy scenario (by supposing the opposite) shows that it is quite likely that the truth of the actual guilt or innocence of the accused defendant is not really an issue in the practice of criminal justice. The entire enterprise is based on adversarialism – who wins and who loses.

This is an example of market thinking being injected into areas not very well suited for it. If the goal of the practice of criminal justice were to arrive at the truth, and this process were aided by mutual cooperation between prosecutor and defence attorneys, the truly guilty would more likely be prosecuted and the truly innocent would not. As for those cases where the result of the trial is indeterminate, the accused could be placed on bail until more facts presented themselves.

The sense of untrustworthiness is endemic in American criminal justice. If the police act improperly in gathering evidence, even the truly guilty – one known to present a danger to society – will be released and all charges dropped, even where this places those not involved in great danger. How is this useful?

Other nations have developed different patterns for solving disputes without having to sacrifice the principles of justice, reward and retribution. It is not evident that these patterns emerged in response to rising tort and litigation costs. Rather, they seem to have developed from national and cultural traditions. On a historical note, many American legal codes began life as the linear descendants of the English legal system but this fails to explain completely why applications of systematized conciliation are as rare as they seem to be.

Perhaps it is due to the truth being always treated as a working hypothesis, accepted conditionally until more information forces a revision, that its basis does not rely on absolute and divine authority for its sanction. This places truth, especially as it is used in the arena of disputes, as forming a paradigm, constructed of working and generally accepted hypotheses. But paradigms can become practically unassailable over time and difficult to alter. The philosophies underlying their formation may have been discredited and their very *raison d'être* may have even been obviated but the paradigm, the shelter of justification for the continuance of practices no longer representing the most advanced thinking, continues unhindered. The longer it exists, the greater the opposition must be for change to occur. If it brooks no questioning of its tenets and resists change, then altering the paradigm to include advances capable of allowing it to respond to developing expectations and thinking about human behaviour and the goals of dispute resolution becomes impossible. In that event the accumulation of inconsistencies and its poor conformance finally result in the collapse of its support and its ultimate abandonment as an acceptable working system.

Historically, the force capable of such directed upheaval, such massive change in social thinking and attitudes and of time-honoured processes, is the formation of new philosophies and paradigms generated from a new prophetic message. The assumptions underlying transactional behaviour are entirely the product of the societal institutions that form the exchange's context, its rules and regulations. These are in turn the product of philosophies of human behaviour which, as has been repeatedly argued, are ultimately wholly derived from prophetic dialogues. We have already analysed statements and other sources demonstrating this truth. At this point we only need to continue the accounting of benefits that accrue from the assumed application of such paradigm changes.

The goal of dispute transactions from zero-sum or even negative-sum arrangements based on adversarialism and balancing opposed tendencies will be changed into discovering the reality of the situation at hand *by referring to the pronouncements of truth as divinely revealed.* This injects into dispute settlements what has been largely absent in the past, and definitely absent from current practices: an independent source for verification, refutation, falsification and testing. The logic is that the world of human exchanges is itself a tautological system unless referenced *from the outside*, hence the necessity for independent verification using prophetic dialogues as a standard.

The Bahá'í writings, as revealed prophetic speech, overcome the main barrier to this procedure that has existed up to now, i.e. the impracticality of obtaining a divine standard for application within a modern context from the arcane dialogues of past Messengers. Those pronouncements, revealed to advance a process of social change, have been largely subsumed by today's global society. But the new dialogues address today's societal conditions and difficulties, difficulties that are often the result of the drying up of the potential of earlier dialogues to effect change. To be clear, this is not to say that personal inspiration and refinement are no longer to be gained from the study of earlier prophetic messages. But it is undeniable and beyond any doubt that their ability to cause wholesale rejuvenation and alteration in social structures and goals is entirely lacking and they no longer contain this power, a power fully evident in the past. Hence the new message from the new Prophet. This new message anticipates current difficulties and challenges and has the latent power to transform society.

Abandoning tort and litigation in dispute arenas as currently practised in favour of systematized applications of the dialogue's principles could result in massive social savings and a freeing of dedicated and sophisticated resources for other productive tasks. This result obtains not only from the acceptance of rules and regulations and the granting of uniform procedures therefrom but also by the change in orientation these rules require. Truth is contained in the divine standard to which all adhere. The objective in conflict resolution shifts to discovering the underlying reality and applying the principles generated from its acceptance. Both contending parties agree to adhere to this binding arbitration and, because it is based on a divine standard, it has the capacity to be used in a myriad of situations. This results from the character of divine speech, which is by nature creative, while all other speech is derivative, even if inspirational.

The idea of presuming the existence of a divine standard – that principles have not originated with human invention – can be a stumbling block to the sceptic but a path to freedom to the applied social scientist. Undeniably, the divine claim has often been turned into political policies that have allowed the subjugation of peoples and classes and been a potent source of human mischief. Also undeniably, standards acceptable to all sides in a transaction are essential for its execution. The broader and more universal these standards are, the easier of acceptance and the greater the range of their application. Given, therefore, that standards are thus essential, the most efficacious standards are the most universal and transcendent. At very least, the claim of a divine source for the prophetic dialogues must be tested with whatever is at hand, so that such a marvellous and all-inclusive teaching not be inadvertently or capriciously dismissed.

***

This chapter has finished the sketch of societal transformation from individual development begun in previous chapters. It has analysed the characteristics of social gains and losses from the presence of certain assumptions about individual behaviour using a loose and associative benefit–cost analysis. It did not quantify the values that result from such a transformation but perhaps it did not need to. Much of the theoretical work in economics hopes only to attach the appropriate sign to arguments, positive or negative, because there is no hope of expressing a social or personal transformation in closed mathematical or statistical form. Mathematical expressions representing a social tendency can and are made, and their first derivatives taken where possible to linearize them. The slope is then analysed to see if it increases or decreases.

Here, however, simple arithmetic of gains and losses was suggested and higher level systematic representations were not needed. Utility function transformations occur in the nexus of society and the individual recursively and associatively, with the direction of the causality running both ways, from individual to society and from society to individual. The gains to the collective whole from applying the divine standard are fairly straightforward. Evidence that such gains will be experienced is given by the historical record and is logically arguable. If there is no way to dispute the claim of a divine source for the prophetic dialogue and the teachings of Bahá'u'lláh, the latest claimant and revealer of verses of unprecedented sweep and compass, then we can expect a shift in all social paradigms within and without science and religion.

The next chapter looks at the changing of the *status quo* that accompanies the revelation of a new prophetic dialogue. It particularly investigates the change in valuations resulting from the relentless impingement of the new teachings on the intellectual foundations and justifications supporting the existing order of things.

12

The Divine Messenger and the *Status Quo*: A Model of Value Redistribution

This chapter summarizes many of the themes developed in previous sections and briefly analyses the process of the alteration of the social and economic *status quo* in terms of value changes brought about by the appearance of a new prophetic dialogue. By identifying some of the existing social and intellectual structures in which we live and develop it might be possible to imagine socio-economic changes that would be apparent with the advent of a new prophetic message.[1] At any one time a *status quo* exists in any particular field or activity. It could be political, religious, scientific or artistic. Its presence does not preclude change existing within that field or activity but it does ordinarily limit the change either to extending the range of the *status quo* or opposing it. The *status quo*, or *paradigm*, as it is more frequently called, thus remains the centre of focus for theoretical development and practical work.

Shoghi Effendi, Guardian of the Bahá'í Faith, has in his books and letters, traced the process of social transformation in the presence of a new divine message from indifference to opposition, to grudging tolerance and finally to full acceptance. What is offered here is specificity in terms of its economic consequences, where 'economic' includes all aspects of human transactions and their supporting institutions.

This chapter also offers a straightforward approach to the changes brought about and expected by the appearance of a historical divine Messenger and discusses who loses power and who gains it as a result, who loses wealth and who experiences an increase and why. This is done in the context of changes in valuations underlying the 'prices' discovered in the exchange process. The written record, and the prophetic dialogues themselves, offer enticing predictions concerning these results but utilizing their literal sense, as we saw in an earlier chapter, is not entirely appropriate, nor would it accord with historical facts in all cases. Nonetheless, we will pull some of these statements out from the Qur'án and analyse them for this characteristic as far as is feasible. This is interesting in its own right and can also direct our investigation of power structure changes arising from the new message.

***

Depending on the context, a *status quo* specifies different constructions of institutions. One is as a *paradigm*, a term popularized after the appearance of Thomas Kuhn's book on scientific development, discussed below. Another is of a 'school' of thought, comprehensive and sharing a common subject of inquiry and a common methodology. The school's work and output itself, carried on over years, experiences developmental stages over time that reflect the development and changes of the practitioners themselves but in an unexpected way. Rather than following the science to wherever it may lead, it is the changing proclivities of the school's leading lights that are followed, dynamic in the beginning and ossified in the twilight of their career path. When youthful, insights are discovered and developed over a lifetime and careers are established in the security of that particular arena's continued existence. Thus science, politics, industry, religion, etc., move forward much as the ancient guilds[2] did in the past, providing a structure in which to work and pass on vital knowledge from one generation to the next. The practice of medicine is very much this way, the practice of other disciplines within and without science, more or less so. But this comforting and supportive structure in the end actually stands in the way of new discoveries and research, turning into an exclusive club presuming to speak for all science, giving pronouncements rather than theories, decrees allowing for no debate rather than hypotheses to be vigorously tested.

Today these virtual guilds and the practice of guildship are present in many sectors of modern societies, working in a self-defensive manner. They are averse to new ideas, especially those having the capacity to overturn the generalized *status quo* of social structures.

The guildship of scientific thought is an example of the power of the *status quo* defending itself against change and is emblematic of how the *status quo* in societies works to oppose change. In the following summary we will analyse the anticipated changes brought about by the advent of a new prophetic message, including some elaboration of those aspects generally seen to have economic content, in the way we have defined this in the previous pages. That is, which areas of human activity would be altered by a new revelation of God appearing in our midst today? Here is a suggested list.

Economic and Social Sectors Likely to be Impacted by a New Divine Revelation

Here is a list of the areas of human society likely to be impacted by the advent of a new divine revelation. Obviously, others might create another list and another context. This is just one possible list devised to highlight those subjects discussed in this volume. We begin with scientific orthodoxy because it is the nexus of many of the social forces directly challenged by the appearance of a new divine message.

1) *Scientific Orthodoxy*

Since the appearance in 1962 of Thomas Kuhn's description of how science changes over time in his seminal book *The Structure of Scientific Revolutions*, a scientific *status quo* has been termed a paradigm. The term has been used often in this text because of its facility in conveying the idea that a systematic body of thought takes on a life of its own, even being ready to defend itself from encroachments or diminution. It maintains a sort of intellectual sovereignty within which researchers feel free to work. With the appearance of a new divinely-inspired message, all or part of this sovereignty is immediately in danger of being nullified as a result of the creative influences released and the associated discoveries and re-evaluation of past – and now largely outworn – models of behaviour with their outmoded assumptions.

Perhaps another and simpler description of scientific *status quo* construction could explain all this behaviour just as well or even better. A more parsimonious way to model a paradigm is as a *guild*, i.e. a syndicate of craftsmen having specialized knowledge. Their beneficial qualities have just been referred to, as they provide a sheltering structure in which to develop the science or craft and apprentice the young, so the knowledge can be carried on by succeeding generations, etc. But there is another role guilds play, that of extracting payments for their knowledge from the public in order to fund the guilds' work and guarantee their continued existence. They do this by controlling their knowledge by making its use a legal monopoly, with which they attempt to extract rents from the market. Rents are payments to a production input greater than what is actually needed to maintain it in its present use and greater than what a competitive market would provide. For example, imagine that you are applying for a job and you have decided you will not work for less than, say, $58,000 a year. The interviewer announces, 'We can only pay you $65,000 a year; take it or leave it.' You take it and do not say, 'Actually, I will accept $58,000 and you can keep the rest.' So you are hired for $65,000 and collect $7,000 in *rents*, since you would have worked for $7,000 less. It is the same thing with any other resource in productive use. The guild is like a supply cartel, which endeavours to enhance its supply control over the market and thus earn high rents for its members. The American Medical Association is an example of such a cartel-guild, operating since its inception to maintain medical standards which its members must assume, essentially locking out – for good or ill – others from practising medicine through use of the AMA's power to control government licensing procedures.

Thus science, in order to create an environment for research and achievement, may actually be cutting off some promising lines because they do not coincide with established practices. Scientific and religious hierarchical structures have strong similarities owing to their having the same intellectual origins, divine inspiration and scholasticism. In ancient times both were elitist, exclusionary and discriminatory and were strongly associated with an existing revelation of God.

2) *Religious Orthodoxy*

This is another hierarchical structure whose leaders derive their power and authority from the body of knowledge they maintain and over which they assert unchallenged control. Often this control, like scientific knowledge, is written into civic laws and ordinances. Also, it has been argued earlier in this book that science and religion have a common root, the revelations of God. It is natural, therefore, if both elements – the two most powerful forces in society – were to follow the same trajectories from their initial impulse to their full maturation and finally their subsequent revision and renewal by forces they deem to be from the outside and therefore illicit in character.

However, unlike in science, orthodoxy in religion is far more brittle because its ideological corruption is more complete. As previously argued, ideologies have no independent existence and are threatened with extinction as soon as belief in them ceases. Also, the dedicated capital and tools of a craft developed over centuries of concentrated study and sacrifice have practically no value in any alternative employment (zero-salvage value, zero opportunity cost). The defence of the *status quo* by practitioners of religious orthodoxy is thus likely to be more determined and more desperate than that of scientists since they see the new knowledge as a direct and mortal threat to their livelihood and power, and see in its acceptance their own demise, while scientists, after adjustments, would simply begin researching and developing the new paradigm. As history shows, with the appearance of a new divinely-inspired message and the subsequent overthrow of outworn orthodoxies, the separation of science and religion disappears and these two most powerful forces in society are again drawn together as analysis becomes unified, ideologies are temporarily refuted and fields of study are reformulated around new identities.

Religious leaders see no professional afterlife such as what might be possible for scientists. With much of their so-called knowledge being composed of outworn and refuted ideological constructions, it is only natural to expect the existing religious power elite to use any tool at their disposal to stop the development of the new cause. What tools they employ are shown by the historical record surrounding the appearance of every divine revelation through the ages, accounts carefully recorded in all the holy books and discussed below.

3) *Political Orthodoxy*

The political *status quo* also bequeaths to its leaders perquisites valuable enough to be defended against their diminution from the spread of new assumptions on collective behaviour, and particularly, on the redistribution of wealth stores. In the short run political exchanges are zero-sum, with each appointee displacing the current office-holder. Specific issues and disputed ground shifts a great deal. But the will to retain power and leadership raises social difficulties where atavistic appeals are made to the public as a means to stay in power. This is, however, just business as usual for politicians, although with the appearance of a new divine revelation they face a wholesale revision of their operational procedures.

4) *Economic/Commercial Orthodoxy*

Throughout history buying and selling has not changed in its essentials. But what gets produced and what gets demanded changes with the appearance of a new divine teaching because of its direct impact on tastes and preferences and its inculcated standard of morality and righteousness in personal and collective endeavours. The activity of marketing, manipulating and feeding the tastes of consumers who have been moulded and nurtured to be insatiable consumers of whatever is the 'next new, new thing' will not go undisturbed. Along with this shift is an even larger shift in what people may choose to do for a living. Even as technology sets are altered with our understanding of science, many professions retain their groupings, i.e.

arts and literature, science and engineering, the healing arts, fundamental research or philosophy, agriculture and food science, transportation, commerce, entertainment, marketing and public relations, civil order, law or national defence, etc. At the appearance of a new divine message some tasks will not be encouraged as much as they once had been, while others will take on a new importance.

Also, the whole question of industrial justice, the rights of capital and labour, the role of technology, job tenancy, compensation, resource allocation – all this will undergo alteration under the influence of the new teaching.

Finally, financing practices would likely be altered, including attitudes towards different types of debt, different levels of debt and how debt must be paid back. Whether this will lead to embracing more joint ventures and venture capital or to straight debt financing is not clear. But it will certainly inform what happens to world financial markets over the next few decades.

5) *Social Institutional Orthodoxies*

Emanating from these causal structures are various institutions of pivotal importance. The impact of the new message on these is secondary and derivative but their changes and subsequent influences on the direction of social development are of the first importance. The following acts as a summary of some of these impacts from the advent of a new divine message.

- The institution of the family has undergone radical changes in the last 50 years, mostly of the deconstructing sort. This has made child-rearing a chancier business than in the past in the sense that the child is basically a reflection of the parents' will for it and the ability of parents to influence their children is being eroded by the forces of modern life. Today, many exogenous forces, some positive, some not and most uninvited, have intruded into the process to such a degree that, as a force in the child's life, parents are discounted at a chronologically earlier point than ever before. The coming of a prophetic message can be expected to fulfil its historical precedent of re-establishing the primacy of parents and parenting in the development of children and in society's fundamental responsibility to do everything necessary to support family life and defend the family unit against all threats to its continuation, be they economic, cultural or commercial.

- Schooling and formal learning is at the nexus of social science, religion and politics. With expected radical changes in these orthodoxies, what is taught and how it is taught will also undergo change. There may be greater emphasis placed on character development and conformal socialization standards than now exists. Subjects chosen for attention might also change, as would pedagogical techniques.

- Civic order, the forceful and enforceable reflection of public standards of decorum and interpersonal action, will not be left unchanged. How will these standards be altered under the influence of a new prophetic message?

- Work and leisure will be changed both in their qualities and perhaps in their mutual proportions. Here is meant not the experience of work, which is a topic of industrial psychology and justice, but rather what type of work is chosen, which reflects changes in tastes and preferences. The new divine message will certainly alter existing tastes, encouraging some activities and discouraging others. The aggregate of these private decisions will profoundly affect the economy's output, both in the type of goods produced and their number.

These constructions comprise the main transmitters and stores of knowledge, understanding, power, social welfare and economic output mentioned and discussed thus far in the context of the essential harmony of divine revelation and economic science. Whatever effect these elements have impacts the direction of collective and individual life. We have already discussed the interrelatedness of prophetic influence and how its causality is multi-directional once dispersed[3] and we have suggested the direction of changes forced by the impact of a new divine revelation. Now we discuss this in more detail.

Expected Changes in Orthodoxies from a New Divine Revelation

Scientific Orthodoxy

It has been argued in this book that scientific inquiry and prophetic dialogues share a common analytical structure. The structure was perhaps taught by the Prophets themselves, since without it the people would not have had the means either to challenge or to credit the validity of what they were hearing. It also would have been essential for their purposeful spiritual and material advancement, required for enabling them to understand the message of the 'return' once it had appeared. This ability to handle and analyse abstractions and to incorporate the advanced ideas contained in the prophetic dialogue led directly to a dramatic strengthening in the foundations of civilization and all the arts, culture, commerce, jurisprudence and scientific excellence pertaining to its inner and outer structure.

Over time the common analytical structure between natural and supernatural investigations was lost sight of. Science, at least as a systematic approach, more closely resembled a path of inquiry initially established by the Prophets and their derivative philosophers, while religion became incapable of separating itself from impinging dogmatism and ideological associations.

As argued at length in a previous chapter, having inherited the analytical tools from the Prophets and metaphysical philosophers, science began a concentrated analysis of the material universe, the phenomenological world and its laws. This *most great rift* between science and religion in the world of logical and rational analysis, therefore, seems for the most part not to have harmed the emerging sciences. The character of this harm might possibly be understood by what science often decided was a legitimate subject for analysis, including the science of war and other anti-humanitarian enterprises, for example, or pseudo-scientific pursuits largely discredited by scientists of following generations.

However, denying science's metaphysical and epistemological roots did not guarantee that it would remain wholly untainted by ideological inroads or from political manipulation. Even ruling out these tendencies, science habitually established orthodoxies for itself wherein generations of scientists could safely work and make their living, as explained above, a practice having a long career as guildship. But, as previously argued, while sheltering its work and workers it is undeniable that orthodoxy made it difficult to accommodate changes in thinking and novel ideas. New techniques and new results could be accepted as new branches of inquiry and thus increase the number of working scientists within the discipline; new theories and findings that refuted older ones meant new persons replacing established ones in a zero-sum process. Naturally enough, this was opposed by those most likely to have their work overturned and their support withdrawn. This is common sense and no elaborate model of how science develops is needed to explain it. Even the corporatization of scientific research in modern times has not altered this picture very much in its essentials, except to diffuse risks and responsibility.

Not having this metaphysical ground to defend frees it to follow its well-worn path of investigating whatever seems of interest to it and for which financial support can be found. This last point about financial support is of great importance. After all, research costs money and needs the dedication of scarce and expensive capital to its exclusive use. This was just as true in ancient times, when kingly patronage was needed, as it is today, when research proposals and lines of inquiry and investigation are in open competition for available corporate and trust research funds. Graduate schools in public universities have not altered this situation very much, as the graduate student soon finds out[4] when it is time to choose what to research. Then s/he learns that the choice must be made from a limited menu of possibilities for which funding exists. This is only natural; economics teaches that while our wants are not limited we must live and work within available means.

More evidence of funding primacy in determining what to research is shown by the First World's initial refusal to develop and market a cure and treatment for river blindness, blindness caused by a parasite common in certain central African regions that causes damage to the optic nerve. It turned out that the cure was ready at hand but the user-population had no funds for it so the drug would not be developed. The First World had the cure but no need for it while the Third World had the need but not the means to develop and provide it. Finally, a benefactor was found that could fund the required large-scale start-up and distribution costs and the cure was made available by the 'big pharma' company Merck to those communities otherwise devastated by this disease. This is an example of the problem, where one group has the means but does not need them while another needs them but does not have them. Here is where the exclusivity of property rights fosters a sub-optimal result for the community as a whole, where pooling of responsibility and inclusion of otherwise foreign elements could have dramatic effects on social welfare. But this is a problem of public goods and externality and a way must be found to link a unit of cost with a unit of compensated benefit. There are many more such examples.

As just explained, it is the need to shelter a living within the scientific establishment that finally and inevitably leads to intellectual stagnation, even as it once led to the development of cutting-edge research. This phenomenon occurs over the life cycle of the individual scientist and over the development life of sciences themselves. It also falsely justifies the need for new dedicants to learn what might be characterized by objective outsiders as useless material and 'a marring of the days of one's life', as 'Abdu'l-Bahá called this practice.[5] To the extent that *guildship* can fully explain the behaviour and character of scientific evolution through time, it can act as a replacement for other, more complex theories, such as paradigm shift, etc.

Crediting the scientific community's opposition to promising new theories and its refusal to give them a fair trial to *guildship-science* signifies that whatever opposition it raises against the implications of a new prophetic message *will be quite ordinary and of no unusual character.* For the daily practice of science does not concern itself with metaphysical arguments any longer. It has ceded this ground to philosophers and occupies itself (with the exception of cosmology) to practical material research applications and theoretical model-building.

On this basis it would seem that science would not be expected to vociferously oppose a new prophetic or divinely-inspired message because the character of the new proposal's source is of less concern than its presence. Whether atheistic, materialistic or metaphysic, what seems to be of concern is the cogency and discipline the contending theory is capable of putting forth since therein lies its real threat to the establishment. The more formalized and ordered, the more it is underpinned by irrefutable logic and rational evidence, the more difficult it will be to dismiss the contending theory.

For this reason prophetic dialogues are not generally seen as a threat to scientific orthodoxy, even while inspired, derivative research lines might very well be. Also for this reason, the changes brought about by the appearance and initial spread of the divine message into the minds of the intellectually prepared are actually under way before the community of science as a whole is made directly aware of it. Thus science, being generally free of entrenched ideologies and largely unconcerned with metaphysical struggles, begins to reflect the new divine light before other orthodox structures are able to do so and scientists are often in the vanguard of the associated movement's new and brave adherents.

Religious Orthodoxy

To religious orthodoxy the new divine message is direct and confrontational and therefore represents a threat to its very existence. The dwellers within are certainly aware how their own emergence represented the death of an old order, of an *ancien régime.* They are also aware of the thousands of lives lost on battlefields, the kingdoms toppled, the religionists done to death by adversaries within and without such structures.

That there will be opposition from established religions is beyond any doubt and not worth debating. The historical record will show that not one Prophet appeared who was not fiercely opposed by the religious establishment He was sent to spiritually revive. One has only to be exposed to the prophetic dialogues of the Qur'án or the irrefutable logic of the Kitáb-i-Íqán to be convinced of this. And still today not even a truce exists between the militant branches of the established religions and their perceived enemies, from without or within. Religious fanaticism still claims its thousands of victims and is on the increase, even as this is written and as you read it. In India, Pakistan and South Asia, Iran and the Middle East – with Iraq displaying its most revolting and loathsome manifestations – Sudan, Egypt and the Maghreb, the Levant region, Indonesia, Europe and even New York City, the victims of religious fanaticism are adding up.

Little wonder that some national governments have decided to vigorously oppress *all forms* of religious expression except those they directly sanction and control. This is the case in China, increasingly in Russia, for many other Asian nations and the Middle East. Some nations, such as Turkey, have tried to ban religious political parties altogether. Such strong reaction would not have been necessary had it not been for the actions of certain religionists who took their religion as ideology and believed that the goals of their sect justified whatever means were at hand and that God Himself sanctioned such behaviour. This belief, of course, finds no support in the dialogues of their Prophet. But little matter: the religious priest-class assured the people that it was so.

This is proved by examining the statements of radical religious movements and comparing these with the teachings laid down by the Prophet-Messenger they nominally follow. For example, His Holiness Muhammad stated clearly that there is no compulsion in religion and that kindly speech should be employed when discussing religious controversies. He also said that if one witnesses misbehaviour that person should pass by in dignity and not get involved. He even stated that prayers should not be offered in a voice loud enough to disturb others, that the true follower, in other words, should say or do nothing that would lessen the religion's exalted character in the eyes of the public or create any barrier to its acceptance. Armed combat was to be defensive and taken up as a nation (*'ummah*) in defending its national interests. But all that careful teaching has not stopped Islamic terrorism and Islamic fascism.

Another example is Jesus admonishing one of His followers who had struck off the ear of an opponent with his sword. Jesus stated that whoever lives by the sword shall die by it. Although there may be teachings of Jesus about collective security that were never recorded, many other verses that *were* recorded exalt an attitude of individual forgiveness and a pacific standard of personal conduct. Notwithstanding all these recorded pronouncements utterly rejecting contention and conflict, it has somehow been possible for leaders within Christianity to raise armies from the mass of followers for purposes of religious conquest and persecution. Nor have those exalted words kept those who nominally subscribed to them and were bound by their tenets from slaughtering each other in the millions over the centuries. The same rejection of the divine verses by the followers of all the world's religions has led to this endless bloodshed we see today. 'And their unbelief shall only increase for the unbelievers their own perdition.'[6]

There can be no doubt, therefore, that the appearance of a new prophetic or divinely inspired Messenger will cause the repetition of whatever has happened at similar times in the past.

Yet how could someone ignore the clear instructions of the holy books which s/he passionately believes to be divinely inspired and freed from all error and corruption and follow instead murderous instructions formulated by mere mortals that directly disobey and contradict the divine word? Personal self-interest is insufficient as an explanation for such behaviour. If one believes in God and that He revealed a book of teachings, how could s/he wilfully fail to submit to them, knowing as s/he must that the punishment for such behaviour is dire, that God is all-powerful to fulfil whatsoever He chooses and that all opposition to Him is useless?

Again, the logical explanation for this behaviour is that human ideologies have been allowed to supersede and completely subsume the divine message and to subvert its legitimate goals. Initially, there may have been a legitimate political explanation for introducing such a practice. The newly emerged religion needed to be properly organized and its teachings propounded systematically to an illiterate public. Short-cuts may have been taken, and it may have seemed necessary to arrogate absolute powers to its professional ranks for the unity of the cause.

But such an enterprise obviously held the seeds of its own destruction. No authority or sanction for such practices was given anywhere in the writings of the religion's Prophet-Founder. All the complex ceremonials, the authority of the clergy class, the carefully worked-out laws and jurisprudence, etc. – these were all human inventions justified by vague and inconclusive statements open to broad and conflicting interpretations. Until now, the successorship of authority has not been established in the revealed prophetic text of any of the existing world religions.

Of greatest importance was this: once the mighty bulwark of religious orthodoxy was firmly established, by what means or process could Gnosticism be differentiated from the necessarily revisionist teachings of the promised Return to which all pledge fealty? By what process could the structure be modified? There seemed none. It stood 'as is' or was toppled, with no intermediate line possible. We have this general result: *ideologies, in contrast to true knowledge cannot be reformed, only overthrown.* That is because they exist only in the minds of their believers and have no independent existence beyond this. Ideologies vanish when no adherents uphold their tenets or propound their ideas. But truth and true religious revelation, like all universal laws, require for their existence no belief in them from mortals, angels or any other created thing. They exist independently of us. It is for us to align ourselves with these laws in order to exist and thrive but the laws themselves are indifferent to our acceptance or rejection, since they exist in the mind of God.

What is perhaps most fascinating is the denial of the Prophet's return by the professional clergy to whom He has been sent. We have previously discussed rational preferences and the choices that the rational agent can make. We established that if two things have identical attributes and qualities it is irrational to accept one and reject the other.[7] In light of this, look at two possibilities for an explanation of the clergy's rejection of this returned Prophet.

- They had become literalists and discarded rational analysis altogether. Having abandoned the idea that findings be either falsifiable (in the Popperian sense) or verifiable (in the Kuhnian sense), the clergy more and more gave themselves over to the elaboration of structures of their own creation for which neither authority nor antecedent knowledge could be found in any of the prophetic statements themselves. They had made a dogma – an ideology – of the religion, a tautology not susceptible to evidentiary procedures or any further questioning of its tenets. Since none of the promised prophecies had ever been literally fulfilled, they were free to reject the new Prophet as an impostor and heretic. But, of course, this explanation requires that the priest-class had never really understood the true meaning of the teachings to which they swore obedience. Is institutionalized ignorance on such a scale possible?

- The priests do not actually believe in the Prophet as being sent by God, nor in a God who successively sends revisions as they are deemed necessary by Him, nor, perhaps, even in the idea of a God who does as He pleases. This explanation has the clergy-class ministering to the needs of the people as paternalistic totalitarians. They could be sceptics, agnostics or even atheists who believe that the primacy of the established religion must never be assailed lest it place the people in danger of insidious Gnosticisms that will wreck their lives. Thus the clergy must lead and bear the burden for the masses, which are incapable of comprehending the inner meaning of the prophetic verses. The clergy will instruct the masses 'not to play God' by studying the divine writ for themselves, as this could be dangerous for them. Where this is the case, the return of the Prophet, or a new Prophet, must be opposed

> and His teachings banned as dangerous heresy for the good of society. Indeed, the returned Prophet shall be branded a worker of sedition and mischief and a corrupter of the young.

This second hypothesis explains the murderous actions of religious followers who rub out whatever cause or teaching or people their leaders tell them to. It explains the wars, the terrorism and religious fanaticism that has covered with smoke and sullied the fair name of the established religions and subverted their legitimate goals. Follow these words by Fyodor Dostoyevsky from 'The Grand Inquisitor' in *The Brothers Karamazov*. The scene is Ivan soliloquizing to his brother Alyosha, as the Grand Inquisitor of the Church to whom the resurrected Jesus has been brought for examination. The Grand Inquisitor is addressing Jesus and explaining why they will, once again, crucify Him as before:

> No, we care for the weak, too. They are sinful and rebellious, but in the end they too will become obedient. They will marvel at us and look on us as gods, because we are ready to endure the freedom which they have found so dreadful and to rule over them – so awful it will seem to them to be free. But we shall tell them that we are Thy servants and rule them in Thy name. We shall deceive them again, for we will not let Thee come to us again. That deception will be our suffering, for we shall be forced to lie . . . We have corrected Thy work and have founded it upon *miracle*, *mystery* and *authority*. And men rejoiced that they were again led like sheep, and that the terrible gift [freedom] that had brought them such suffering, was, at last, lifted from their hearts.[8]

Then follow these words, which give the author's view of the totalitarian and fascist tendencies of the Church, to which might be added that they could also be used to describe the thinking of at least a portion of the professional priest-class in most, if not all, hierarchical orthodox religious structures.

> They will become timid and will look to us and huddle close to us in fear, as chicks to the hen. They will marvel at us and will be awe-stricken before us, and will be proud at our being so powerful and clever, that we have been able to subdue such a turbulent flock of thousands of millions . . . Oh, we shall allow them even sin, they are weak and helpless, and they will love us like children because we allow them to sin. We shall tell them that every sin will be expiated, if it is done with our permission, that we allow them to sin because we love them, and the punishment for these sins we take upon ourselves. And we shall take it upon ourselves, and they shall adore us as

> their saviours who have taken upon themselves their sin before God . . . The most painful secrets of their conscience, all, all they will bring to us, and we will have an answer for all. And they will be glad to believe our answer, for it will save them from the great anxiety and terrible agony they endure at present in making a free decision for themselves. And all will be happy, all the millions of creatures except the hundred thousand who rule over them. For only we, we who guard the mystery, shall be unhappy . . .[9]

This book has been quoted at length for its spellbinding description of totalitarianism and its perfect-sounding justification for it. History unfolded subsequent to this book's publication in the manner these words prophesied but with secular fascism ruling in Italy and Germany, the heart of Roman Christian religious orthodoxy and the remnant of the Holy Roman Empire, and anti-religious communism in the heart of Eastern Christian orthodoxy and the remnant of Byzantium.

Certainly the professional religionists must have harboured such thoughts on some level, as demonstrated by their actions down through the ages at the appearance of each subsequent Prophet. It is, of course, only a characterization and not refutable. No volume of words can hope to contain a description of all the damage the misuse of religious devotion has caused. But the purpose of quoting these passages is to suggest the *character* of the defensive forces that will be called upon by religious powers in fending off the new message.

We unavoidably return to ideology as an explanation for a lot of intellectual mischief and human misery. Freed from this force there would remain only personal self-interest on the part of the clergy-class as a reason to oppose the new message. Is this potent enough alone to explain the existence of radicalism and fanaticism in religions? Perhaps not. It can explain sporadic and bloody treatment of the adherents to a new message but if the clergy truly believed in the God they serve they must logically come to the inevitable conclusion that opposition to His will is not wise and places them in mortal danger. Eventually they would give up their opposition. This leaves as active opponents only those who do not believe in an all-powerful and sovereign God. To the extent this applies to the clergy and professional religionists of the world, it is an ironic conclusion at the very least. 'And when it is said to them, "Believe in what Allah has sent down," they say, "We believe in what was sent down to us." And they disbelieve in that which came after it, while it is the truth confirming what is with them. Say: "Why then have you killed the Prophets of Allah aforetime, if you indeed have been believers?"'[10]

Economic Consequences

The economic consequences of the advent of a new prophetic message can be gauged by recalling the consequences of the eventual acceptance of an earlier message as recorded by history. The difference in experience today compared to earlier times is that today science is liberated from any subservience to religious orthodoxy. Therefore, with the coming of a new divine message, material developments would be expected to move apace in the very midst of social retardation and spiritual underdevelopment. *And this is exactly what we observe*. There is a doubling of knowledge every decade or less, even while our social institutions, which rely so heavily on divinely-inspired teachings, fail to develop. Science advances to the extent that the World Trade Center in New York City is built but religion, refusing to advance and therefore defenceless against cultist intrusions co-opted by radicalism, destroys those buildings and all inside in a few hours. Having turned its back on its creative divine source and refused to acknowledge the progressiveness in all things, religious ideology could only corrupt and oppose. With respect to its pronouncements Besançon states,

> This [ideological] language becomes magical as its powerlessness becomes apparent. Incapable of modifying the real according to its ends, unable to create another reality which conforms to what it has promised, its function is to *evoke*, in the magical meaning of the word, that is, to suggest the nonexistent reality. In order to do so, it borrows from the two magics which have traditionally grafted themselves into religion and science, that is, the black mass and quackery. It is formulary, because its power is linked to the letter, and it is incantatory . . . [11]

'*Miracle, mystery and authority*', as Dostoyevsky stated. At last, as history has repeatedly confirmed, the new message must make its own structure and compete for the attention of the masses. No new religious expression has successfully banished an older one it was sent to replace. Judaism exists alongside Christianity, and Islam stands in their midst. Hinduism remains after Buddhism claimed to be its fulfilment, while Zoroastrianism retains a portion of the spiritual ground. But it can be asked, what would the reaction be of someone studying all of these disciplines successively? Would s/he be led to conclude that they are all related, and bearing in mind their time of revelation, that each fulfils the one existing before it on some level? Why all this strife?

Such a question presumes a logical process at work. The truth is that once a religion's leadership refuses to accept the actuality of the religion's fulfilment existing in the dialogue of the successor Prophet, of His 'return,' it cuts that religion away from the search after truth and from the study and analysis of reality for the purpose of comprehending existence, and contents itself with dogma, magic and anti-intellectualism.

What is left is ideology, which maintains an unquenchable thirst for power, a will to power in order to make over reality in its own image. Standing opposed to the real, it faces immediate extinction as soon as its temporal power and authority are weakened. No wonder so much blood has been spilt at the advent of every new divine revelation!

Political Orthodoxy

In order not to stray too far from the core elements of our analysis, this will be a brief sketch only of the character of representative politics and how this structure accommodates certain practices better than others. In addition, most of the ideas related here have been covered in more depth earlier in the text. So we will avoid undue repetition by emphasizing the character of the elements involved in the political system and forgo a careful, detailed analysis of its specifics. There are few new points to make here, so this permits its cursory treatment.

A representative governmental form, where officials are elected to serve specified terms and are answerable to the electorate, will limit the planning horizon of proposed enactments to the time between elections. It is precisely for this reason that the central bank officers in the United States, for example, serve six year terms that overlap presidential elections most of the time. This minimizes the effect of outside, narrow political influences and their ability to generate a 'political business cycle', where money is pumped into the economy just before the presidential election, inducing a grateful public to re-elect the incumbent, even though the economy would then soon experience price inflation.[12] Thus the government itself is fully cognizant of the tendency of public servants to think of their own short-term interests first and the national interest second.

In what follows a characterization of current practices and mentalities in politics will be drawn and act as a bench mark for calculating what the response of political structures might be to the advent of a newly authored divine message. A brief discussion of the expected changes in such structures will follow.

The current diminution of political discourse

The conflation of television and political election campaigning has meant a dramatic increase in the cost of running for public office. This has led to corruption in the form of moneyed interests having easy access to public servants while the masses have little to none. One result has been the general perception that powerful and wealthy forces are able to buy lawmakers and force them to craft laws giving these groups advantages, even at the cost of the common good.

The economic term for such behaviour is *rent-seeking*, where *rent* is any payment to a resource that is greater than necessary to maintain it in its current employment, as explained above. In other words, economic actors seek from the government's largess benefits for themselves beyond what the market is likely to give them under conditions of competition. They may want prices fixed, competitors kept out or laws inimical to their private interests defeated. This is also known as 'crony-capitalism' and no one doubts that it is practised in most nations to some extent. In fact, there is no serious challenge to the accuracy of this commonly held view.

The other result is seen in the *laissez faire* character of the laws that have come out of this process and the free-market ideologies used to justify many of them. This is especially ironic when the intention of the lawmakers is so obviously to negate the workings of the free market and to obtain rents for themselves from the government. If such rents are paid – and they usually are for reasons carefully explained by the Nobel Laureate economist James M. Buchanan[13] – it reduces available funds for truly public expenditures.

Granted that matters such as industrial and military policy, the quantity and nature of wealth transfers, support for the poor, educational expenditures and environmental responsibilities are extremely complex and their treatment by representatives can never, or almost never, be the reflection of any single practice, selfish or public-spirited. Nonetheless, it is beyond doubt that, at least in America, the egalitarian standard that reflected the public will since the Great Depression of the 1930s has been set aside in favour of *laissez faire* economic policies which have encouraged a return to extremes of wealth and poverty not seen since the American gilded age over a century ago. In a recent study on marginal tax rates and income inequality in the United States, Altig and Carlstrom found that about one half of the large and disturbing increase in income inequality in the United States in the last decade of the 20th century was the result of tax policies pursued in 1985 that reduced taxes on the rich.[14] There has therefore been a transfer of wealth from the poor to the rich as a result of taxation changes generated by wealthy Americans who exercised their unlimited access to elected officials, who themselves are among the richest of the population.

In addition, economic life in the United States has become far more financially risky for most individuals and families, and certain moral hazards for those given vast fiduciary and strategic corporate responsibility have become more pronounced. Twenty-five years ago few Americans made the list of the world's richest individuals; now they fill the highest ranks,[15] while an ever-larger percentage of the middle class slips into poverty.

The situation nominally necessitating the reduction of the highest brackets of the graduated income tax – high inflation – was eliminated more than 20 years ago and shows no sign of re-emerging. Yet further tax cuts are championed, even by some who are most disadvantaged by them, so thorough has been the planting of anti-government sentiments by politicians themselves.

Such persons claim to work 'for the people' and to protect them from the inroads of government interference. But this is clearly disingenuous: they are mostly rich themselves and would therefore benefit directly from such tax policies. Further, they are accepting vast sums for their own re-election campaigns from other wealthy interested parties who also want to have taxes lowered. At this point, rather than stimulating business investment, low taxes rob the poor and the middle class by reducing funds available for public goods. The middle class especially seems not to realize how different things are today from previous decades, that the threat of too much government has been replaced by the threat of too little and the public is thereby placed increasingly in danger from a radical rollback of not just onerous and burdensome regulation but even useful and productivity-increasing regulation as well. Ask yourself, how many bicyclists would you expect to see using a highway system totally unregulated and what type of vehicle, in that case, would likely be the vehicle of choice for those attempting to utilize it?

WHEN GOVERNMENT REFUSES TO ACT

Again, using America as an example because of its economic might and its tendency to display extremes in capitalistic economic matters, an inspection of one area of American life that is in need of government intervention and political will can illustrate the point that politics in America is a captive of vested interests whose goals are inimical to the public good. The purpose of detailing this is to offer a clear indication of the nature of political opposition to the new divine message and something of the changes to be expected after the general acceptance of that message. Some of this has been detailed above in another context but the present cross-sectioning puts it in a new light

According to an article in *The Financial Times*,[16] American medical services are the most costly in the world while being ranked *37th in quality*, way behind other nations paying far less for their healthcare. France had the highest ranked healthcare in quality, while only costing French citizens about one-half what Americans must pay for their lower quality of care.

America is the only advanced nation on earth lacking a single-pay, government regulated healthcare infrastructure. Medical services in the United States are unaffordable for all but a few and there is no movement in the government to redress this glaring lack in social well-being. Medical costs in the United States are primarily a function of legal expenses, not new technology (which reduces costs in many cases), from suits and litigation and from settlements and jury awards of millions of dollars to complainants. When allowed to assume extreme values, these bankrupt medical professionals and hospitals alike. Doctors are leaving the profession because they can no longer afford liability insurance, which continues to rise annually, in excess of 50 per cent for some practices. Emergency rooms are closing their doors because they cannot staff them with enough doctors. Half of all workers in America may have no health insurance, either for themselves or their families. A simple 20-minute appendectomy may cost you more than $10,000 and a 30-second draining of a mammary cyst with a hypodermic needle in a doctor's office more than $1,300.

Owing to the ever-present threat of litigation (see the discussion on adversarial jurisprudence above), doctors are practising 'defensive medicine', ordering batteries of tests to cover themselves from having missed some unsuspected condition in their patients and getting sued for it months or even decades later. As a result, prices have skyrocketed, forcing individuals to practise self-medicine, not being able to afford any other.

Tort reform, limiting judgements for 'pain and suffering' and providing some statute-of-limitation for certain situations, is needed. The legal profession, however, makes hundreds of millions of dollars annually from medical tort business and will not work to eliminate what has become for some their very bread and butter. Lawmakers are, of course, mostly drawn from the ranks of lawyers, so they have no interest in making the necessary changes that could make medical care affordable again. Furthermore, law firms specializing in medical malpractice contribute millions of dollars towards re-election campaigns.

Beyond this, the absence of a single-pay system has added 40 per cent to medical costs. In other words, medical costs are estimated to be 140 per cent of those that would be experienced under a single-pay system such as that found in practically all other advanced economies, even allowing for the presence of the current tort system.

Drug companies, heavy donors to the re-election campaigns of both parties, have resisted all efforts to make their needed products more affordable. Their high and rising costs – often a reflection of nothing more than marketing expenses – mean that seniors and others cannot obtain insurance to cover them.

An obvious need exists for a government-led effort to redress a clear market failure, where there is evidence of blatant market power and political corruption existing for more than a decade, and the market cannot make the necessary adjustments or provide the right signals no matter what it does. Yet, in spite of over a decade of continual pleas from the public for political action, nothing is done to alleviate the situation. And this while America is the richest economy in the world and while virtually every other developed nation, rich and poor, has found the way – and the will – to solve this problem.

But the damage does not stop there. Major corporations, especially in heavy industry, are leaving the United States and settling elsewhere owing to the high cost of medical insurance. Recently America lost out to Canada in wooing a major car maker because Canada, with its universal single-payer medical system, reduced employee medical insurance costs enough to reduce manufactured automobile and truck prices significantly.

As noted at the beginning of this section, the primary reason this situation continues is the need of elected officials for money to pay for re-election campaigns and the public's general inability or unwillingness to foot the bill for expensive TV spots. This leaves the door open for those who can and, by this means, get favourable treatment for their personal interests. Nothing new here.

In fairness, however, there are true believers who actually think that this situation, though more costly, providing poorer performance and causing doctors to flee the profession, is preferable to others because it eschews collectivism and governmental control. That is, they would rather see the population suffer needlessly if it achieves an ideologically pure result.

Political discourse is not the force it once was – if it ever was – even on its best days. Images have taken the place of dialogue and feelings have replaced analysis. A small, well-financed interest having undue influence over the elected representatives of a republic has been carefully analysed in *public choice economics*. It has established that people will remain ignorant of those things for which their effort will either have negligible effect or where the issue does not directly concern them, a situation called *rational ignorance*. This leads to voters only caring about issues which impact them significantly and for which they are willing to get involved. All other issues are ceded to those who care about them. Thus, the Sugar Producers Group and the food-processing conglomerate Archer Daniels Midland Corporation will work to maintain the American sugar quota because it raises the domestic price of sugar to *four times the world price*. This means more income for American sugar producers and a continued market for its liquid corn-based substitute, high fructose corn syrup (HFCS). It also means poverty for western hemisphere countries which grow little but sugar cane and continued environmental degradation for the Florida Everglades. Higher prices in baked goods and confections are passed on to the consumer but the amount of this, when dispersed across the millions of purchasers with a sweet tooth, is deemed negligible.

Thus gun enthusiasts will elect those guaranteeing no new gun restriction laws will be passed, even while the city of Chicago alone suffers more gun deaths than the entire nation of Canada whose population is 30 times greater. Members of family planning agencies will elect those who agree not to challenge the Roe vs. Wade Supreme Court decision legalizing abortion. Media moguls will fight restrictions on violent and sexual content in their products even as there is growing evidence that such content is harmful to young minds who access it, while environmentalists will vote only for those candidates favouring strong environmental regulations, no matter what their positions might be on abortion rights, gun laws or any of the other 'hot-button' issues setting off the electorate's alarm bells.

In each of these examples the *common* interest is dispersed and disorganized, incapable of mounting a cohesive opposition to these special interests, while private interests are organized and effective in getting what they want. This *Balkanization* of the political arena makes it difficult to build a consensus for more general social welfare initiatives because no identifiable group will be made sufficiently better off to champion them with time and money while those disadvantaged by such moves will organize and effectively lobby for their defeat.[17] Among the millions of people who pay a few pennies more for candy bars, who will be motivated to fly to Washington and lobby for the termination of the sugar quota? At the same time sugar producers are directly affected by such legislation and can be expected to pour thousands into the re-election campaigns of those representatives who guarantee to fight for the quota's maintenance.

The extremes of wealth and poverty now evident in the world's largest economy, the growing disenfranchisement and diminution of its middle class and the reduction of employment security and tenancy for workers, all this has not existed for long in past eras without political upheaval and reorientation of national domestic goals and policies.[18] A new divinely-inspired message, having a strong commitment to social justice and the elimination of income extremes could very well fire up people to work for some changes to the *status quo*. Vested interests, who would be disadvantaged by the call for the elimination of the 'gross accumulation of wealth' and an end to political corruption and rent-seeking behaviour, may try to form opposition, if it cannot co-opt such tendencies. Thus we see the nature and likely tactics that could be employed to oppose the dispersion of a new divine message. It is unnecessary to go beyond this; history will surely repeat itself in this regard.

This sub-section has looked in depth at how the collective will is blocked by the efforts of vested and wealthy interests. While perhaps too detailed and narrow in focus, it is a simple exercise to find other similar examples containing practically all the cited elements. The purpose was to give immediacy to the well-known belief that politics is easily corrupted and its service to the people's will subverted. This is an uncontroversial statement. But it sometimes helps to see one particular example examined in some detail.

Economic/Commercial Orthodoxy Based on Existing Consumer Preference Sets

Now consider what might be the reaction of the commercial sectors to a new divinely-inspired message, including corporate media, which profits by guiding an increasingly sophisticated consumer-oriented population towards ever greater expenditure of personal wealth to acquire the next new thing. Their first question might be, 'How does this new divine message treat commerce and marketing? Is it Luddite or anti-commerce? Is it aesthetic and anti-materialistic?' Operating in a post-industrial economy and heavily emphasizing the pursuit of leisure activities and entertainment possibilities, consumer interests might feel threatened. Certainly those in the gambling industry, the sex trades, the liquor and intoxicant sectors, would likely feel threatened by a divine message with its age-old antipathy towards such enterprises. And to the extent that the divine message eschews hedonism and the pursuit of pleasure for its own sake, the prostitution of art, unnecessary expenditure and excessively frivolous behaviour, other sectors will also make common cause in opposition.

However, some sectors would stand to gain from the expected re-emphasis on work, productivity and the cultivation of attitudes encouraging personal temperance. Top management would certainly embrace it, at least for their workers if not for themselves, as would the ranks of industrial engineers, as a way to reduce actual or perceived shirking, pilfering, petty sabotage and workplace indolence on the part of managers and workers alike.

Economists would warn of serious 'dislocations' in the economy if the new message became the standard thinking of consumers and their aggregate demand shifted in response to a new set of preferences. Politicians would take heed and work to shore up support for the *status quo*, lest the expected changes reduced employment in their districts and they were turned out of office as a result. Individual sectors negatively affected by altering tastes in line with the newly advocated standard would lobby for protection and appeal to their bought-and-paid-for legislators for relief using general revenue transfers to support their eroding income streams.

The commercialization – Shoghi Effendi has termed it the 'prostitution'[19] – of art and literature common today will be scrutinized more closely. For example, literary art, or art in general, is an expression of beliefs, a personal and emotive response to the human condition expected both to stimulate feeling in others and to record the feelings of the self. Of course, it is not guaranteed that what is forthcoming is *good* art, which is contextual and relative. But *that it is art is determined by the motive behind its creation.* The result of writing TV scripts on demand and according to a weekly episode schedule for a specified salary is *not* art, even while it is craft and may be *artistic*. Rather, it is a commercial enterprise and should be treated as such. The difference is one of intent. In the former, the idea was the thing, whether or not others wanted it or cared. In the latter situation, profit is the thing and TV scripts are seen as a means to that end.

Back in television's formative years, much of the programming was a presentation of performance art – basically, placing a camera before a stage – and the challenge for producers was to figure out a way to pay for it with advertising revenues. But now, almost without exception, the goal is to maximize advertising revenues and network profits, and what is shown is judged solely on its ability to sell advertising time at the highest possible price. Thus performance art is prostituted to serve this objective, as are athletic contests, for that matter.[20]

A separate section of this book would be needed to discuss the use of art in advertising to sell goods and services. This also includes profaning exalted national, religious and heroic images and symbols to sell something. The recent use of the Statue of Liberty, with her arm holding the torch of freedom above her head, to sell underarm deodorant comes to mind as a particularly tasteless example of such profanity.

It is probably this prostitution of art and the commodification of all things that leads many to decry the injection of 'market values' into everything. Actually, this characterization is inaccurate; it is the *commercialization* of everything that creates offence. It is the idea that *value in trade* is all that matters, that everything must be profitable in the very narrow sense of being capable of generating current period financial gains. Today a working artist does not merit respect or consideration in many regions unless s/he is a financial success, as if this imprimatur is necessary and sufficient to bestow validity on the work itself. But commercialization forces all endeavours into the Procrustean bed of current period pricing and ignores values accruing over decades or longer or values accruing to other, non-commodified sectors of life. The Prophets and Messengers of God have always thrown out such thinking and given short shrift to its exponents. Indeed, it is a central purpose of every divine dispensation to purge such thinking and recreate a true sense of value and valuation in hearts and minds. It is likely at this point that a cynical and dehumanizing social science electorate would register its strongest rejection of the divine message.

Economics takes a more circumspect view of artistic enterprises, maintaining that market value is changeable, only contextually relative and is certainly not an indicator of a thing's complete or absolute value. Even in a material sense, price as an indicator of absolute value can be very misleading. Isn't water less expensive than gemstones even though life itself depends on an uninterrupted supply of clean water and gemstones for jewellery are completely non-essential? This distinction is an example of the difference between *value in trade* and *value in use*. Artistic merit may take a century or more to be uncovered and appreciated. Indeed, its greatest importance lies more with its external effects on society over time than with its immediate marketable possibilities. Prices function merely as an acceptable system of rationing scarce resources and even in this role do not always produce a desirable result.

This is true for many other elements in society that are essential for a full and developing life. Mírzá Abu'l-Faḍl gave one criterion for determining individual worth: the degree of complexity of the problems a person can solve. The more complex the problem, the greater the worth to society of the person who solves it. However, to determine accurate and appropriate compensation, another criterion must be added: the demand for such problem-solving by the marketplace. But we already know that where significant values that are external to the market's immediate interest exist, the price signal from the market will be an inaccurate indicator of a thing's true worth.

Consider the difference, briefly discussed above, in compensation for a star athlete or film star and a public school teacher or a family crisis counsellor. Over the 20-year working life of that teacher or counsellor hundreds or thousands of children will have been influenced by him or her and that influence will have had a lasting effect on a generation of people, and on their offspring in due time. Yet the star athlete or movie star is paid far more. At least in the present valuation of things, the ability to act in film or kick a round ball into a net on a grass field better than anyone else is of greater value in the public's mind than the work of the school teacher. This is market valuations at work, looking only at a thing's marginal revenue product rather than its total intergenerational value. But people must choose among a range of possibilities to teach or counsel others. Counsellors could become scarce as people turn away from this profession.

And what could be potentially more valuable than the work of at-risk family counsellors? These people are responsible for rescuing family units in danger of dissolution and of insuring the safety and welfare of involved children. Yet these workers are generally overworked and underpaid. Turnover is high and we never hear much about them unless they make a mistake resulting in child abuse or worse. This and other examples indicate that *what benefits society's children is presently considered of less importance than what entertains its adults*,[21] the direct result of applying market values to everything, even things with long-term consequences impossible to price marginally by any acceptable formula.

Preference orderings that pay enormous treasure to entertainers and a pittance to valuable social workers such as teachers, agriculturalists and counsellors would naturally be expected to change with the advent of a new prophetic message, with its reemphasis on the importance of children, healthy families, achievements in art, science, literature and applied technology, and a dignified and temperate lifestyle. External valuations, the public benefits and costs of a privately marketed entity, would be given full importance and would no longer be discounted as not being 'the market's concern'. If the new message did little more than lead to full accounting of externalities and an abundant supply of public goods humanity would be far better off than at present. If it also led to a reversal of the commercialization of all things and the reestablishment of intangible valuations where appropriate, we might see a return to valuing pursuits based on large and inclusive measures of social contribution and a diminution of purely commercial valuations, as further discussed below.

In sum, the extent to which the new divine teaching rejects the commercialization of all things is the extent to which it will be opposed by those who only count *value in trade* and refuse to deal with complexities engendered by broader valuation measures.

***

Another aspect of economic/commercial orthodoxy affected by the advent of a new prophetic message is the area of work and employment. What people choose to do for a living is a function of their tastes and preferences in combination with a clear evaluation of their talents and abilities and compensation possibilities held out by the market. Work is chosen from a menu of available possibilities. Different paths can lead to success, not just one. But leaving aside technology-induced job developments, with changing standards come changing work choices. So certainly these choices will change with the advent of the new message.

Some jobs will no longer be considered 'choice' while others, previously undervalued, will increase in status, and hopefully, remuneration. The pattern of this change will closely follow the prophetic dialogue's valuations of various social functions and tasks. This will remain a question of personal choice but the menu entries could be expected to change over time.

Perhaps of greater interest are the expected changes in workplace orthodoxy brought about by the influence of the social justice aspects of the new message. Most of what can be said in an introductory text such as this has already been discussed. The following attempts to tie previous statements together and place them in the present context of industrial and post-industrial economies.

Data from many nations will show that most of the world's workers saw their lot worsen during the last decade of the 20th century. In North America and Asia, Latin and South America, and Africa workers have lost both income and security. Falling real wages (where the wage received is adjusted for inflation rates) mean a drop in the standard of living for workers.

But perhaps of greater importance is the wholesale loss of any job security. Indeed, in the United States the increase in feelings of insecurity can be related to the seemingly anomalous rise in fertility rates when compared to those in Europe.[22] While falling wages can be adjusted for, albeit painfully, the threat of losing one's job and income cannot.[23] Workers all over the world have become more and more contingent. As far as possible, corporations have shifted the risks and uncertainties of the market completely onto their workers, who are by nature of being small-holders, ill prepared to face income loss. Even while they are far better equipped to balance these uncertainties, corporations have made it plain in their stated personnel policies and stockholder annual reports that they regard their human resources as expendable.

Economists would argue, without needing recourse to moral persuasion, that just on efficiency grounds this attitude and management practice of treating human and nonhuman resources identically is inefficient (the closest economists come to branding something a sin) and will cause the economy to underperform and not to grow as it could.[24]

While there are many similarities with respect to their treatment in economics and finance, and while it is obvious that corporate managers have almost entirely conflated them, human resources are fundamentally different from nonhuman varieties. For one thing, they can revolt and overthrow the existing order if pushed far enough, something a copper ingot, a CAD-CAM program or a letter of credit cannot. What keeps this from happening is the tacit psychological contract of employment requiring certain actions from both sides. But if there is persistent reneging by one of the parties, events may take a radical turn. Certainly the appearance of a dynamic prophetic message enfranchising the oppressed could trigger it, as has already been witnessed in the world.

This, in general terms, is what can be expected from commercial structures caught up in the market changes arising from the appearance of a new prophetic message.

***

The nature of the expected impacts and reaction of specific social and economic segments to a new divine dispensation suggests how redistribution of resources will result from the spread of a new divine message. Valuations will be altered; what was considered in the past to be great value may be considered practically worthless and relegated to historical flotsam, while new ideas and teachings are valued highly and seen as holding the key to our continued advancement as a species.

How Values Shift

What is the instrumentation of shifting values? What are the mechanics of such a shift? Recall that price is the relative value of a good or service being exchanged, that it is discovered by resolving supply and demand forces and that it informs all interested so that resources will be used to make goods of the highest possible value. If this is further deconstructed it provides the context for analysing the expected effects of a divine message. We have already seen something of such a message's appeal and the aggregated effects that has on societal development over time. Immediately above we looked at some of the social structures and their natural response to a realigning divine message of accelerating influence. This part treats the process of what Schumpeter called 'creative destruction' and some of its aftermath.[25]

Institutions represent investments, the standing constructions of scarce resources. They must provide, must earn their keep, so to speak. If they cannot do this then it is essential for the future of the community that such constructions be brought down, taken apart, decomposed and their resources made available for other, better uses. A society can certainly not afford to tie up scarce resources in enshrining past methods and practices. A divine message, similar to what was capable of transforming the Arabian Peninsula and the Middle East, the Levant and the Maghreb, will necessarily start by freeing up resources for their rededication into institutions of service to its cause.

This superficially describes the destruction and re-creation of institutions, a painful process, ordinarily. As we have seen, institutions have two choices in the presence of unavoidable change: adaptation and metamorphosis or resistance and destruction. Of the institutions just discussed we can conclude with the following essential points:

- Science will not resist what it does not take seriously or consider a threat to its guilds. Its *status quo* changes as it develops according to its own needs and is generally unperturbed by events outside its sphere of influence. The abandonment of metaphysical analysis by most branches of science has insulated it, so to speak, from direct confrontation with the force of a newly authored divine revelation and freed it from having to battle it. Science will therefore continue its work. The things it chooses to work on will be altered as the perceptions of its practitioners are altered. As some of the best minds of their generations are not in the habit of ignoring evidence, they can be expected to embrace the new teachings in large numbers, if, and only if, they are capable of distinguishing between divine truth and religious ideology.

- Religious orthodoxy is, by nature and habit, irremediably opposed to the establishment of a new divine standard. In the past the new prophetic message represented the fulfilment of a particular faith and it was that faith in its latter days that most opposed the new one. In doing so the established faith became somewhat weakened and discredited for its ideological position in opposition to what was obviously a continuation of the same message. However, if a new message begins as a universal cause rather than as the fulfilment of a particular historical faith, opposition from all existing religious ideologies can be anticipated. If the historical record continues to provide a standard against which to comprehend the character of current events, then the opposition of existing religions to the newly revealed teaching will only accelerate its establishment and their own discreditability and demise. But before that time, however, much as the varying religious structures and sects may loathe each other, they are expected to make common cause against this new divine cause as it represents to all of them their own temporal diminution.

- Political orthodoxy trades in the products – the ideas, symbols, myths and superstitions – of all these orthodoxies. Its objective is otherwise to incorporate the will of society in its actions. Politics is operated by people drawn from the society it serves and reflects contemporary standards and expectations in its representatives. A new divine message exercising its effect over time will result in reduced corruption, an increased emphasis on public goods provision and social justice, and a greater willingness to adjudicate external effects. As far as directing behavioural change in the community, this cannot be expected of it. Political orthodoxy changes rapidly when it must but it does not lead, it follows. It will, however, offer focused expression and attempt to organize the resources of the community to fulfil the divine teaching's potential when sufficiently marshalled by the people's will.

- In areas of commercial/economic orthodoxy great changes can be expected. Tastes and preferences will radically change as the impact of the new divine message exerts its influence. The effect on markets would result in extensive dislocations. Employees working to supply no-longer-demanded products will be laid off while industries supplying what is newly demanded will be seeking more workers. Entire industries will wither as others are formed. The pattern of these changes will follow the dictates of the divine teaching. Industrial justice will result in better working conditions, increased security for workers' lives and greater production efficiencies from worker–management cooperation. Corporations will seriously consider their role as being largely responsible for the livelihood of their workers and their workers' dependents and maturing children and will formulate strategies in keeping with the reality that human resources are distinct from nonhuman types. This might mean developing methods of management that maximizes worker–family welfare rather than corporate shareholder profits. This is not to minimize the need for corporations to be profitable; what is referred to here is economic – or pure – profits and their use after all resources have been compensated and expected returns paid out. Shareholder values will be transformed into stakeholder values wherein long term benefits and losses to the community hosting the corporation will be given more consideration.

- The family unit, nuclear or extended, which has been under serious attack from various forces, will be rejuvenated. This has been the case with the appearance of every prophetic message. Each has regarded the family as the building block of society and its very foundation. Thus their teachings are designed to promote family unity and eschew its disintegration.

- Other expected changes can be gleaned from the writings of Shoghi Effendi.

- *Status quo* changes begin with changes in the valuation standard, the pricing system that signals something's worth. A truly divine standard is, by definition, an expression of reality. When it is revealed it forces all else to respond to it and orient around it. Past religions, upon refusing to acknowledge their interrelatedness and dependence on the new divine teaching for their own validation, have become overshrouded with dogmas and changed into closed systems of ideological thought, no longer capable of transforming society or even of changing themselves. But they have become the *status quo* and, naturally, the *status quo* will defend itself, even if it must destroy all else in doing so. As asserted above, ideologies opposed to the new reality exist only so long as people follow them and believe in them. That is, they have no independent reality. This is not the case with the natural laws of gravity, optics or the law of reciprocity, of trustworthiness, etc. What the Prophets would have us understand is that r*ational laws pertaining to metaphysics and spiritual logic are just as immutable as God's natural laws and are also not reliant on our belief in them for their validation or existence.*[26]

Analysis, the most potent force for change in humanity and the human enterprise's guarantor, is again seen as a single realm of investigation by the acceptance of commonly understood evidentiary procedures and hypothesis testing, as it had been in the past before the *great rift* caused by the submergence of analytical and rational religion under a drowning sea of dogma and ideology. And this by the essential facilitative instrumentality of a divine revelation. According to the historical record there were great results in all aspects of civilization in the days before this intellectual rift, when there was just rational analysis as applied to both the material and the super-material world. There is every reason to believe that such a productive unification in analytical thinking will be repeated to the inestimable gain and glory of whatever civilization experiences it.

> But by religion is meant that which is ascertained by investigation and not that which is based on mere imitation . . . [27]

13
In Sum

This inquiry has attempted to do a number of things, using as its vehicle and main focus the economic content of divine speech. In addition, it has attempted to show that rational analysis is as essential in religious explorations as in material ones. In fact, it is perhaps of even greater importance to maintain the highest standards of logical argument and rational analysis in the arena of religious discussions since, as history has shown, it is more profoundly and systematically affected by ideological incursions and corruption than is science. *'But by religion is meant that which is ascertained by investigation and not that which is based on mere imitation . . .* '[1]

The character of this book is of a formally argued set of propositions, supported with logic and authoritative references from science and the sources of divine revelation. The hope is that it will stimulate a long overdue discussion among social scientists and others as to the unified nature of rational analysis. The appearance of a new divine revelation has repeated a pattern established with similar past appearances: the reunification of all analytical disciplines under a single set of procedures. With this unification should come new discoveries and applications in science and spirituality undreamed of in past epochs, especially in the area of social science. Let us hope this happens soon.

Appendix

Islamic Contributions to Economics and Finance, in Brief

Discussing the extensive and sweeping contributions the Islamic dispensation has made to modern economics and finance in an appendix to a book is presumptuous, to say the least. However, this appendix will concentrate on just two of those contributions and their effects on modern finance: 1) risk management and 2) the implications of prohibiting the collecting and paying of ordinary interest. God willing, another volume will deal with Qur'ánic economics in detail and discuss its still unexplored aspects, now coming to light and prominence with the appearance of the dispensation of Bahá'u'lláh.

The intense light shed by the Bahá'í dispensation has illuminated all previous dispensations, not least the Islamic dispensation. Witness the surge in Islamic finance and Islamic banking products over the last few years. This is a market segment that did not even exist 30 years ago, even though all the requisite teachings and principles have been in place for 1,300 years.

Why has it taken until now to develop these financial instruments based on Qur'ánic teachings? Considering the repetition of previous historical divine cycles and bearing in mind that God does not change His ways of dealing with mankind, it seems that such development awaited the strong influence of a new dispensation for its true character to be revealed. As has been argued throughout this book, a new dispensation sweeps away established anti-analysis, anti-rational and anti-intellectual ideologies associated with previous dispensations. As the character of the *status quo* ruling, influential dispensation in society goes, so goes that society in material and intellectual pursuits. At the beginning of all divine revelations a vast increase in intellectual pursuits and a fresh analysis of existing paradigms is seen throughout the world, causing the abandonment of false and artificial barriers in knowledge-based entities. The result is the founding of new sciences and a reinvigoration of existing ones.

This is what appears to have occurred with the emergence of Islamic finance and its commercialization in international money centre markets and beyond. Naturally, expected profits are the motivating force behind many of the new Islamic finance bank product offerings, such as index-tied bonds, insurance products and rent-to-own consumer purchase contracts. But this profit push has forced Qur'ánic scholars to research the efficacy and compliance of these products, exposing for the first time the full panoply of Qur'ánic teachings on finance, risk management and modern economics, none of which was possible, it seems, until the relative power of the new divinely-sourced light had increased enough to illuminate the previous holy books more fully.[1]

Several good texts of Islamic scholarship in finance and dealing with Islamic economics already exist. They include *Towards a Just Monetary System* by M. Umer Chapra, published by the Islamic Foundation. This book is written for economists and non-economists alike and explores many aspects of modern finance and monetary systems, their drawbacks and how Islamic finance addresses them.

Another book by the same author and publisher is *Islam and the Economic Challenge*, which provides readers with a fairly good characterization of the limitations of western economics and how Qur'ánic teachings address them. The analysis is comprehensive and systematic.

Students of the Bahá'í teachings are aware that the dispensation of Bahá'u'lláh does not enter a spiritual or intellectual void but follows on previous dispensations and divinely authored teachings; that it does not eliminate them but, as the Guardian of the Bahá'í Faith states, unites, connects and fulfils them.[2] Specifically, many teachings in the Qur'án are confirmed and re-established in this day and many more are now being utilized for the first time as a direct result of the Revelation of Bahá'u'lláh. And these include – with just some slight alterations – Qur'ánic economic teachings, the latent power of which, now that they are confirmed and linked for all time with the Revelation of Bahá'u'lláh, are taking centre stage in the financial and economic worlds.

One of the most important and well-known Qur'ánic teachings on finance is the prohibition against paying or charging interest – *ar-ribá* – on borrowed capital. But it is only in the last several decades that its implications in modern finance have been understood to any extent. This prohibition has two immediate effects: 1) it requires that business enterprise start-ups utilize investment partners for initial funding and 2) it all but prohibits consumer lending. Consumer lending can only occur using non-recourse, zero-interest loans; or the purchaser can enter into a 'rent-to-own' agreement, whereby s/he rents the product under contract and ends up owning it after some specified time period. This arrangement is common in Islamic countries. Instead of quoting low interest rates on the loan, a low 'profit' rate is advertised for the 'lease'.

The larger implications of the prohibition against interest are far-reaching and profound, affecting finance, risk management, portfolio analysis, futures and options markets, derivatives and other financial instruments, spending and saving decisions, the generation of new business enterprises and the balance of production and consumption in the economy. Indeed, it is no overstatement to say that the Qur'án, in the full implications of this prohibition, fully encouraged the formation of the modern joint stock corporation and stock trading, the existence of a corporation as a legal, independent entity, futures and options markets, modern portfolio theory and the efficacy of financial derivative markets. It also created the impetus behind the use of limited investor-partners and the establishment of venture capital markets, and bankruptcy and financial reorganization laws now prevalent as tools of modern finance. We will look at just one of those areas here, risk management in enterprise start-ups.

Treatment of Market Risk in Islam

The core concept associated with the prohibition against interest payments and charges is that risk must be fully apportioned among a broad base of participants and that it must reflect market prices, costs and values as they change over time. By prohibiting fixing the value of obligations and rewards it allows valuations to reflect their true worth across time as economic realities change. It is a dynamic system, which mitigates the negative effects of constantly changing valuations in an economy. This is in sharp contrast with conventional interest-based systems, whose weakness is in fixing the value of obligations and rewards for different enterprise participants in an economic regime of continuous valuational changes.

A practical alternative to borrowing start-up capital requirements is to enlist partner-investors. As with any investment, these will share in the risks and the rewards of the enterprise. If it fails, all lose in proportion to what has been invested and no further payments are due. If it succeeds, all investors share in the rewards proportionately, just as their losses would have been shared. This system spreads enterprise risk from one individual to the enterprise-entity, reducing entry and start-up costs with respect to risk premiums being born disproportionally by any one party. Recall 'Abdu'l-Bahá's exploration of the implications of profit-sharing, of which this is one example.

Contrast this financial structure to a simple loan at interest. No matter what happens to the object for which the loan was obtained, the loan must, in any case, be paid back, even if the generator of future funds – the enterprise – has been lost. This is a disincentive for businesses and invention commercializations because the risk premium on both sides is simply too high.

The effect of investor-partner funding is to push risk up the hierarchical management chain and place the greatest risk on the broadest shoulders, those of the enterprise as a collective form. Not only is partnering with others in enterprise start-ups necessitated, which spreads risk among partners in proportion to their importance to the enterprise, *it broadens the human capital employed by the enterprise*, greatly increasing its chances of survival. This supports another teaching of the Qur'án – reiterated by Bahá'u'lláh – that we should consult on matters of importance with all those affected. (This translates indirectly into the economic principle that cost and benefit externalities should be internalized.)

Now consider the broader implications of this teaching on the economy in its entirety, using a simple example.

Imagine that you have a new invention, which could conceivably cause a revolution in, say, information technology. But you are in need of funds to get it off the ground. You go to a bank but it has little interest in your dream. You have no track record as a business operator and your new idea is hard for the bank to evaluate. How much could it be worth? What about collateral? What is a likely pay-out term? What would its price/earnings ratio be? None of the established analytical finance ratios are of any help to the bank. So your new idea gets no loaned funds.

You are now introduced to a venture-capital investor. This person arranges investing for new ideas by finding partners, limited or full, who will give you the financing needed in exchange for a share of the ownership of the business. Whatever it makes in future, the partners now own a share and get paid from its profits. They retain ownership of their shares until they want to sell out.

This scenario is from history and describes the personal computer and Internet revolutions in the 1980s and beyond. Left to bank financing, none of that could have possibly got a start. This is not to say that Silicon Valley and Redmond, Washington, consciously followed Qur'ánic teachings to fund a new industry but that what occurred was in complete accordance with Qur'ánic economic and finance teachings and in fact could not have happened without the financing structure the Qur'án requires.

Even without the requirement to be Shariah compliant in financial activities (to accord with Islamic law, as distinct from purely Qur'ánic implications), the result of following these teachings enabled the appearance of a market sector employing millions of workers and paying billions in taxes for infrastructural improvements, created jillions of useful and convenient devices and made the entire economy more efficient, reducing costs for all of us and enhancing our living standards.

The reason why venture capital finance – promoted by the Qur'án – succeeds where bank financing fails is that *bringing new things to the market is risky* and neither the borrower nor the lender is prepared to bear the full impact of fixing the assignment and the value of that risk if things go wrong. For the borrower, if the venture fails, all the funds must still be paid back. Few are so confident, or so crazy, to take this risk lightly. For the banker, which lends out other people's money at interest, it risks never getting repaid. If that happens a few times too many, the bank becomes insolvent and its doors are shut. That is because many commercial banks routinely have only about six per cent of assets available for depositors' redemption at any time. If just some of the borrowers fail to repay, the bank fails.

The Qur'ánic teaching on financing enterprises leading to venture capitalism has other implications all aimed at assigning risk loads in proportion to reward prospects. It enables hiring needed workers at a low current wage while the new start-up is cash strapped, by promising to pay stock options, which give workers the right to buy company stock at a price below market, then sell them back to the market to recoup the price difference if they choose. That way, workers become worker–owners, partners in the enterprise and dedicated to its success in a way that an ordinary employee, who is paid a wage or salary and has no stake in the business beyond a desire for job security, can never be. Again, risk management utilizing Qur'ánic teachings is a win–win: employers get dedicated workers and workers get a shot at some real money if the business takes off. And again, this is in line with the explanations of profit-sharing made by 'Abdu'l-Bahá and promoted by the Bahá'í Faith, thus reaffirming the teachings on profit-sharing in Islam.

Many businesses today offer stock options in conjunction with a lower initial salary or higher pay and no stock options. Most times, the options are chosen rather than the higher initial pay. Of course, the chances of a new business succeeding are not usually good and the stock options could end up being worthless. But losing a job is the real economic setback, far more serious than having worked for less, because all income is now lost and the worker must go through the materially and psychologically costly process of marketing him- or herself. Being a better-paid worker or holding worthless stock options does not change that. However, the dream of future riches is there and everyone remembers the story (possibly true) of Bill Gates moving out of his mother's garage and into office space and his neighbour helping him but insisting on being paid cash rather than accepting several thousand shares in his brand new company, Microsoft.

Further Economic Implications

Not only has this prohibition on interest spawned venture capitalism and stock options, it has also led indirectly to the creation of other instruments designed to allow producers to offload their risks in exchange for a variable fee or percentage of profits. That keeps producers producing, adding value to our lives, and giving the risk to those who, by training, desire or constitution, choose to bear it in the hope of making a profit. Assuming such risks is never easy. A study of commodity participants found that while hedgers gained clear advantages in being able to offload their price risks, 90 per cent of the risk-assumers, that is, the speculators, lost money in their associated trades.[3]

In the short run this is a zero-sum game; what the speculators lose is exactly what the hedgers gain. But in the long run it is a positive-sum game, where all win over time. Even if the hedgers lost, their losses would have been scheduled, known quantities and offset by opposite positions in cash and futures markets, rather than the unknown chance of a non-hedged business-ruining loss. And the presence of willing participants who desire to assume price risk makes hedging possible, thereby reducing risk premiums for all.

In an economy there are always two sets of activities in production: 1) activities that directly add value in the form of better goods and services to end users and 2) activities that do not add value but rather facilitate value-adding activities. The venture capitalist, the limited partner, the speculator and investor, add no actual value to anything but because they are willing to invest and share the risk, the enterprise can commence. Without it, owing to prohibitive risk premiums, the enterprise, with all its promise, never happens. Facilitative activities are just as important as those activities that directly add value to what we consume.[4]

The producer must always worry that for some unforeseen reason prices might turn against him, resulting in unexpected and potentially devastating losses. The farmer wants a great harvest but, unfortunately, that will mean everyone else will likely have a great harvest also. That might mean that the value of his harvest is not worth much because the market now has more than it wants.

If the farmer can pre-sell his crop before harvest time at an acceptable price which covers all costs and offers acceptable profit, then all he needs to worry about are the usual things like weather, labour, machinery breakdowns, water, energy, etc. but not what price he will receive for his production. This is obviously a great benefit to any producer. And it is the reason why we have the modern, securitized futures market, where contracts for the future delivery of numerous goods can be bought and sold.

In fact, the Qur'án allows – indeed, encourages – risk market diversification because it enables investors and producers to offload unwanted price risk onto willing speculators, just as insurance protects against non-price economic losses. (Aren't insurers also speculating that the unforeseen will not occur?) All forms of securitized futures, options and derivative contracts are acceptable just as long as their values are not tied to a guaranteed payout amount based on a fixed return or valuation of the underlying economic entity. Valuations change with time and returns must be allowed to fully reflect that reality. The Qur'án does not allow return fixity as this has the effect of divesting the economic entity of this dynamic reality.

***

Qur'ánic teachings on economics support production and producers by encouraging venture capital investments and securitized futures, options and derivative markets where price risk can be offloaded and sold to those dedicated to its management. All these forms are allowed in Qur'ánic finance as long as they are not tied to any form of value fixity and are allowed to fully reflect underlying valuation changes through time.

Qur'ánic economic structuring of risk is far more modern and efficient in this regard than loan-based conventional forms, which usually fix valuations at some point and therefore increase risk when dynamical changes in valuations no longer reflect such fixed obligations. If we observe carefully, it is seen that much of the economic dislocations in currency, bond and other markets today are due to dynamic valuation changes occurring within a regime of fixed financial obligations. Such a system will inevitably pile up risk on one side of the transaction while benefiting the other side in a zero-sum scheme, bringing fabulous wealth to some while leaving others in ruin. Such fixity within inherently dynamic systems is responsible for most of the financial damage from speculative bubbles.

The Qur'ánic teachings on economics and finance impose risk sharing on all enterprise participants and do not allow fixed obligations in the face of dynamic valuation changes. They fully allow assets to reflect underlying values as economic and financial realities change and insist that all rewards and penalties arising from such changes be borne by all in proportion to their investments and levels of responsibility. This is a system tailor-made to enhance production opportunities and the creation and commercialization of new goods and services by forming a facilitative financial regime that efficiently assigns risks and rewards from economic endeavours in a world of constant change.

What, then, is implied by legalizing interest payments, as the teachings of Bahá'u'lláh allow? It has yet to be seen but one suggested effect is to allow easier consumer financing. Above, it was stated that Qur'ánic teachings, by disallowing *ar-ribá*, make no provision for consumer lending. This has the effect of emphasizing production over consumption. Consumer lending allows balancing production with consumption leading to increased supplies of consumer products and services.

To show the degree to which Qur'ánic economic and financial teachings have been deemed complete by the Bahá'í dispensation, consider that the Ḥuqúqu'lláh of 19 per cent is just one per cent different than the 20 per cent Zakat in Islam, which performs the same function. Tax laws are virtually unchanged; and the only other financial change of note is in inheritance laws of personal stature.

The Revelation of Bahá'u'lláh has been entrusted with enlarging people's understanding of the economic implications of spiritual attributes. For example, trustworthiness is discussed and analysed in depth, wherein it is revealed that it is the source of wealth for the world and the guarantor of every transaction. Other attributes are also so analysed, including how to gauge our own worth to society and what the goal of economic structures must be. It is imperative that Bahá'ís understand that while much of the analysis of previously revealed laws is new with this Faith, the underlying teachings, with the permission of God, have been established by His Holiness Muhammad and reaffirmed by His Holiness Bahá'u'lláh, thereby eternally affixing them in the galaxy of constellations that guide our way in the heaven of the knowledge of God, until the next Sun of divine knowledge rises above the horizon of revelation.

Bibliography

The following list covers most of the information sources used in the preparation of this book.

Primary Bahá'í texts have gone through many editions and printings but are largely in the public domain. The scriptures are mostly standardized in the American editions so whatever edition is obtained, the pagination is identical. For example, the *Kitáb-i-Íqán* published by the American Bahá'í Publishing Trust uses the same pagination in all editions. This is true for most other American Bahá'í Publishing Trust publications, including, for example, *The Bahá'í Proofs*.

The older economics texts referenced or used as general sources have been reprinted many times by various publishing houses. For example, *Capital* (*Das Kapital*) by Karl Marx, or *Principles of Political Economy* by John Stuart Mill, or even the more recent *The General Theory of Employment, Interest and Money* by John Maynard Keynes have all been published by a number of houses and in many different formats. The publications and the years given in the bibliography correspond to the texts I have used but many other editions of these older or more famous texts commonly exist.

Books

Formal and Technical Economics Books

Blanchard, Olivier and Stanley Fischer. *Lectures on Macroeconomics*. Cambridge, MA: MIT Press, 1989.

Browning, Edgar and Jacqueline Browning. *Public Finance and the Price System*. New York: Macmillan, 3rd ed. 1987.

Ehrenberg, Ronald and Robert Smith. *Modern Labor Economics*. Boston: Addison-Wesley, 7th ed. 2000.

Garis, Dalton. 'Human Capital: An Analysis of the Intergenerational Investment Decision'. Ph.D. dissertation. University of Florida, 1996.

Henderson, James and Richard Quandt. *Microeconomic Theory: A Mathematical Approach*. New York: McGraw-Hill, 3rd ed. 1980.

Kaufman, Bruce and Julie Hotchkiss. *The Economics of Labor Markets*. Mason, OH: Thomson South-Western, 6th ed. 2003.

Krugman, Paul and Maurice Obstfeld. *International Economics: Theory and Policy*. Boston: Addison-Wesley, 5th ed. 2000.

Mishkin, Frederick. *The Economics of Money, Banking and Financial Markets*. Boston: Addison-Wesley, 6th ed. 2001.

Rosen, Harvey. *Public Finance*. New York: Irwin/McGraw-Hill, 5th ed. 1999.

Stiglitz, Joseph. *Economics of the Public Sector*. New York: W. W. Norton, 3rd ed. 2000.

Varian, Hal. *Macroeconomic Analysis*. Ann Arbor, MI: University of Michigan Press, 3rd ed. 1992.

Theoretical and General Economics

Eatwell, John, Murray Milgate and Peter Newman (eds.). *The New Palgrave: The World of Economics*. New York: W. W. Norton, and Basingstoke, Hants.: Macmillan Press, 1991.

Galbraith, John Kenneth. *The Affluent Society*. Boston: Houghton Mifflin, 1958.

— *Economics and the Public Purpose*. Boston: Houghton Mifflin, 1973.

— *The Great Crash, 1929*. Boston: Houghton Mifflin, 1954.

— *The New Industrial State*. Boston: Houghton Mifflin, 1967.

Hausman, Daniel (ed.). *The Philosophy of Economics: An Anthology*. Cambridge: Cambridge University Press, 2nd ed. 1994.

Heilbroner, Robert. *The Crisis of Vision in Modern Economic Thought*. Cambridge: Cambridge University Press, 1995.

— *Teachings from the Worldly Philosophers*. New York: W. W. Norton, 1996.

— *The Worldly Philosophers: The Lives, Times and Ideas of the Great Economic Thinkers*. New York: Simon and Schuster, 1953.

Hodgson, Geoffrey. *Economics and Utopia: Why the Learning Economy is Not the End of History*. New York: Routledge, 1999.

Keynes, John Maynard. *The General Theory of Employment, Interest and Money*. San Diego, CA: Harcourt Brace & Co., 1936.

Mandelbrot, Benoît and Richard L. Hudson. *The (Mis)Behavior of Markets: A Fractal View of Risk, Ruin, and Reward*. New York: Basic Books, 2004.

Marx, Karl. *Capital* (*Das Kapital*). Ed. Frederick Engels. Chicago: Charles Kerr & Co., 1906 (English edition) and New York: Modern Library.

Mill, John Stuart. *Principles of Political Economy*. London: Longmans, Green & Co., 1929.

Smith, Adam. *The Wealth of Nations* (*An Inquiry into the Nature and Causes of the Wealth of Nations*). New York: Modern Library, 1937.

Thurow, Lester. *Head to Head: The Coming Economic Battle Among Japan, Europe and America*. New York: Morrow/Avon, 1992.

Industrial and Labour Relations

Gordon, David. *Fat and Mean: The Corporate Squeeze of Working Americans and the Myth of Managerial 'Downsizing'*. New York: Martin Kessler Books, The Free Press, 1996.

La Boz, Dan. *Rank and File Rebellion: Teamsters for a Democratic Union*. London: Verso, 1990.

Moody, Kim. *Workers in a Lean World: Unions in the International Economy*. London: Verso, 1997.

Murray, R. Emmett. *The Lexicon of Labor*. New York: The New Press, 1998.

Yates, Michael. *Why Unions Matter*. New York: Monthly Review Press, 1998.

The Philosophy of Science

Concise Routledge Encyclopedia of Philosophy. New York: Routledge, 2000.

Kuhn, Thomas. *The Structure of Scientific Revolutions*. Chicago: University of Chicago Press, 1962; 3rd ed. 1996.

Popper, Karl. *The Poverty of Historicism*. New York: Harper Torchbooks, 1961.

Social Criticism, Political, Demographic and Economic Histories and Analysis

Abrahamian, Ervand. *Khomeinism: Essays on the Islamic Republic*. London: I. B. Tauris & Co., 1993.

Ayittey, George. *Africa in Chaos*. New York: St Martin's Press, 1998.

Besançon, Alain. *The Rise of the Gulag: Intellectual Roots of Leninism*. New York: Continuum, 1981.

Goldman, Marshall. *The Piratization of Russia: Russian Reformation Goes Awry*. New York: Routledge, 2003.

Greider, William. *Secrets of the Temple: How the Federal Reserve Runs the Country*. New York: Touchstone Books, 1987.

Heller, Michael and Aleksandr Neckrich. *Utopia in Power: The History of the Soviet Union from 1917 to the Present*. New York: Summit Books, 1986.

Kennedy, David. *Freedom From Fear: The American People in Depression and War, 1929–1945*. Oxford: Oxford University Press, 1999.

Kids Count Data Book: http://www.aecf.org/kidscount/ (accessed 22 February 2007).

Marx, Karl and Frederick Engels. *The Communist Manifesto*, 1848 (many modern editions).

Murray, Charles. *Losing Ground: American Social Policy, 1950–1980*. New York: Basic Books, 1984.

O'Brien, P. J. *Forward With Roosevelt*. Philadelphia, PA: John C. Winston & Co., 1936.

Postman, Neil. *Amusing Ourselves to Death: Public Discourse in the Age of Show Business*. New York: Viking Penguin, 1985.

Schirmacher, Wolfgang (ed.). *German Essays on Science in the 20th Century*. New York: Continuum, 1996.

Schumpeter, Joseph. *History of Economic Analysis*. Oxford: Oxford University Press, 1954.

Soros, George. *On Globalization*. New York: Public Affairs, 2002.

Stiglitz, Joseph. *Globalization and its Discontents*. New York: W. W. Norton, 2002.

Religious and Spiritual Texts

'Abdu'l-Bahá. *The Promulgation of Universal Peace*. Wilmette, IL: Bahá'í Publishing Trust, 1982.

— *The Secret of Divine Civilization*. Wilmette, IL: Bahá'í Publishing Trust, 1990.

— *Selections from the Writings of 'Abdu'l-Bahá*. Haifa: Bahá'í World Centre, 1978.

Abu'l-Faḍl, Mírzá. *The Bahá'í Proofs*. (Facsimile of the 1929 edition). Wilmette, IL: Bahá'í Publishing Trust, 1983.

The Báb ('Alí-Muḥammad al Báb). *Selections from the Writings of the Báb*. Haifa: Bahá'í World Centre, 1976.

Bahá'í World Faith. Wilmette, IL: Bahá'í Publishing Trust, 2nd ed. 1976.

Bahá'u'lláh (Mírzá Ḥusayn 'Alí). *Gleanings from the Writings of Bahá'u'lláh*. Wilmette, IL: Bahá'í Publishing Trust, 1983.

— *The Hidden Words*. Wilmette, IL: Bahá'í Publishing Trust, 1990.

— *The Kitáb-i-Aqdas*. Haifa: Bahá'í World Centre, 1992.

— *Kitáb-i-Íqán*. Wilmette, IL: Bahá'í Publishing Trust, 1989.

— *Tablets of Bahá'u'lláh*. Wilmette, IL: Bahá'í Publishing Trust, 1988.

Chapra, M. Umer. *Islam and the Economic Challenge*. Leicester: Islamic Foundation, 1992.

— *Towards a Just Monetary System*. Leicester: Islamic Foundation., 1985.

The Holy Bible (King James Version). New York: National Bible Press, 1944.

Lights of Guidance: A Bahá'í Reference File. Compiled by Helen Hornby. New Delhi: Bahá'í Publishing Trust, 5th ed. 1997.

The Noble Qur'án in the English Language. Trans. Dr Muhammed Taqi-ud-Din and Dr Muhammad Mushin Khan. Dar us Salaam: Alharamain Islamic Foundation, 1996.

Principles of Bahá'í Administration. London: Bahá'í Publishing Trust, 1976.

Shoghi Effendi. *The Advent of Divine Justice*. Wilmette, IL: Bahá'í Publishing Trust, 1990.

— *Guidance for Today and Tomorrow*. London: Bahá'í Publishing Trust, 1953.

— *Messages to the Bahá'í World*. Wilmette, IL: Bahá'í Publishing Trust, 1971.

— *The Promised Day is Come*. Wilmette, IL: Bahá'í Publishing Trust, rev. ed. 1980.

— *The World Order of Bahá'u'lláh*. Wilmette, IL: Bahá'í Publishing Trust, 1991.

Miscellaneous Topics

Appleman, Philip (ed.) *Darwin: Texts, Backgrounds, Contemporary Opinion, Critical Essays*. New York: W. W. Norton, 2nd ed. 1979.

Caro, Robert. *The Power Broker: Robert Moses and the Fall of New York*. New York: Vintage Books, 1974.

Chayefsky, Paddy. *Network*. 1976.

Dostoyevsky, Fyodor. *The Brothers Karamazov*. New York: Random House, 1950.

Gladwell, Malcolm. *The Tipping Point: How Little Things Make a Big Difference*. Boston: Little, Brown & Co., 2000.

Hobbes, Thomas. *Leviathan*, 1651 (many modern editions).

Jacobs, James, with Coleen Friel and Robert Radick. *Gotham Unbound: How New York City was Liberated from the Grip of Organized Crime*. New York: New York University Press, 1999.

Kahan, Stuart. *The Wolf of the Kremlin: The First Biography of L. M. Kaganovich, The Soviet Union's Architect of Fear*. New York: William Morrow & Co., 1987.

Kelling, George and Catherine Coles. *Fixing Broken Windows: Restoring Order and Reducing Crime in our Communities*. New York: Touchstone Books, 1996.

Koestler, Arthur. *Darkness at Noon*. New York: Macmillan, 1941.

Medvedev, Zhores. *The Rise and Fall of T. D. Lysenko*. New York: Columbia University Press, 1970.

Schulberg, Budd. *What Makes Sammy Run?* New York: Random House, 1941.

Steinbeck, John. *The Grapes of Wrath*. New York: Viking Press, 1939.

Stroheimer, John and Peter Westbrook. *Divine Harmony: The Life and Teachings of Pythagoras*. Albany, CA: Berkeley Hills Books, 1999.

Velikovsky, Immanual. *Ages In Chaos, Volume I: A Reconstruction of Ancient History from Exodus to Akhnaton*. New York: Doubleday, 1952.

Journals and Periodicals

Aghion, Phillipe, Eva Caroli and Cecilia Garcia-Penalosa. 'Inequality and Economic Growth: The Perspective of the New Growth Theories'. *Journal of Economic Literature*, December 1999.

Altig, David and Charles Carlstrom. 'Marginal Tax Rates and Income Inequality in a Life-Cycle Model.' *American Economic Review*, vol. 89, no. 5, December 1999, pp. 1197–1215.

Becker, Elizabeth. 'The New Villain in Free Trade: The Farmer on the Dole'. *The New York Times*, 25 August 2002.

Becker, Gary. 'Crime and Punishment: An Economic Approach'. *Journal of Political Economy*, vol. 76, no. 2, 1968, pp. 169–217.

Benabou, Roland. 'Unequal Societies: Income Distribution and the Social Contract'. *American Economic Review*, March 2000.

'Canada's Healthcare Set to Remain in Public's Hands'. *The Financial Times*, 5 December 2002.

Cassidy, John. 'The Decline of Economics: John Maynard Keynes was one of the most revered men of his time. Fifty years after his death, where are his successors?' *The New Yorker*, 2 December 1996.

— 'The Greed Cycle: How the financial system encouraged corporations to go crazy'. *The New Yorker*, 23 September 2002.

Cheng, Ian. 'Barons of Bankruptcy, Part I: Survivors who laughed all the way to the bank'. *The Financial Times*, 31 July 2002.

Collier, Paul and Jan Willem Gunning. 'Why Has Africa Grown So Slowly?' *Journal of Economic Perspectives*, Summer 1999.

Crews, Frederick. 'Saving Us from Darwin'. *The New York Review of Books*, 4 October 2001.

Diamond, Jared. 'Darwin's Cathedral: Evolution, Religion, and the Nature of Society'. *The New York Review of Books*, 7 November 2002.

Elwood, David. 'Anti-Poverty Policy for Families in the Next Century: From Welfare to Work and Worries'. *Journal of Economic Perspectives*, Winter 2000.

Epstein, Helen. 'Time of Indifference'. *The New York Review of Books*, 12 April 2001.

'Face Value: How to Pay Bosses. Michael Jensen still thinks he has the answer'. *The Economist*, 16 November 2002.

Flannery, Tim. 'A New Darwinism?' *The New York Review of Books*, 23 May 2002.

Franklin, Benjamin: http://fierce.jnfr.com/archives/2006/01/a_republic_mada.html (accessed 5 February 2007).

Garis, Dalton. 'A Fertile Subject', in 'Letters', *The Economist*, 7 September 2002.

— 'Poverty, Single Parent Households and Youth At-Risk Behavior: An Empirical Study'. *Journal of Economic Issues*, December 1998.

Gladwell, Malcolm. 'The Televisionary: Big business and the myth of the lone inventor'. *The New Yorker*, 27 May 2002.

— 'The Tipping Point: Why is the city so much safer? Could it be that crime really is an epidemic?' *The New Yorker*, 3 June 1996.

Granger, Clive. 'Investigating causal relations by economic models and cross-spectral methods'. *Econometrica*, vol. 37, no. 3, July 1969, pp. 424–38.

Hardin, Garrett. 'The Tragedy of the Commons'. *Science*, vol. 162, 1968, pp. 1243–8.

Ibsen, David. 'It's a banking business, but not as the Japanese know it'. *The Financial Times*, 5 August 2002.

Jennings, Kate. 'The Hypocrisy of Wall Street Culture'. *The New York Times*, 14 July 2002.

Kangas, Olli. 'Self-Interest and the Common Good: The Impact of Norms, Selfishness and Context in Social Policy Options'. *Journal of Socio-Economics*, vol. 26, no. 5, 1997.

Krueger, Anne. 'Are Preferential Trading Arrangements Trade-Liberalizing or Protectionist?' *Journal of Economic Perspectives*, Fall 1999.

Krugman, Paul. 'The End of Middle Class America (and the Triumph of the Plutocrats)'. *The New York Times Magazine*, 20 October 2002.

Lee, Eddy. 'Globalization and Labour Standards: A Review of the Issues'. *International Labour Review*, Summer 1997.

Lewonton, Richard. 'The Politics of Science'. *The New York Review of Books*, 9 May 2002.

Massing, Michael. 'The End of Welfare?' *The New York Review of Books*, 7 October 1999.

Myrdal, Gunnar. 'How Scientific are the Social Sciences?' *Bulletin of the Atomic Scientists*, January 1973.

Ndulu, Benno and Stephan O'Connell. 'Governance and Growth in Sub-Saharan Africa'. *Journal of Economic Perspectives*, Summer 1999.

Rohatyn, Felix. 'The Betrayal of Capitalism'. *The New York Review of Books*, 28 February 2002.

Ryan, Alan. 'Schools: The Price of "Progress"'. *The New York Review of Books*, 22 February 2001.

Schumpeter, Joseph A. 'Science and Ideology'. *The American Economic Review*, vol. 39, no. 2, March 1949, pp. 345–59.

Soros, George. 'Who Lost Russia?' *The New York Review of Books*, 13 April 2000.

'A Tale of Two Bellies'. *The Economist*, 24 August 2002.

Traub, James. 'Common Talk: In Enron-ized America, why is populism such a dirty word?' *New York Times Sunday Magazine*, 13 October 2002.

'What Ails Japan: A Survey of Japan'. *The Economist*, 20 April 2002.

'The Wickedness of Wall Street'. *The Economist*, 8 June 2002.

Notes and References

Introduction

1. All Qur'ánic references are from *The Noble Qur'án* unless otherwise noted.
2. 'Abdu'l-Bahá, *Promulgation*, p. 455.
3. Qur'án 43:51–4.
4. Qur'án 34:34.
5. Bahá'u'lláh, *Kitáb-i-Íqán*, p. 125.
6. By prediction is not meant prophecy. A prediction can be based on analysing present conditions and projecting that, if the trend is not altered, certain results will assuredly be forthcoming. A prophecy, however, is a pronouncement concerning the nature of distantly future events or conditions based on transcendental spiritual awareness or direct revelation and is not obtainable from critical analysis of present conditions.
7. Qur'án 17:23.
8. Qur'án 51:47.
9. Qur'án 50:15.
10. Qur'án 44:36.
11. Qur'án 25:7.
12. Qur'án 2:81.
13. Qur'án 22:7.
14. Qur'án 39:68–9.
15. Qur'án 14:48.
16. Qur'án 40:34.
17. Qur'án 26:5.
18. Qur'án 10:74.
19. Qur'án 34:43.
20. Bahá'u'lláh, *Kitáb-i-Íqán*, p. 26.
21. Qur'án 17:51.
22. Qur'án 41:53.
23. Qur'án 51:52.
24. Qur'án 46:7.
25. Qur'án 42:24.
26. Qur'án 28:48–9.
27. Granger, 'Investigating causal relations'.
28. Qur'án 14:28.
29. Besançon, *Rise of the Gulag*.
30. Heller and Nekrich, *Utopia in Power*.

31. Kahan, *Wolf of the Kremlin.*
32. Besançon, *Rise of the Gulag*, p. 209.
33. ibid. p. 281.
34. ibid. p. 282.
35. Qur'án 34:49.
36. Dostoyevsky, *Brothers Karamazov*, pp. 305–9. Emphasis in original translation.
37. Qur'án 2:256.
38. Qur'án 23:52.
39. Qur'án 36:38.
40. Qur'án 2:101.
41. Qur'án 2:85.
42. Qur'án 2:285.
43. Qur'án 2:91.
44. Qur'án 23:71.
45. Qur'án 23:52–3.
46. Qur'án 7:101.
47. Qur'án 2:170.
48. Qur'án 7:35.
49. Qur'án 18:55–6.
50. Qur'án 33:62.
51. Qur'án 2:106.
52. Qur'án 42:13.
53. Qur'án 34:49.
54. Qur'án 2:1–2.
55. Qur'án 36:12.
56. Bearing in mind the sequence of time, 'recent' Islam corresponds in this characterization to what obtained under middle Christianity and middle Judaism with respect to the loss of temporal influence and intellectual leadership.
57. Qur'án 25:30.
58. Qur'án 8:53.
59. Qur'án 13:41.
60. Qur'án 3:86.
61. Qur'án 13:41.
62. Qur'án 10:49.

Chapter 1

1. Some new mathematical and scientific techniques can be of help here. Chaos theory says, among other things, that what exists is the result of all things preceding it. Nothing – however trivial – can be ruled out as having had an effect on the present situation and condition. While these elements can never be truly catalogued and their effects measured, the result that all of it matters coincides with the Prophets' assertion that all things, however miniscule, are noted down in a book and that nothing is ever lost; hence, conservation of actions and their traces in both worlds.
2. Qur'án 46:7.
3. Kuhn, *Structure of Scientific Revolutions.*

4. In fact, the modern calculus textbook, laying out what a one and two semester university course should cover, first appeared with a book by Angus Taylor in the early decades of the 20th century. But this lack did not stop early scientists and mathematical practitioners from accessing whatever they needed of calculus techniques for various scientific applications.

Chapter 3

1. Blake, 'Proverbs of Hell', in *Marriage of Heaven and Hell*, p. 252.
2. Hardin, 'The Tragedy of the Commons'. *Science* 13 December 1968, vol. 162, no. 3859, pp. 1243–8.
3. Bahá'u'lláh, *Gleanings*, p. 328.
4. Qur'án 29:64.
5. Qur'án 29:57.
6. Qur'án 4:78.
7. Bahá'u'lláh, *Kitáb-i-Íqán*, p. 194.
8. Qur'án 4:77.
9. For a complete discussion of this topic and its extensive use in economics, see Blanchard and Fischer, *Lectures on Macroeconomics*, ch. 2, p. 39.
10. 'Abdu'l-Bahá, *Secret*, p. 96.
11. Qur'án 4:128.

Chapter 4

1. Another possibility is that it is genuine and not stolen but the person selling it is not in his right mind or needs the money in a hurry. But be careful!
2. Formally, exploitation is when a resource is paid less than its marginal benefit to the enterprise where employed. This resource could be anything from labour to lumps of sugar and includes returns to management as well as to any other input. A firm employs an amount of a resource until its marginal cost just equals its marginal benefit in use. This is the basic saddlepoint solution for the theory of the firm. In an exchange, exploitation is when a good returns less than its value in trade, based on the equalization of its value in production and its value in consumption; again, the saddlepoint solution.
3. This is not a defence of current medical market practices in the United States, as shown below.
4. In fairness, the Nobel prize was granted for their surpassing contributions to the science and to our understanding of the world. As individuals they may hold whatever views they please, of course. And being capable and forceful writers in their languages, they will convince many of the goodness of their viewpoint whether scientifically validated or not.
5. There is, of course, a 'market' for laws, just as for everything else. But the medium of exchange is not just money but political power and votes. Within the government monopoly of the United States a great deal of market trading take place, since money is essential for election campaigns, but most of this is the subject for another book. We will investigate the nature of this market in some detail here, however.

6. The Most Great Public Good is arguably the revelatory dialogues of the historical religious Prophets.
7. In fact, the complete lack of evidence disputing this result provides some proof of the assertion that all exchanges require exogenous regulating for optimal outcomes to be realized. It is spurious to maintain that since both parties agreed to the exchange, therefore mutual benefits were achieved and the exchange was successful. The very nature of exploitation means that possible coercion or fraud exists. It would then not be considered an 'open-eyed' exchange and would not fit the definition of a freely entered exchange.
8. Does this suggest a possible motive for certain terrorist acts? By enlarging transactions to include such things the weak party attempts to nullify institutionally concentrated power. This has been the case since before Goths invaded Rome. (Here we do not refer to ideological terrorism having as its goal little beyond pathological destructiveness.)

   The negative results for weak traders in this event are exacerbated further if the people cannot freely choose their trade representatives and there is enough of a benefit accruing to the weak side to make the trade representatives themselves quite wealthy. They may act to 'sell out' the common interests of their side if a sufficiently large payment can be made to them as an inducement to do so or where the trade benefits will in any case be seized and controlled by them. This is the case with many sub-Saharan African governments, for example, where countries having fabulous natural wealth, such as Angola or Nigeria, also have the highest rates of poverty on earth, while their leaders, dos Santos and Obasanjo respectively, are numbered among the richest persons on earth.

   In fairness, economics characterizes such situations as 'inefficient' or as 'market failures' needing third party intervention and adjudication.
9. The law of demand states that, all things being equal (no changes in income, tastes and preferences, prices of other goods, number of demanders or expectations), where the unit price of a normal good rises the quantity of units purchased will decline.
10. But not always. If the good is a necessity then the per cent change in the quantity purchased will be less than the per cent change in its price (price inelastic in demand). Suppliers of these goods experience a rise in revenues for a rise in price within a broad range. This is also why necessities are usually heavily taxed, e.g. petrol, tobacco products and liquor (for those using tobacco or alcoholic beverages on a regular basis). Such items are also slow to see price declines, e.g. fluid milk or residential rents. Other goods that are *non-necessities* show the opposite tendency: the per cent change in the quantity purchased is greater than the per cent change in the price (price elastic in demand). For these goods supplier revenues increase when the price is reduced. Examples are consumer electronics and soft drinks.
11. Are decisions always made 'at the margin'? Let's hope not. The distinction between wisdom and foolishness is precisely the ability to discriminate between what has a large positive total value in utility but a small or even negative marginal value, and what has negative total utility but a high mar-

ginal utility. The fool uses dangerously addictive drugs since their marginal utility is extremely high but the wise avoids them because their absolute and total utility is negative.

12. Problems arose, however, when scientists attempted to assign motive to what they observed, such as that markets functioned efficiently when each person did nothing more than follow his own personal interests, then generalized this assertion to say that 'greed is good' or whatever. Classical economics was very much the nexus of philosophy and science. Considering its newness and the inchoate theories it still throws up for analysis, it is too soon for cutting off philosophical and metaphysical links until its own identity and character are more developed. Perhaps in a few centuries its position among the sciences and its relationship to existing philosophies will no longer be in such fundamental doubt but presently economics has not reached that stage.
13. Another problem with the rigid egalitarian pay system of the soviet model was that extra effort was rarely rewarded and could even get you arrested if it raised the jealousy and ire of other workers who would then work to have you eliminated.
14. This logically forces the conclusion that time series analysis, which generally outperforms structural econometric model predictions and forecasts, is grounded in theory, that macroeconomic processes are random.

Chapter 5

1. Economics today seems to be experiencing something of an upheaval in its theoretical modelling. For years it has been under the sway of an influential but ultimately misleading modelling formula in which assumptions matter little but the ability of the model to narrowly predict behaviour matters a lot. A model would correctly predict behaviour *as if* actors were fully cognizant of certain economic or financial verities, when in fact this cognizance was never proved. Over time, the ability of a model to correctly predict results in this way was construed as affirming the truth of the model's assumptions, which is fallacious and illogical. Now this methodology is being questioned as some of its resulting assertions appear ever more ridiculous and absurd. The trap of a model's predictive ability thereby validating its assumptions is being recognized.
2. Some results will be thrown out, of course, if they do not hold up under scrutiny using the improved tools of analysis and some of those overturned results are quite well known and underpin important social policies.
3. Hobbes, *Leviathan.*
4. See http://fierce.jnfr.com/archives/2006/01/a_republic_mada.html
5. This section is ordinarily treated in advanced economics and decision theory textbooks under the heading 'preference theory'. It is included here because it underpins later assertions and because it completes the picture of economics as analysing how transactions are made and how societies maintain themselves over time.
6. In Bahá'u'lláh's writings we read that among the things investing a message

with authority is the purity of motive and spirituality of the one delivering the message. For a message to be transcendentally powerful it must therefore have been delivered by a soul more pure and detached than that of ordinary people. This fact rules out a good message being delivered by a bad person or a bad message being delivered by a good person and severely limits the circle of those capable of delivering a truly transcendental message. It would seem that only those chosen or otherwise specialized in some way unimaginable to most of us would qualify for the task.

7. 'Abdu'l-Bahá, *Promulgation*, p. 83.
8. John 3:6.
9. Bahá'u'lláh, *Hidden Words*, Persian no. 10.
10. Apparently love alone is capable of uniting both worlds. But it is obvious that our current understanding of this force is incapable of analysing this possibility.
11. 'Abdu'l-Bahá, *Selections*, pp. 193–4.
12. 'Abdu'l-Bahá, *Secret*, p. 96.
13. In continuous form it would be the sum of two integrals, the inside one limited by birth and death and the outside one from death to infinity. This different form allows consideration of the suggested transversality condition where infinity is a limit of the integration.
14. This is from Lazar Moiseyevich Kaganovich, as quoted by his nephew, Stuart Kahan, in his biography of his uncle, *The Wolf of the Kremlin*.
15. We can certainly understand how people would object to these sentiments and would be revolted by the complicity of any section of religion with them. We can also understand how some people would declare that it is time for man to play God, that if God decrees the systematic suffering of children and the poor on the very doorsteps of the rich then it is high time that the earth be seized by man and in the name of man and that God's throne upon it be demolished. *The Communist Manifesto* by Karl Marx and Frederick Engels attempted to do just that.
16. Schumpeter. 'Science and Ideology'.
17. ibid.

Chapter 6

1. See a letter written on behalf of Shoghi Effendi to an individual, 10 June 1930, in *Lights*, pp. 548–9, no. 1862.
2. 'Abdu'l-Bahá, *Selections*, p. 135.
3. ibid. p. 140.
4. 'Abdu'l-Bahá, in *Bahá'í World Faith*, p. 377.
5. ibid. p. 375.
6. Bahá'u'lláh, *Kitáb-i-Íqán*, pp. 144–5.
7. 'Abdu'l-Bahá, *Selections*, p. 68.
8. ibid. p. 67.
9. This is not to say that God's purpose can ever be thwarted by anything we might do but our deeds can certainly delay the coming of His law into our lives and there are alternative scenarios for us. 'Now that ye have refused

the Most Great Peace, hold ye fast unto this, the Lesser Peace, that haply ye may in some degree better your own condition and that of your dependents,' Bahá'u'lláh states (*Gleanings*, p. 254), indicating that different endings are the result of different actions. If this were not so volition would have no value as all things would be entirely predetermined and the burdens of life would be Sisyphusian.

10. Bahá'u'lláh, *Kitáb-i-Aqdas*, paras. 124–5. It is inescapably clear from these words that the standard of government for this day is paternalism. Individual licentiousness, the goal of market consumerism and libertarianism celebrated in the United States, is strictly proscribed.
11. 'Abdu'l-Bahá, *Secret*, p. 96.
12. Kelling and Coles, *Fixing Broken Windows.*
13. See Gladwell, 'Tipping Point'. He argues that the reason is simpler but less obvious; that crime acts like disease where small changes can act to suddenly increase it like an epidemic or cause it to collapse like a depensating population of whales. The reasons are not mutually exclusive. Community policing as envisioned and practised by Commissioner Bratton was the *cause* of the steep crime reduction experience and the tipping point/contagion process gave it its essential acceleration.
14. This is not an apology for unions, as none is needed. Unions populate economic space along with other organizations such as cooperatives, corporations, sheltered workshops and multinational companies. As to the use of strikes for achieving their ends, note that 'Abdu'l-Bahá states that a war can be the source of good if waged for a righteous purpose ('Abdu'l-Bahá, *Secret*, pp. 70–1). If this can be true for such a great evil, then it must also be true for the far lesser evil and injury to the fabric of society caused by a work strike by labourers in an attempt to receive fair compensation for their toil. Can strikes be exploited to demand more than a fair share for labour to the injury of the public good? Certainly, just as powerful business interests can and do influence the passage of legislation favourable to themselves and injurious to the public good. At least in the United States, exploitation by labour is practically non-existent today. The obscene growth in executive compensation over the last 15 years and the fall in real wages earned by their labouring counterparts is a matter of record and beyond dispute (see Gordon, *Fat and Mean*). In many parts of the world corrupt businesses and their bought-and-paid-for governments oppress workers atrociously. Until the right of labourers to receive just compensation and a share of enterprise profits is admitted, it is wholly disingenuous and hypocritical to disparage union attempts to better the lot of workers while refusing to acknowledge the presence of worker exploitation warranting such activity.
15. In the whole story of union corruption in a longshoreman's union (ILA or ILWU) in the movie *On the Waterfront* (Elia Kazan, director, with Marlon Brando, Eva Marie-Saint, Karl Malden, Rod Steiger and Lee J. Cobb), I do not recall a single scene that shows any police presence. But that's Hollywood!
16. See La Botz, *Rank and File Rebellion.*
17. 'Abdu'l-Bahá, *Selections*, p. 137.

18. Qur'án 4:128.
19. See Garis, *Human Capital*, ch. 2, 'Investing in the Future'.
20. ibid.
21. For a picture of the degradation of United States's public schools see Murray, *Losing Ground: American Social Policy, 1950–1980*.
22. 'Abdu'l-Bahá, *Selections*, p. 98.
23. Bahá'u'lláh, *Hidden Words*, Arabic no. 31.
24. Bahá'u'lláh, 'Words of Wisdom', *Tablets*, p. 156.
25. Bahá'u'lláh, *Hidden Words*, Persian no. 19.
26. Qur'án 4:32.
27. Qur'án 4:77.
28. Bahá'u'lláh, *Hidden Words*, Persian no. 39.
29. ibid. Arabic no. 56.
30. Qur'án 2:254.

Chapter 7

1. Perhaps this gives us some additional insight into understanding what is meant when Bahá'u'lláh relates the episode of the clergy in Iraq demanding that He work a miracle. '"Choose any matter ye desire, and ask your Lord, the God of Mercy, to reveal it unto you. If He fulfil your wish, by virtue of His sovereignty, believe ye then in Him, and be not of those that reject His truth." . . . He arose and returned unto them that sent him, *at the bidding of God*, the All-Glorious, the Well-Beloved' (Bahá'u'lláh, *Gleanings*, p. 132). The italics are mine, to emphasize this relationship between the Creator of laws and their intrinsic operational capacity.
2. Mark, 10:18.
3. If imagining an independent Being is hard, no problem: just imagine whatever it is that that Being relies upon. Repeat until you give up and can say, 'Fine; so it's out there somewhere and I can't chase it down.' You have reached the acme of true understanding.
4. It also means that it can be depreciated using commonly accepted accounting practices.
5. This gives us an obvious way to judge the efficacy of all activities. The result, based on what we have learned about pricing, is an increased awareness of how much some things should be compensated if their only value is entertainment. It doesn't make us exactly ready to determine if the contract for some baseball player paying him $250 million over ten years is excessive or likewise a contract paying a movie actor $25 million a movie but it at least allows us to order such decisions as 'better' or 'worse'.
6. Of course, this scoring is not on display very often. Rather, economics discusses steady prices, rising GDP, labour efficiency, etc. That is because, for some economists, these metrics are as close as we can come to measuring anything like benefit to mankind.
7. In the United States land held in common was not recognized as having the same right of protection as land privately owned. Therefore the clearing of

vast tracts of 'Indian land' of Native Americans for use by the new Europeans in the 18th and 19th centuries in North America was not legally troubling. Treaties would be formed then broken with a probability approaching one. The American emphasis on private property as the basis of legal recognition was received from European jurisprudence that had developed since the Middle Ages and before.

8. 'Abdu'l-Bahá, *Secret*, p. 72.
9. In fairness, the possibility that compensation could be reversed to block a project must have been considered because there is a symmetry here, called 'path independence', meaning that things could work in reverse. In contrast, path dependent moves are harder to reverse as their solutions tend to be unique.
10. Business and economics have a theory–application relationship, similar to physics and engineering. The goal of business is to create wealth or make a profit while the goal of economics is that of a pure science, that is, to explain the world in its own terms. In fact, some economists are not even sure that only profit maximizing companies survive and that those that do not maximize profit always disappear. That is, some companies might win by maximizing market share rather than profit or may have other types of maximizing behaviour. Nonetheless, over time only companies that can make a profit will survive. A model looking at survival rates for all businesses over a ten year period might find a lot of profit maximizers being rubbed out and a lot of companies less dedicated to the bottom line surviving. Luck and consumer sentiment have a lot to do with business success. In bad times even the smartest often lose and in good times companies whose spending patterns are lavish may do well. Would a model of businesses treating their ten year survival rates as random provide significantly different results?
11. 'Abdu'l-Bahá, in *Bahá'í World Faith*, p. 384.
12. See Galbraith, *Economics and the Public Purpose* and *The New Industrial State*.

Chapter 8

1. Matt. 6:21.
2. 'Abdu'l-Bahá, *Secret*, pp. 96–7.
3. ibid. p. 98.
4. ibid. pp. 97–8.
5. See Murray, *Losing Ground: American Social Policy 1950–1980*.
6. For a couple in America in 2002 with no children, the family earning income cut-off level to be eligible to receive benefits was $945 a month, while in New York City a typical one-bedroom apartment rented for $1,600 a month and a studio apartment was $985 to $1,185 a month.
7. Let us not forget that the reason most people are on welfare is because of a combination of economic non-viability with dependent individuals to support. If these dependent individuals are children from a dissolved marriage or have a widowed parent, then this regrettable circumstance is mostly unavoidable. But if they are the result of careless sexual activity and the sole parent is

the 'natural' parent, then this situation certainly could have been avoided with institutional intervention, e.g. family, religious structure, education, etc. If this situation is the result of a married couple having more children than they can afford to raise on their own, then again, social institutions could intervene to mitigate. In the United States the single greatest cohort on welfare is mothers who have never married with young children. Such mothers are often very young themselves and possess virtually no economic, social, cultural or formalized intellectual capital to invest in their children. The second largest cohort is divorced women with young children. Having children, therefore, absolutely increases the chances of poverty. Presently the largest cohort of the population in official poverty are children. See Garis, 'Poverty, Single Parent Households and Youth At-Risk Behavior: An Empirical Study', *Journal of Economic Issues*, December 1998.

8. The effects of incentives are not always easy to follow and their results are not always obvious. Poverty would seem to induce persons to have fewer children since little is available for their support. The opposite is true, however. With respect to uncertain economic and financial conditions leading to increased fertility rates, see Garis, 'A Fertile Subject'.
9. Matt. 6:21.
10. Bahá'u'lláh, *Gleanings*, pp. 8–9.
11. Bahá'u'lláh, *Kitáb-i-Íqán*, pp. 3–4.
12. Qur'án 2:106.
13. Qur'án 23:62.
14. The emotional content of divinity is not lessened by this and Bahá'u'lláh makes many statements where He warns various miscreants that God is angry with them. ' . . . yet the rod with which I can chastise the wicked is grievous, and the fierceness of Mine anger against them terrible' (Bahá'u'lláh, *Gleanings*, p. 325).
15. Here also, however, it might be that this was latently available to us from earlier prophetic dialogues. For example, Muhammad revealed this: 'Or think you that you will enter Paradise without such trials as came to those who passed away before you? They were afflicted with severe poverty and ailments and were so shaken that even the Prophet and those who believed along with Him said, "When will come the help of God?" Yes, certainly, the help of God is nigh!" (2:214). This suggests that the difficulties of life *are* the help of God, in that these purge us from those things that would hinder our entrance into Paradise and develop in us those abilities required for a successful life in the next plane of existence.
16. Bahá'u'lláh, *Kitáb-i-Íqán*, p. 192.
17. ibid. p. 211.
18. His fears were well founded, of course. Every Prophet has invariably prophesied the appearance of his own return in the person of another Prophet after the fulfilment of certain signs and historical events. Notwithstanding, each of these Prophets was in turn denied and vilified by the people who had reduced the abstruse and mystical doctrines of these teachers into a narrow set of literal meanings, just as Pythagoras feared would happen to his own multifaceted lectures.

19. Strohmeier and Westbrook, *Divine Harmony.*
20. Let's be clear: More important than just about anything is knowing the general direction of prices and the sentiment of the buying public. It happens very often that a good idea marketed at a good price, where the supplier keeps costs low and otherwise does everything correctly, still can lose if the economy is in a downturn and people concerned with rising unemployment rates are too scared to spend very much. Conversely, certifiably dumb ideas can make their creators rich and generate high returns for years if launched during economic boom times that last for a few years, no matter how ineptly the business is run. Prices tell on which side of the market you should be but they cannot time propitious exits and entrances.
21. Assuming in practical terms, of course, that patronage can be obtained to support it where needed.
22. Another way of thinking about the inability to delay gratification is the network trap. Imagine a situation where you must get from one place to another through a network of city streets. Having made the trip many times before you know that the street directly in front is clear but only until it veers to the left, where traffic becomes congested and you may sit for an hour. Avoiding this costly situation you take another street that begins badly but soon clears up and is fastest overall in getting you to your destination. But today your friend insists on driving and takes what appears to be (but you know is not) the best route, starting with the good-becoming-bad route. This is the network trap and is similar to life in that we must use our earlier years to build for the future (hard-becoming-easy), even while wanting to do nothing beyond having some fun (easy-becoming-hard).
23. By this is primarily meant the extent to which media channels and other communications platforms allow one kind of message rather than another. For example, a town may only have the local public school for meeting places. But laws may proscribe religious discussions, even while allowing commercial activities in public buildings. Or there might be a large volume of brand advertising in the school but no religious advertising would be tolerated. A society might see nothing wrong with commercial advertising campaigns targeting children while other nations might prohibit it.
24. Garis, *Human Capital.*
25. Shoghi Effendi, *Advent*, p. 30.
26. Qur'án 3:185.
27. Qur'án 3:186.
28. Qur'án 11:11.
29. Qur'án 20:131.
30. Qur'án 39:73.
31. Qur'án 41:53.
32. Qur'án 46:20.
33. Mark 10:24–5.
34. Matt. 6:33.
35. Matt. 19:29–30. This does not mean that you should physically abandon children if they depend on you, as is demonstrated by verses elsewhere that say

you should support them and should treat your parents with marked respect and deference.

36. Matt. 25:31–46.
37. Matt. 25:34.
38. The image of fire is interesting for at least two reasons. First, trees yielding actual fruit are cultivated so that their fruit-bearing is increased. Trees no longer yielding fruit are harvested for their fuel value. This is well understood and accessible to most listeners, especially those who until recently had to spend some of each day acquiring fire fuel, often wood. Another interesting thing about this image is in conjuring the flame of remorse. Muhammad explains in one line that hellfire is constructed from regrets. 'And God will show them their deeds as regrets for them. And they will never get out of the fire' (2:167). Such a haunting prospect! Most of us have already, at one time or another, experienced this sensation. Only the continuation of life's demands and daily requirements force movement away from it. But what if that were not possible and there was nothing to offer some distance? Fire, indeed.
39. Qur'án 23:115. The plain logic of this argument has the overall effect of one being swept aside by a large and powerful ocean wave. Even if one feels scepticism for a particular line, after reading the entire discourse, the effect is overwhelming.
40. Bahá'u'lláh, *Gleanings*, p. 226.
41. ibid. p. 171.
42. ibid. p. 329.
43. Qur'án 55:60.
44. Bahá'u'lláh, *Kitáb-i-Íqán*, p. 125.
45. Bahá'u'lláh, *Tablets*, pp. 145–6. As to Socrates, Bahá'u'lláh states in the same Tablet, 'He is the most distinguished of all philosophers and was highly versed in wisdom. We testify that he is one of the heroes in this field and an outstanding champion dedicated unto it (ibid. p. 146).

Chapter 9

1. 'Abdu'l-Bahá, *Selections*, p. 288.
2. Bahá'u'lláh, *Kitáb-i-Íqán*, pp. 194–5.
3. 'Abdu'l-Bahá, *Promulgation*, p. 468.
4. Solving this situation should represent a challenge and an opportunity to economic science. But if judged by the lack of general concern, as measured by the dearth of research papers in the major journals analysing this subject, economics seems strangely indifferent. As stated in an earlier chapter, economics must avoid appearing to advocate any particular point of view ('preaching'), however worthy the cause. The research must be carried out as dispassionately as possible. However, the choice of subjects is governed solely by the tastes and preferences of the scientist. Unfortunately, research is expensive and must be funded somehow. Thus research directed towards purely social and humanitarian issues tends not to be of interest to paying parties.
5. Qur'án 9:34.

6. Bahá'u'lláh, *Hidden Words*, Persian no. 5.
7. Bahá'u'lláh, *Kitáb-i-Íqán*, p. 194.
8. Bahá'u'lláh, *Hidden Words*, Arabic no. 25.
9. 'Abdu'l-Bahá, *Selections*, p. 133.
10. ibid. pp. 140–1.
11. Qur'án 23:7.
12. Qur'án 25:30.
13. Mark 7:9.
14. Qur'án 10:79.
15. Qur'án 5:104.
16. Bahá'u'lláh, *Kitáb-i-Íqán*, pp. 240–2.
17. Qur'án 37:173.
18. That is, people of reprehensible behaviour, great and insignificant, are a common fact of life. These people do not seem to be 'judged' by God, in the sense of being punished for their behaviour in such a way that we could witness it. So the literal meaning of this verse does not conform to reality.
19. Qur'án 6:62, 14:51.
20. Bahá'u'lláh, *Kitáb-i-Aqdas*, para. 64.
21. It is thus sadly apparent the extent to which modern labour and management practices diminish such wealth earning possibilities. By the establishment of standardized jobs scope for personal specialization taking full advantage of individual strengths is lessened since all are expected to do much the same thing. This disadvantages most workers and gives management the ability to influence wages in a way, and to an extent, not otherwise possible.
22. 'Abdu'l-Bahá, *Promulgation*, pp. 216–17.
23. The demise of the American consumer electronics industry and its replacement by mostly Japanese products is an illuminating story involving American corporate misdirection and the rise of Japanese manufacturing based on superior quality control. The quality control in question was developed in 1947 by an American, W. Edwards Demming, who could not interest US manufacturers in the method he had perfected. The Japanese were indeed interested, however, and its application could make a product consistently superior in quality to anyone else's. Combining this with the Toyota Production System and an export-driven national manufacturing policy took Japan from a developing nation to a super-rich nation in just one generation (see Thurow, *Head to Head*).
24. This does not leave aside what happens to all the people – labourers, managers and the retired drawing pensions from the company – who are displaced when their production is no longer wanted. But this is a separate issue requiring societal intervention to assure a smooth transition into new productive areas.
25. Verses in the Qur'án indicate that everything that happens to us, which would include success and failure in business or anything else, is related to some level of divine intervention. His Holiness Muhammad criticizes people who say that bad things are from God but that whatever success they have is due solely to their own actions and has nothing to do with God. This could mean

that everything we do is the result of divine intervention and that therefore talent and ability are not necessary. However, it is more likely to mean that talent is necessary but not sufficient for success and that we are entirely dependent on the sanction and permission of God. This understanding is consistent with prophetic statements made elsewhere, such as Bahá'u'lláh's statement that results depend upon means (Bahá'u'lláh, *Hidden Words*, Persian no. 80). Means become a necessary condition, even if not a sufficient condition, for success.

26. Bahá'u'lláh, *Tablets*, p. 155.
27. Bahá'u'lláh, 'Words of Wisdom', *Tablets*, p. 156. How extraordinarily apt for economic discourse are the words revealed by the Prophets! 'No vision taketh in Him but He taketh in all Vision. He is the subtle, the All-Perceiving' (Qur'án 6:104) and 'Neither is there a thing green nor sere but it is noted in the unerring Book' (Qur'án 6:59).
28. Let us not also forget the working planning horizon for an elected official. His or her professional life falls entirely between elections and the only thing the electorate will see, character issues aside, is what s/he did during those years.
29. 'Abdu'l-Bahá, in Shoghi Effendi, *World Order*, p. 37.
30. One problem in the United States is that the official government policy is, and has always been, to provide 'cheap food'. In this it has been wildly successful. The United States now has the cheapest food in the world, and in the history of the world, as a per capital percentage of expenditures. The citizens of no other nation, now or in recorded history, have paid less, as a percentage of household expenditure, for food than do Americans today. But the cost of this has sometimes meant environment degradation and the food itself has not always been of the highest standard of wholesomeness, flavour, nutrition or quality, especially compared to what might be available in some European nations.
31. This has been called the Coase theorem. It also relies on the absence of transaction costs. But in fairness, pollution rights auctions have been successfully used in cutting overall pollution levels across state boundaries. For example, it is estimated that one old, out-of-tune car is 47 times as polluting as a new car. At least in the short run, it reduces more pollution to buy these cars from users and give them new cars to use, rather than to spend millions trying to squeeze another mile per gallon from the newer car fleet.
32. Bahá'u'lláh, *Kitáb-i-Íqán*, pp. 111–12.

Chapter 10

1. Recall our admonition, made in an earlier chapter, concerning the concept of utility. Worthwhile discussions of utility fall within the extremes of 1) a functional mathematical closed form utility, an absurdity, and 2) something that can explain every action, a useless tautology.
2. Societies have generally decided to support human capital formation by various policies that aid higher education, research and development firms and training institutes. But at least in America educational costs beyond the 12th grade are the responsibility of the individuals desiring education. Since the presence in society of educated and highly trained individuals increases the

economic output, order, tax revenues and public goods and decreases many kinds of crime and many forms of public corruption, it is hard to fathom why America collectively refuses to bear a greater share of the expense and risk burden of higher education purchases. A US citizen, having purchased tens of thousands of dollars of higher education and having graduated with the requisite degree or professional certification, is burdened with this huge personal debt no matter what. This means that volunteer work or poorly paid but needful employment helping the disadvantaged is impossible because the student loans must in any case be serviced. If the economy shifts and employment cannot be obtained, not even personal bankruptcy can discharge the loans.

3. Shoghi Effendi, *Bahá'í Administration*, p. 66.
4. Schumpeter, *History of Economic Analysis*, pp. 73–142.
5. 'Abdu'l-Bahá, *Secret*, p. 92.
6. We allow for the interactive nature of the individual–institutional relationship and the extent to which people within this relationship are thereby influenced from an early age. But granting this, the Twelve Apostles of Christ were the products of their society and were yet entirely transformed by Jesus, to the extent that they overturned time-honoured traditions and social forms then extant.
7. This points to an obvious line of economic research – how to promote useful and fulfilling living for those people otherwise incapable of financial self-support. Perhaps private *and* public worth could be paid to individuals, allowances for social work in the form of negative income taxes, for example, to augment meagre or non-existent wages from their private market earnings.
8. A bequest always exists in some form for the exclusive use of the developing individual. It can have the form of natural ability and environmental inputs unique to that individual. This is the *factor* endowment form and is what is actually developed within the individual. The other form of an endowment is something like money which can be used to purchase or otherwise arrange for needed development of factors.
9. If, therefore, it now appears that at least two years of post high school education is necessary to produce individuals capable of economic and financial viability, then the state should clearly provide this at no charge and even make attendance compulsory, as was done in the past.
10. The fixity of tastes and preferences has been asserted by the Nobel laureate Gary Becker in 1968 ('Crime and Punishment') and followers have left this assertion basically unchallenged.
11. An interesting technical sidebar to this argument is that technology clearly changes over time as is commonly experienced. In the United States, in all but the market for medical services, whose costs are driven more by litigation and legal considerations, technology unambiguously reduces production costs, and therefore supply prices, over time. What this means is that U-shaped long run cost curves are impossible since the lower envelope or lower contour of aggregated short run and quasi-long run cost curves must be falling and negatively sloped. The obviousness of this has somehow not found its

way into economic principles classes, which still use the (incorrect) U-shaped curve to describe long run costs.

12. Gladwell, *Tipping Point*.
13. This opens up a philosophical question. In material terms, it is possible to borrow the money you intend to invest – investing on the margin, it is called. Is it possible to do this in spiritual terms? It seems not. Spiritual investing would seem to offer no scope for investing on the margin since credit is not accepted. In economic terms we do borrow time and we do borrow from the future to buy and spend today. But it does not seem possible to do this in a spiritual sense.
14. Not to be confused with the birth–death process in balancing equations from queueing theory.
15. This can be taken too far, of course. There is the joke about the two economists spying a 50 dollar bill on the street, then grandly shaking hands and complimenting each other on not picking it up, assuming, in accordance with neoclassical economics, that if it were real it would have been picked up already!
16. Interestingly, while intellectual capital compounds in the same way as financial capital, it depreciates in the same way as physical capital does. It must be constantly maintained to avoid becoming useless. On the other hand, the more it is used, the greater its capacity to solve difficult problems.
17. Qur'án 24:35.

Chapter 11

1. Qur'án 12:53.
2. 'Abdu'l-Bahá, *Secret*, pp. 84–5.
3. Qur'án 36:12.
4. Qur'án 8:50.
5. Bahá'u'lláh, *Gleanings*, p. 254.
6. Shoghi Effendi, *World Order*, p. 204.
7. Bahá'u'lláh, Ishráqát, *Tablets*, pp. 121–2. Emphasis added.
8. The amount of this burden on each trader depends on their respective elasticities of supply and demand.
9. Certainly there are fools who think their untried scheme will work and just need a loan from a bank to start up the new enterprise. We are not talking about this situation. But if the banker offers the loan because, well . . . we are insured, after all, then this is called a moral hazard, as now explained.
10. Allow it to be said here, however, that Americans are seething with anger and wonder loudly why these corporate officers, responsible for the ruin of so many lives, are not at least being tried for grand larceny which carries serious penalties upon conviction. What is needed, perhaps, is a code that treats each worker who has been ruined and impoverished as a direct result of the corporate officer's malfeasance as a count in the indictment, so that to be found guilty of one is to be found guilty on all similar counts. This would multiply the resulting penalty to a degree that would give pause to many of even the most arrogant, brilliant and dishonest corporate officers. This could

also apply to government bureaucrats, many of whom face the same temptations and also work in the unstructured world of executive decision-making where comprehensive oversight is impracticable or impossible and where a large amount of personal trustworthiness is demanded.

11. 'Abdu'l-Bahá, *Selections*, p. 249.
12. It is a recurring phenomenon that after a country is freed from an oppressive strongman or regime the nation's unity is tested in uprisings and revolts and the settling of old inter-community scores, sometimes generations or even centuries old.
13. The reason manufacturing jobs pay more than most service sector jobs has to do with the amount of capital each worker can manipulate and control on the job. Generally speaking, the greater the value of the capital, intellectual, financial, asset, a worker controls, the more the job will pay. A store clerk, who is not expected to do much and operates a cash register with others, or a garment worker who sews pieces of cloth together to make a shirt using a Necchi sewing machine, cannot expect to earn as much as a machine operator who handles the controls of a pneumatic press or an assembler who helps to build a $30,000 automobile.
14. This is not mere speculation. See Gordon, *Fat and Mean* for a detailed and further development of these issues. 'US corporations have become fat and mean. They need to become lean and decent – not just for the sake of their workers, but for the sake of their competitive advantage' (from the dust cover).
15. Bahá'u'lláh, *Hidden Words*, Arabic no. 5.
16. 'Abdu'l-Bahá, *Selections*, p. 130.
17. ibid. p. 136.
18. ibid. p. 130.
19. This is true in actual terms but, practically speaking, while Iran uses its increased revenues on national expenditures, it is hard to see that this is the case for Nigeria. It could be that its increased production is going towards current consumption and not towards building up the national infrastructure. If it is being spent for public infrastructure, there is little sign of it. The suspicion is that the increased revenues are either finding their way directly into foreign private bank accounts or are being used for armaments and luxury goods for the leader class.

Chapter 12

1. In the strict sense, the message brought by Bahá'u'lláh is not prophetic. He declared that it fulfils past prophecies and establishes the commencement of a new age within which many successive Messengers will appear to advance the work now established. But the use of the term 'prophetic' is being used owing to its generally accepted connotation of a message that is divinely sourced and not reflective of either the thinking of the Prophet or of any current or past school of thought.
2. As stated earlier, by guild is meant a body of practitioners representing a discipline's store of knowledge. These leaders are responsible for maintaining

and expanding the applicable base of this knowledge and passing it on to new dedicants. Most of the guilds of historical Europe were therefore craft apprenticeships – blacksmithing, baking, saddle making, the needle trades, medicine and apothecary sciences, etc. – but there were also merchant, capitalist and banking guilds whose objectives were mercantilist. In addition, becoming a priest, a rabbi or a monk is clearly guildship, as is certainly the practice of science and obtaining the degree of doctor of philosophy.

3. There is no evidence that the divine Messengers were ever influenced by the world in which they appeared. The historical evidence is that they provided influence to the world but the world was incapable of influencing any of them.
4. In chapter 8 there is a description of higher learning's graduation rituals and how seemingly close in appearance they are to the monasterial practices of Middle Age Europe. It is useful to be reminded of them again at this point.
5. 'Abdu'l-Bahá, *Secret*, p. 106. 'Abdu'l-Bahá continues. 'Not only this, but it also prevents the individual from undertaking the study of those arts and sciences of which society stands in dire need' (ibid.). Thus, guild-science is destructive to the pursuit of useful knowledge.
6. Qur'án 35:39.
7. Recall that we excluded irrelevant differences, e.g. a car's colour to a colour-blind agent, a first edition book compared to a reprint when the agent cares nothing for such a characteristic or the personal differences between one and another Prophet if the message, the actions, the cause and all other necessary qualities of the message are identical.
8. Dostoyevsky, *Brothers Karamazov*, pp. 301–5.
9. ibid. pp. 307–8.
10. Qur'án 2:91.
11. Besançon, *Rise of the Gulag*, p. 284.
12. Although Greider argues that this is exactly what one sitting US Federal Reserve chairman did in an attempt to get himself reappointed midway into a presidential term. Having authority over the American money supply, money was pumped into the economy, giving consumers an instant boost. This was done to appease the electorate and to ingratiate himself with the sitting but now campaigning president (Greider, *Secrets of the Temple*, p. 346).
13. Buchanan discussed the expected results of changing the US Congress's formula for representation. It was changing over from assigning districts geographically (which gives rural dwellers a greater voice) to assigning them only by population density. Many felt this would mean that the interests of rural dwellers would be ignored. But Buchanan said, no, quite the opposite. As a group gets smaller its influence increases, he explained, especially in rent-seeking success. The government cannot afford to hand out favours and benefits to the millions of poor, for example, but can do so for a few hundred or thousand, especially where the process is not well publicized. Thus, farmers today have greater influence than ever before, especially since farmers are viewed with sympathy by urban dwellers, who do not realize that today practically all farms are multimillion dollar enterprises and far removed from the

share-cropping image of Tom Joad in Steinbeck's *The Grapes of Wrath*. Even after Edward R. Murrow exposed the wretched condition of migrant farm workers and Cesar Chavez and the United Farm Workers of America organized a national protest boycott of California table grapes, little has changed in the public perception of the farmer.

14. Altig and Carlstrom, 'Marginal Tax Rates and Income Inequality in a Life-Cycle Model', *American Economic Review*, vol. 89, no. 6, December 1999.
15. See Traub, 'Common Talk'.
16. 'Canada's Healthcare Set to Remain in Public's Hands', *Financial Times*, 5 December 2002.
17. In Robert Caro's biography of Robert Moses, master builder of public transportation and parks in greater New York City and Long Island (*The Power Broker: Robert Moses and the Fall of New York*, Vintage Books, 1974), the point is effectively made that none of the construction projects would have been possible had Moses not been able to override and ignore all public opposition. Of course, the downside of that situation was that it led ultimately to civic arrogance and a total disregard for public needs, also well documented by Caro.
18. Is it the presence of cheap and ubiquitous entertainment sources that is keeping citizens from pondering their worsening economic situation and political impotence? Neil Postman thinks so: '. . . Americans are the best entertained and quite likely the least well-informed people in the Western world. I say this in the face of the popular conceit that television, as a window to the world, has made Americans exceedingly well informed . . . In saying this I do not mean to imply that television news deliberately aims to deprive Americans of a coherent, contextual understanding of their world. I mean to say that when news is packaged as entertainment, that is the inevitable result' (Postman, *Amusing Ourselves to Death*, pp. 106–7).
19. Shoghi Effendi, *Advent*, p. 30.
20. See Budd Schulberg's brilliant and tragically comical book *What Makes Sammy Run?*, about Hollywood and the movie business. Its characterizations can certainly be extended to include the TV business today. See also Paddy Chayefsky's Oscar-winning film *Network*, 1976, with Fay Dunaway, Peter Finch, Robert Duvall, William Holden and Ned Beatty.
21. One supposes that this is the very reason that schools are supported with taxes and not bake sales and that social workers are government employees and not dependent on charitable contributions.
22. See 'A Tale of Two Bellies' in the 24 August 2002 issue of *The Economist* and the author's letter to the editor in the 7 September issue, pointing out that economic insecurity has been shown to be positively related to increases in fertility rates. In secure circumstances fertility rates tend to fall, as they have in Europe. In America they are rising again and no one seems to know why. But the explanation is obvious to anyone living in the United States today. Compared to their European counterparts, Americans face increased risks of economic loss, job termination and getting sick or hurt. As the living experience for American workers comes to resemble that in Third World economies,

then certainly the fertility rate in America will more closely resemble theirs also.

23. This would seem to induce increased family size. Portfolio theory suggests that one way to manage risk is to spread it around, i.e. 'don't put all your eggs in one basket'. Families with several breadwinners are more secure against economic loss than those having only one. But while some population groups in the US have large families, there is little evidence that this is to insulate them from economic setbacks. Some data indicate that today more Americans live alone than at any time in the nation's history.
24. See Gordon, *Fat and Mean.*
25. Joseph A. Schumpeter, Nobel laureate in economics, developed this idea of creative destruction, and it is one of the concepts he is known for.
26. By all accounts a new prophetic and divine message has been revealed by Bahá'u'lláh, author of the Bahá'í Faith. Evidence of its authenticity is to be found in the nature and logical structure of its arguments, especially in close and scrupulous comparison with the verses and surahs of the Qur'án. That is, by whatever proof the Qur'án is deemed a revelation from God, the same argument yields the same result when applied to the writings of Bahá'u'lláh; and whatever argument is used to reject the revelation of Bahá'u'lláh must, without any alteration, reject as divine revelation (God forbid!) the Qur'án. A first best example of this is contained in the book The Kitáb-i-Íqán, every word of which was revealed by Bahá'u'lláh. As in the past, its presence as divine speech in the midst of society will cause great upheaval. The ensuing struggle will be between what is generated by the creative forces of a newly authored and divinely-sourced revelation, and vestigial forms of previous revelations now subsumed and co-opted by tautological ideologies that have not the ability to spawn new life in social constructions. One of the unifying themes of this book is that, stripped of ideologies, science and prophetic dialogues are only different aspects of the analysis of reality. Economics provides the analytical framework to construct a type of spiritualmetrics, as it were, to derive results from the application and testing of spiritual theories just as physics or chemistry does in the material world.
27. 'Abdu'l-Bahá, *Selections*, p. 303.

Chapter 13

1. 'Abdu'l-Bahá, *Selections*, p. 303.

Appendix

1. It was the revelation of the Kitáb-i-Íqán that 'unsealed' the holy books of the past, and most specifically the Qur'án. Over time, enough of the divinely revealed teachings, analysis and rational arguments found in those pages have been dispersed to the extent necessary to cause a reevaluation of established teachings in the Qur'an; its latent forces are now being released, as promised by the divine Prophets.
2. Shoghi Effendi, *World Order*, p. 22.

3. This should come as no surprise because 90 per cent of American business start-ups fail in their first year; so, why should futures speculating be any different?
4. Of course, facilitative activities extract payments from productive enterprises, which is the reason they are resented by those not understanding their essential role in production. How large should the facilitative sector be? Just large enough, and rich enough, to allow the economy to grow at its potential. Any less and the economy cannot grow; any more and it becomes parasitic, extracting too much from productive enterprises.

Index

This index is alphabetized word by word, hence 'global warming' precedes 'globalization'.